LEGENDARY LOCALS

OF

WAYLAND

MASSACHUSETTS

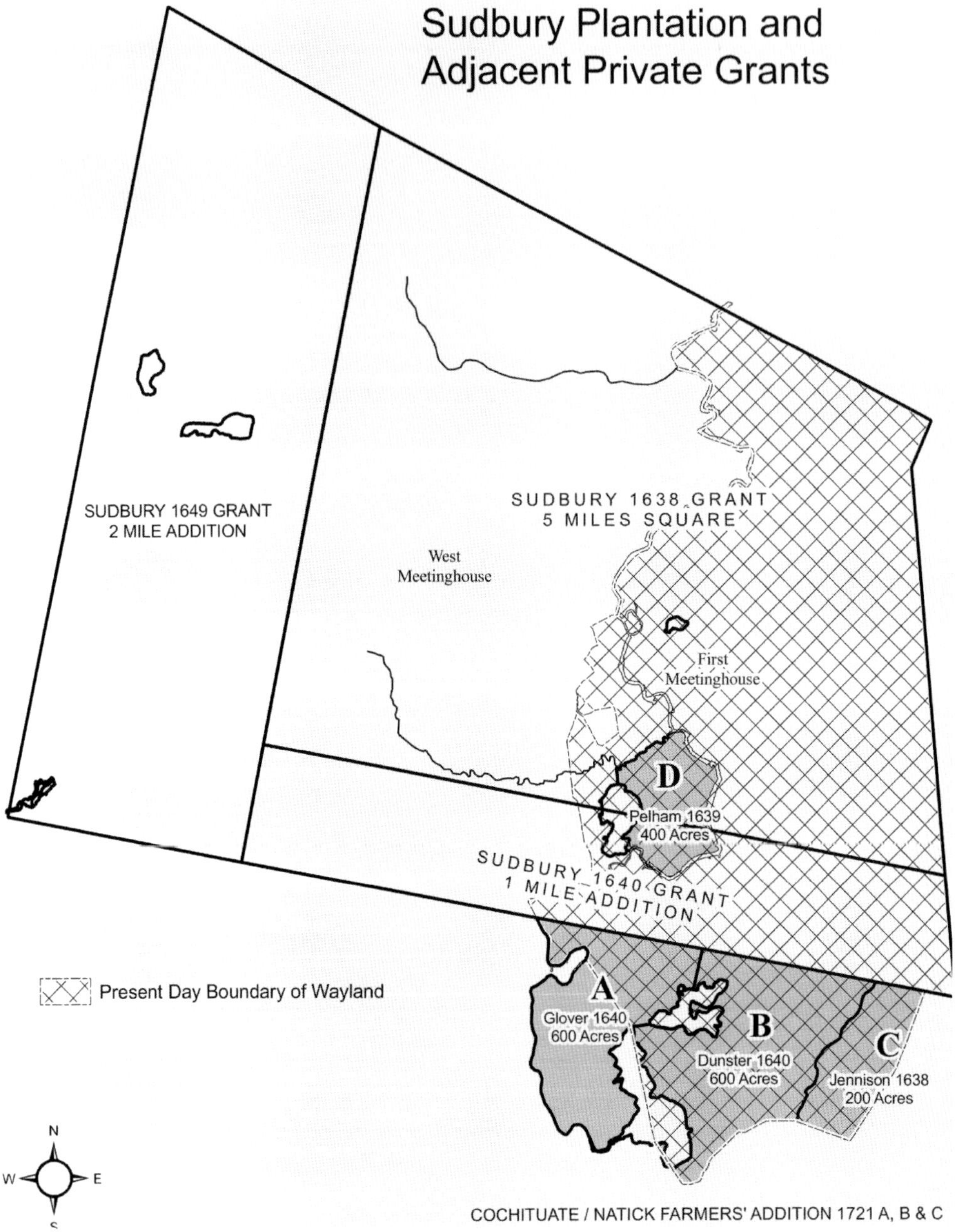

Sudbury Plantation

Pictured here is a map of the original Sudbury Plantation and the adjacent private grants. (Courtesy of Wayland Historical Society.)

Page 1: First Parish Church

First Parish Church, built in 1815, has a three-door entrance, Palladian windows, and gables. A Paul Revere bell hangs in the belfry. (Courtesy of Stephen Engler.)

LEGENDARY LOCALS

OF

WAYLAND

MASSACHUSETTS

EVELYN WOLFSON

LEGENDARY LOCALS

ISBN 978-1-4671-0191-2

Legendary Locals is an imprint of Arcadia Publishing
Charleston, South Carolina

Printed in the United States of America

Library of Congress Control Number: 2014946509

For all general information, please contact Arcadia Publishing:
Telephone 843-853-2070
Fax 843-853-0044
E-mail sales@arcadiapublishing.com
For customer service and orders:
Toll-Free 1-888-313-2665

Visit us on the Internet at www.arcadiapublishing.com

Dedication

This book is dedicated to Lily Schlafer, to whom I am forever grateful.

On the Front Cover: Clockwise from top left:
Roberta Wambolt, Community Nursery children (author's collection; see page 63), George B. Howe, Civil War veteran (courtesy of Wayland Historical Society; see page 77), Dr. Leonard Carapezza, pediatric orthodontist (courtesy of Leonard Carapezza; see page 55), Mabel Draper, first curator of Wayland Historical Society (courtesy of Wayland Historical Society; see page 27), Marilyn Wallin, violin, viola, and cello maker (courtesy of Pierre Chiha; see page 37), Charlotte Russell, triathlon winner (author's collection; see page 93), Richard Turner, World War II veteran (courtesy of Richard Turner; see page 84), Gladys Widdiss, tribal leader, Wampanoag Tribe of Gay Head (courtesy of Dawn Widdiss; see page 104), Juliet Lambert Pratt, Broadway performer (courtesy of Juliet Lambert Pratt; see page 43).

On the Back Cover: From left to right:
Alberto Salazar, 1982 Boston Marathon winner (courtesy of Wayland Historical Society; see page 92), Timothy Skehan, Elizabeth Russell Skehan, Charlotte Russell, and Lewis Russell, owners of Wayland's oldest business (courtesy of Suzanne Shapiro; see page 68).

CONTENTS

ACKNOWLEDGMENTS

This book would not have been possible without the friendship and expertise of John Schlafer, who scanned every photograph, often lugging his laptop, scanner, and power source to the site; Lois Hanssen Davis, curator of the Wayland Historical Society, who gave generously of her time, locating archival photographs and biographies and answering my endless questions; and Jo Goeselt, curator emeritus, whose knowledge of town history is unsurpassed. I could not have managed without Jo's expertise in navigating ancestry.com. I am also grateful to the staff at the Framingham Historical Society for sharing, and especially Ruthann Tomassini, who donated her time researching specific materials. I thank Dacia Callen and Dick Hoyt for reading and critiquing. Finally, I thank the many Wayland citizens who granted interviews and the amateur and professional photographers who gave so generously of their time and expertise.

Unless otherwise noted, all images are courtesy of the Wayland Historical Society.

INTRODUCTION

We are all tattooed in our cradles with the beliefs of our tribe;
the record may seem superficial, but it is indelible.

—Oliver Wendell Holmes Sr.

In 1638, Peter Noyes, Rev. Edmund Browne, and Brian Pendleton headed west out of Watertown with a vision. They hoped to establish a proprietorship, a communal system of farming, unlike Watertown. Not long after crossing the Watertown border, the men came upon acres of green grass watered by a meandering river. Their vision began to materialize.

The men petitioned the general court for "straitness of accommodation, and want of meadow," and were granted five square miles astride the river: approximately 3,000 acres, just upstream from Concord. They named their new proprietorship Sudbury Plantation and the river the Sudbury, after Reverend Browne's hometown of Sudbury, England.

The proprietors established a system whereby families could join the community by contributing services such as milling or smithing, making payment into the proprietorship, or both. The men called themselves free townsmen. Working together, families fenced the cow common and set their animals to graze, planted communal gardens, built a meetinghouse and mill, and established garrison houses. The first meetinghouse was built in 1643, at a cost of £6, at the site of the Old Burial Ground on Old Sudbury Road. That same year, Thomas Cakebread opened his mill at Mill Pond, where Mill Brook and Pine Brook converge. Sudbury Plantation quickly grew to capacity.

Within 15 years, land had become scarce and the proprietors petitioned the General Court for an additional two miles along the west side of the river, which they were granted. However, young farmers argued that the land was too far from the cow common and community gardens, and petitioned the town meeting for individual ownership of the land. The issue was hotly debated in town meetings for two long years. According to Sumner Chilton Powell, "The social, political, and economic philosophy of Sudbury was at stake." In the end, the petitioners won the vote and the Proprietorship was divided among shareholders.

For more than half a century, Sudbury Plantation continued to grow, particularly on the west side of the river. Then, in 1707, west side residents submitted a petition to build a meetinghouse on their side of the river, using the river as a natural divider. But the river was not a fair division, as two-thirds of the land was on the west side of the river, along with a majority of the settlement's parishioners. For the next 16 years, officials sought a solution to the problem. In the end, no solution could be found, and the river became the line of demarcation. The meetinghouse was finally built in 1723, creating the East and West Precincts.

The West Precinct continued to grow over the years, and by 1771, its population exceeded that of the East Precinct by an appreciable amount. That year, a proposal was made to enlarge the West Precinct meetinghouse. East Precinct residents opposed funding the addition since they paid the bulk of the community's taxes. Debate continued during the Revolutionary War period, even as the settlement's militia marched to Concord, Massachusetts. With no solution in sight, East Precinct residents proposed the establishment of two separate towns. That suggestion brought up an older problem—dividing the land fairly. Division by the river remained an unfair solution. For almost another decade, a fair solution was sought. At last, East Precinct residents decided that if they were going to establish a separate town they would have to settle for less land and lose the name. Thus, in 1780, the West Precinct became Sudbury, and the East Precinct became East Sudbury, as the side seeking separation had to surrender the name by law.

For reasons historians have not been able to determine, East Sudbury changed its name to Wayland in 1835. Many believe confusion over the similar names of Sudbury and East Sudbury was the impetus. However, no documentation regarding the change has been found.

In 1815, a fifth meetinghouse, (First Parish Church) was built across the street from Pequod House on the Boston Post Road, and the state's first free public library opened in 1850 on Cochituate Road. Rev. Francis Wayland, president of Brown University, who summered in town, offered to donate the sum of $500 for the establishment of a free library, provided townsfolk would donate an equal amount. James Sumner Draper assumed the task of raising the money, securing donations between $5 and $20 until the goal had been met. In the end, Reverend Wayland's gift was matched with a small amount in excess. In 1878, a Victorian town hall went up next to the library, and a horse car line was installed from the center of town to Cochituate Village. East Sudbury had over a hundred farms by 1870, and when the railroad came through Wayland Center a little more than a decade later, farmers could ship milk to market and receive feed deliveries in return.

But financial successes in the dairy industry never matched that of Cochituate's factory owners. In the southern part of town, the village of Cochituate, named after the lake nearby, grew rapidly. Villagers gradually gave up farming and established industrial operations like those in neighboring Natick and Framingham. The Bent brothers had turned a small shoe shop into a large, steam-powered shoe factory by 1860, hiring workers from surrounding areas as well as immigrants from Europe, Nova Scotia, and Quebec. Cochituate Village's population exceeded 1,000 by the end of the 19th century.

In the latter half of the 19th century, well-to-do businessmen and manufacturers established estates in town, increasing the town's tax base, and contributed time, expertise, and funds to the betterment of the community. Wayland's two villages continued to prosper into the 20th century, thanks in part to the overwhelming generosity of Jonathan M. Parmenter, who left funds for the town to build a hospital and a town-wide water system. In addition, he made bequests to First Parish Church, the library, and Radcliffe and Harvard Colleges to provide scholarship funds for needy students.

When the town began to experience a pattern of unregulated growth, resident Howard Russell began a campaign to do something about it. He proposed the establishment of a town zoning board and was joined by Allen Benjamin, Hugh Morton, Bob Charnook, Bill Bertelsen, and Fred Perry. By 1933, they had devised a set of zoning bylaws as a means of "securing order and good arrangement within the town."

During World War II, a group of Wayland volunteers decided to publish a newsletter for Wayland servicemen, titled the *Village Bugle*. They set up shop in the two-room Mellen law office in town where they typed, edited, and compiled the newsletter, then had it mimeographed in the law offices of Charles T. Morgan in Boston. Later, residents in Cochituate began publication of their own servicemen's newspaper called the *Jeep*. It had more pages and many photographs due to the printing options available to them.

By the 1950s, families were moving to Wayland from the city, and the town was prepared to support developments of all sizes, with lots zoned from one to two-and-a-half acres and homes priced accordingly. Construction of a new high school was completed in 1960, and a decade later, a new junior high/middle school was built. To preserve vital open lands threatened by development, seven Wayland residents established a conservation organization, Sudbury Valley Trustees (SVT), and began to raise money to purchase available lands. The town quickly outgrew its farm community label and become a true Boston suburb.

When I bought my first home in Wayland in 1961, town offices had recently been moved into a new one-story brick town hall building at the northeast corner of the Boston Post and Cochituate Roads, Raytheon was building a new facility near the center of town, and we had a variety of desirable neighborhoods to choose from.

Most important to my husband and me in choosing where to settle was to find a town we believed had good bones. Wayland has a rich history—the town was founded only eight years after Boston and a mere 20 miles away; a town meeting form of government; clean, clear drinking water; and a commitment to preserving open space. Wayland cheerfully celebrated its 375th anniversary in 2014; town meetings remain important to upholding these basic values and have evolved from a stand-up counted vote to state-of-the-art electronic handheld voting devices. Our drinking water, delivered from local wells, remains clean and protected, and citizens continue to vote for funding of open space.

My husband, who supported the mission of the SVT, had become a member while working in an adjacent town. SVT was formed in 1953 by a group of seven Wayland men—Alan Morgan, George Lewis, Richard Stackpole, Roger Stokey, William Ryder, Allen Benjamin, and Henry W. Parker—who had organized to raise money and buy as much available town land as possible before it was lost to development. True visionaries, they were intent upon safeguarding the marshlands, which hold rain as it percolates into the ground, replenishing the water we depend on for drinking; maintaining natural habitats for animals; and containing urban sprawl. Today, Wayland's green spaces continue to add character, charm, and definition to our many neighborhoods.

Since I moved to Wayland 53 years ago, the town has added a great deal of flesh to its bones: a top-ranking school system, abundant recreational facilities, and a solid core of committed volunteers working to ensure a better quality of life for everyone.

I often take visitors to walk some of the original preserved common land, 65 acres of it, where settlers first set their cattle to graze some 375 years ago. Thanks to those early visionaries, the river is still visible in spring, even though the cranberries and the marsh grass are long gone.

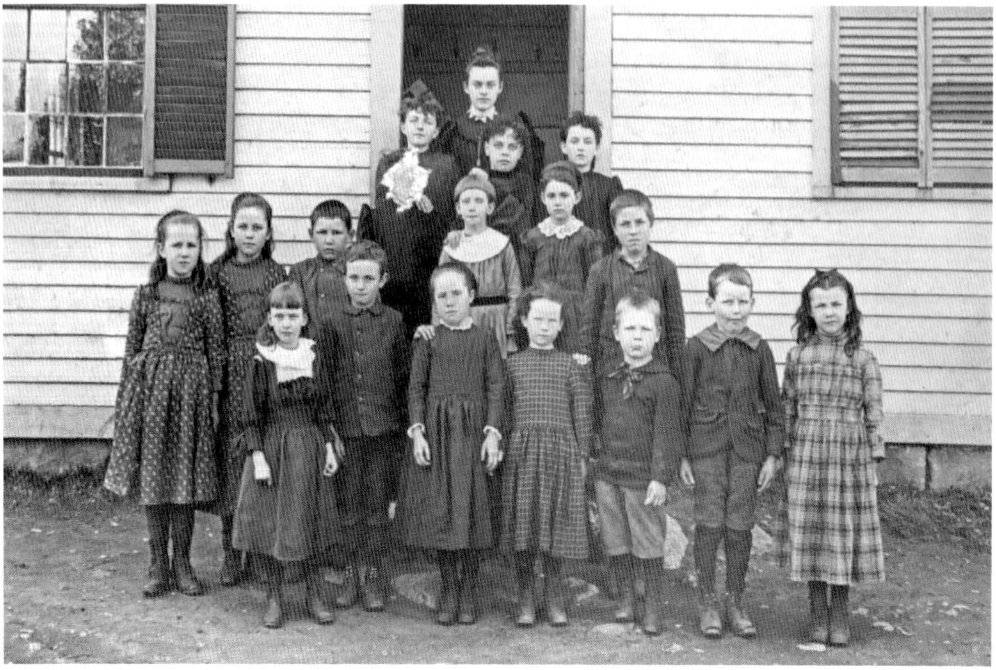

Rutter School Children, c. 1883

The East District Rutter School was located near the intersection of Old Connecticut Path and Rice Road.

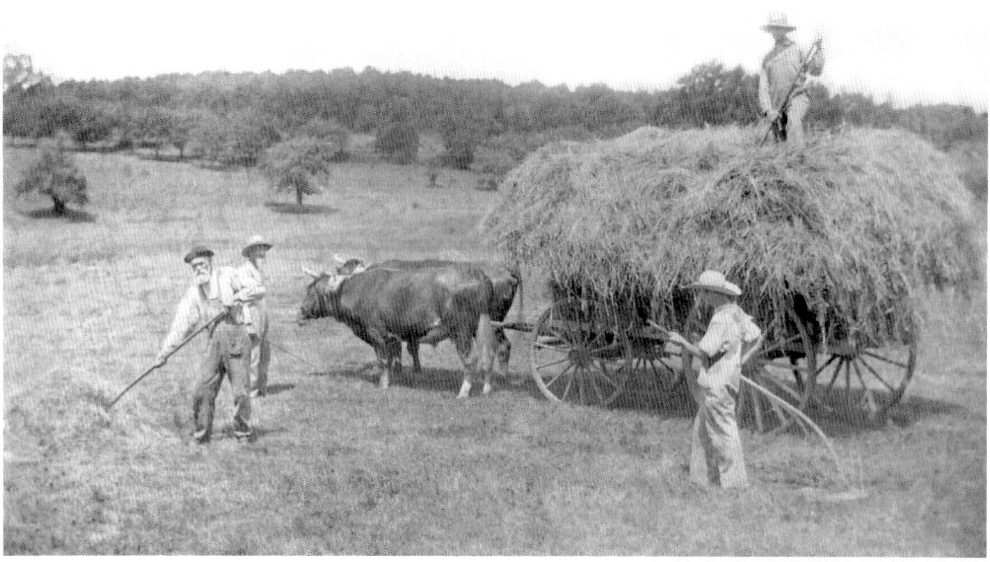

Haying on a Dairy Farm

Here, farmers collect hay by hand and load it onto an ox-drawn cart.

CHAPTER ONE

Past Notables

The future is not an inheritance, it is an opportunity, and an obligation.

—Bill Clinton

Indians Karto (Cato), Jethro, and their families lived peaceably on two nearby hills when Sudbury settlers arrived. Karto and his family, probably from the Massachusetts tribe, lived on Goodman's Hill, and Old Jethro and his family, from the Nipmuck tribe, lived on Nobscot Hill. They were survivors of several epidemics that had wiped out most of the New England tribes. The Sudbury River Valley had never been claimed for permanent settlement but had been a seasonal hunting and fishing ground shared by many tribes. The Wampanoags came from Cape Cod, the Nipmucks from Connecticut and Worcester, the Pawtuckets from New Hampshire, and the Massachusetts Indians traveled from Boston. By the time settlers arrived, the traditional Indian lifestyle had ceased.

Early Sudbury settlers learned from the Indians how to weave weirs (nets) across the river to catch fish, clear forest underbrush for hunting, and plant corn "when the leaves of the oak tree are the size of a mouse ear."

Indians, in turn, learned to attend church. Some even converted to Christianity. Karto converted after hearing a sermon given by Rev. Edmund Browne, who served the congregation for four decades. Old Jethro never converted, but his son, Young Jethro, went to live in Natick, Massachusetts, with the Praying Indians.

By 1835, East Sudbury had been renamed Wayland, and wealthy Bostonians had begun to establish large estates in town. William Power Perkins, who by 1883 had purchased 326.5 acres off Old Connecticut Path, established the first Guernsey cow farm in the state. In 1891, Francis Shaw began purchasing farms around the intersection of Old Connecticut Path and Cochituate Road. He built a 22-room mansion on the hill and called his estate Five Paths. Shaw became a benefactor of the town, pledging substantial funds toward the construction of the Center School.

Residing close to town center, James Sumner Draper and Edmund Hamilton Sears dedicated time and energy to making the town a better place to live. Draper served as town librarian for 20 years, making books available to everyone. He created maps and publications that remain valuable resources today. Edmund Hamilton Sears, a versatile poet and preacher, became an abolitionist and joined his neighbor, Lydia Maria Child, on the Boston Vigilance Committee, formed in direct response to the new Fugitive Slave Act of 1850. The number of residents who became part of the Underground Railroad is not known, but runaway slaves had the sympathies of townsfolk.

Civic-minded men and women have continued to make outstanding contributions to the community over the years. The largest monetary contribution was made by Jonathan Parmenter early in the 20th century. In his will, he donated the bulk of his estate to benefit the town. Howard Russell created town-wide zoning rules in 1933, Alan Morgan initiated land preservation in 1953, and Mabel Draper, following in the footsteps of her famous father-in-law, James Sumner, and his father, Deacon James, helped organize the town's first historical society in 1954.

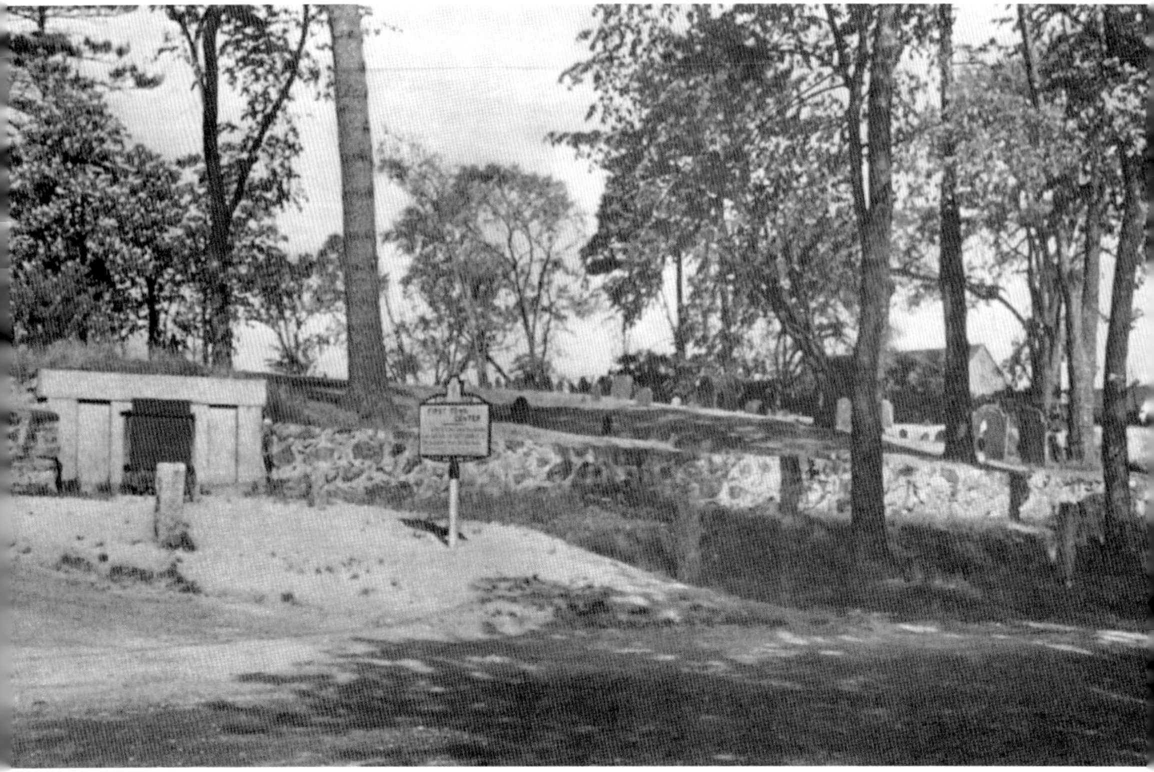

Reverend Edmund Browne (1606–1678)
For more than four decades, Reverend Browne served as minister in the first three meetinghouses built at the site of today's North Cemetery. The church was Congregational in government and Calvinistic in creed and faith. The reverend owned hundreds of acres of land, both in and out of the town. He was an accomplished musician and devoted much of his time to converting the Indians. In his will, he left £50 to the town to build a school.

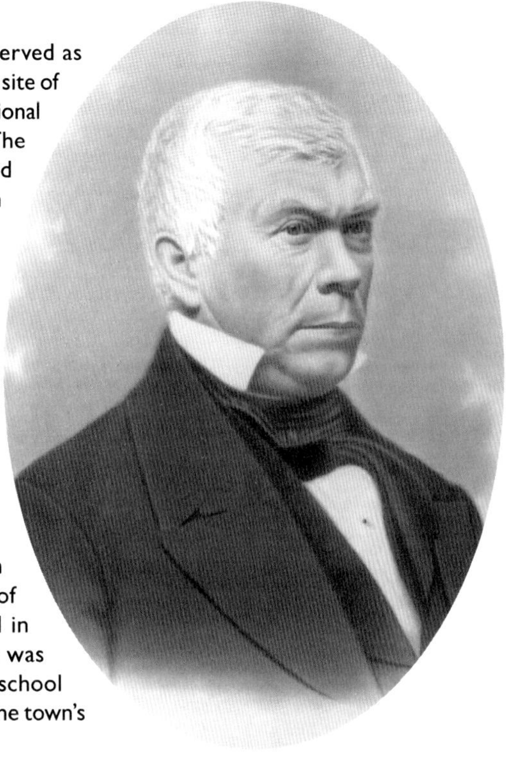

Judge Edward Mellen (1802–1875)
After Judge Mellen purchased the village home and law office of Samuel Mann, he began a law practice in the two-room law office, which still stands on Wayland's town green. The law office, built in 1826, is one of the few remaining two-room law offices in Massachusetts. Mellen was justice of the Court of Common Pleas in Worcester, and in 1855 became chief justice of the same court. He was an advocate of higher education, served on the school committee, and was instrumental in the funding of the town's first public library.

Allen Benjamin (1915–2003)

Benjamin had a passion for trying to make Wayland a better place to live and worked tirelessly for the town. A civil engineer and town planner, he served on the Planning Board, Zoning Board of Appeals, Assessors, and Town Center Committee. He created a veritable farm on his Concord Road property to insure a country-style life for himself and his family. The annual First Parish Church Easter sunrise service was often held in his orchard.

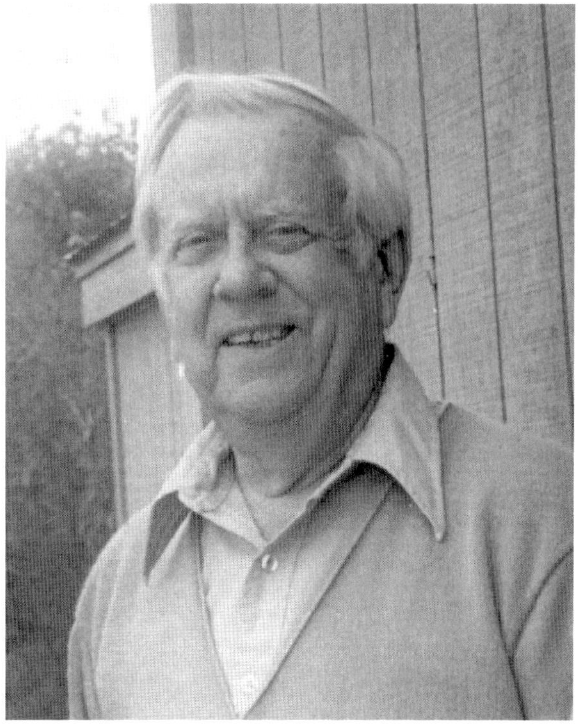

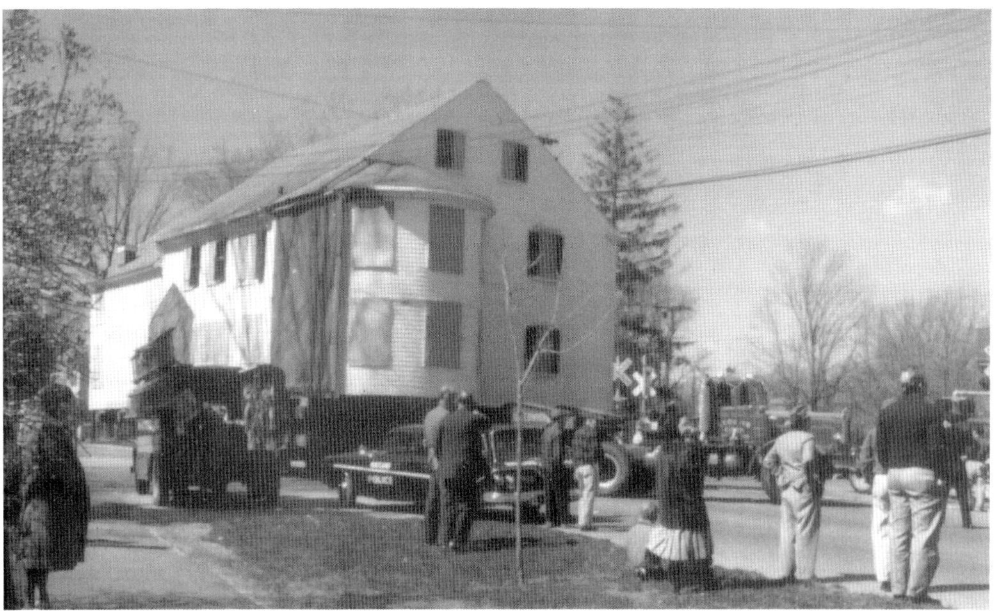

Charles Malcolm Campbell (1884–1969)

Campbell, better known as Malcolm, was a carpenter, mechanic, and pilot. He restored and flew vintage aircraft and served in the Civil Air Patrol. He was one of the town's original firefighters. Malcolm became the Historical Society's first resident custodian, living in the Grout-Heard House after it was moved back to its original foundation in 1962 (pictured). He lovingly restored the old charm and beauty of the house we see today.

Archibald Cox (1912–2004)

Cox was a popular figure in town long before Richard Nixon's famous "Saturday Night Massacre." He had married Phyllis Ames after graduating from Harvard and moved into the Ames's family farm on Glezen Lane. While teaching at Harvard College, Cox served the town on the Personnel Board and the Board of Assessors, as president of the Wayland United Nations Association, and the Wayland chapter of the Red Cross. He served as solicitor general for Pres. John F. Kennedy in the early 1960s. Appointed as an independent counsel to investigate the Watergate affair in 1973, Cox subpoenaed President Nixon's taped phone calls and conversations in the White House. The president refused to comply, and instead ordered that Cox be fired. Attorney general Elliott Richardson and his top deputy, William D. Ruckelshaus, resigned their posts rather than carry out Nixon's order. That firing became known as the Saturday Night Massacre. Former president Bill Clinton awarded Cox the Presidential Citizens Medal for exemplary service in 2001, an award established, ironically, by Nixon in 1969.

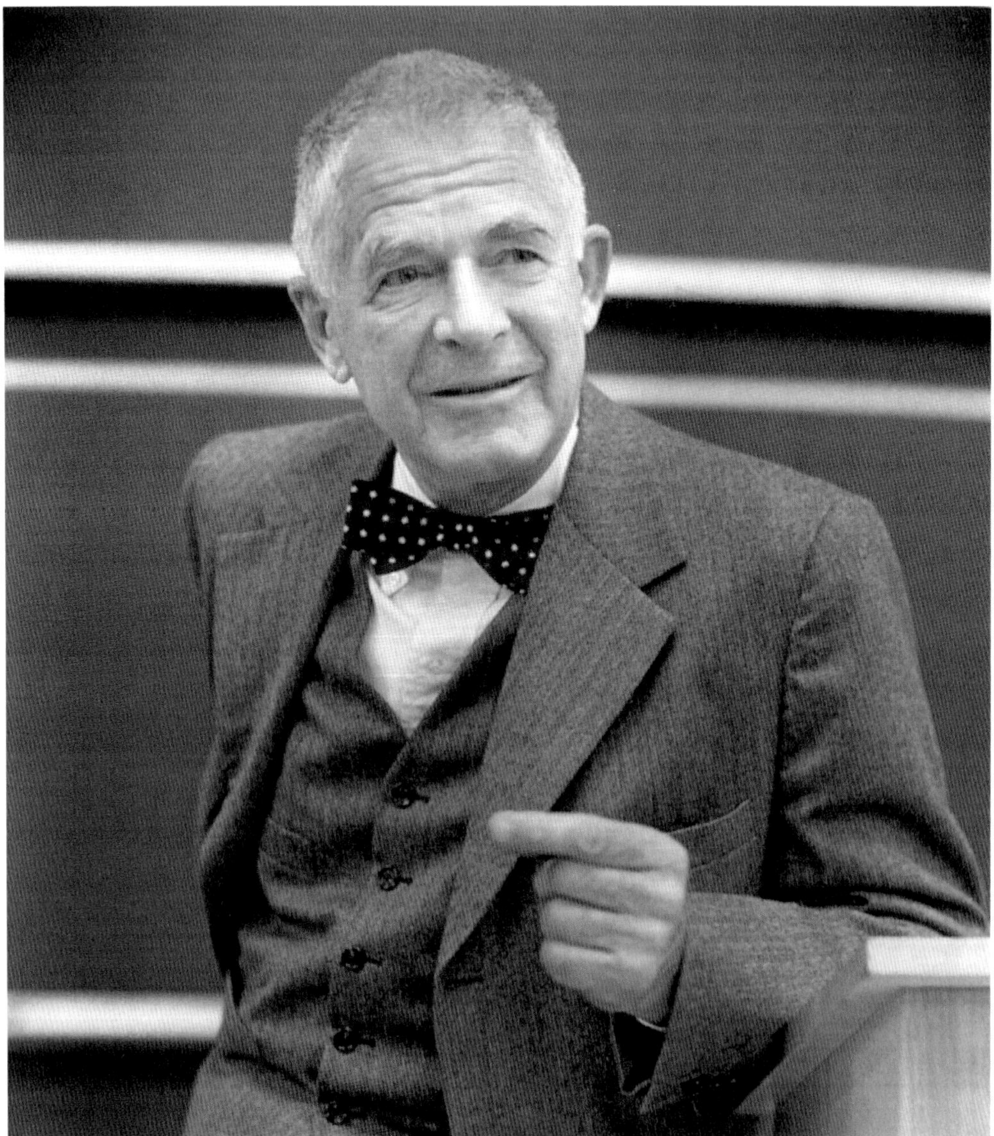

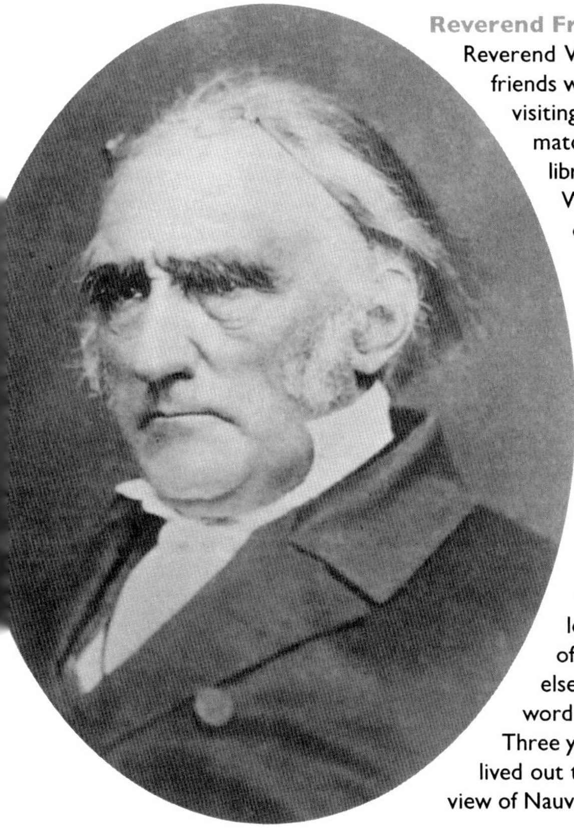

Reverend Francis Wayland (1796–1865)

Reverend Wayland, president of Brown University, became friends with Judge Edward Mellen, a Brown alumnus, while visiting in town. When the reverend offered $500 to be matched by the citizens of Wayland to fund a public library, Judge Mellen set the wheels in motion. Reverend Wayland proudly dedicated the library in 1851. Many citizens have speculated that the town received its name from Rev. Francis Wayland, although it has never been proven, and many are skeptical.

Lewis Abbott (1794–unknown)

Abbott sold his home in Wayland in 1830 to join the Mormon trek westward. The group made several stops before buying the small town of Commerce, Illinois, in 1840. Joseph Smith, who led the Mormons (now the Church of Jesus Christ of Latter-day Saints) to escape religious persecution elsewhere, changed the name of the town to Nauvoo, a word from Isaiah 52. Smith was killed in Nauvoo in 1844. Three years later, Abbott left for Salt Lake City, where he lived out the remainder of his life. Pictured here is an 1855 view of Nauvoo. (Author's collection.)

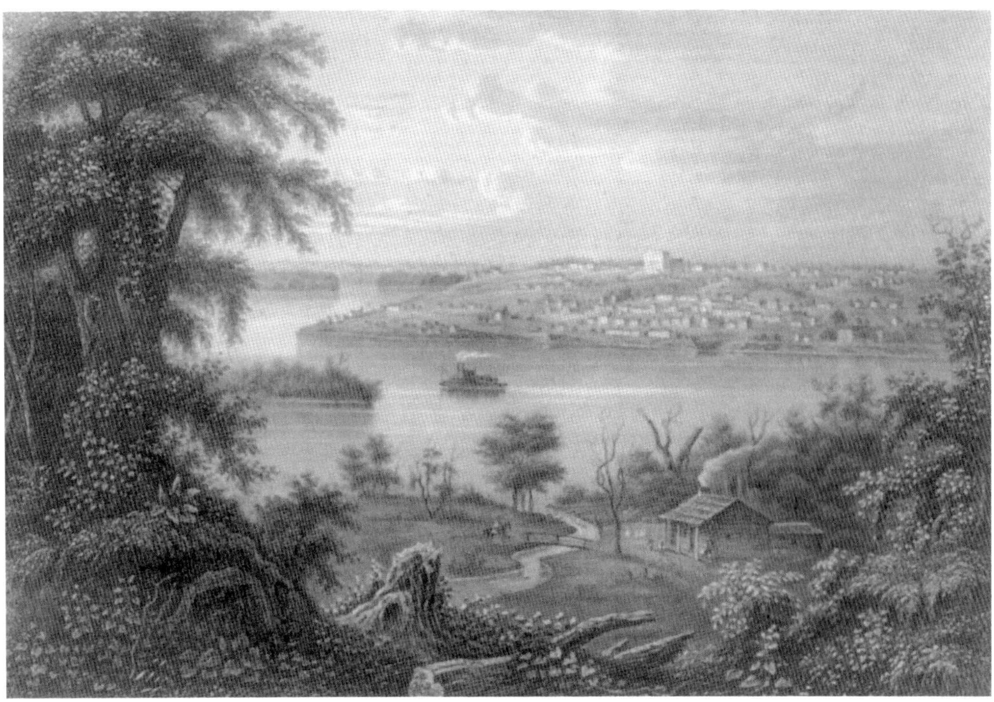

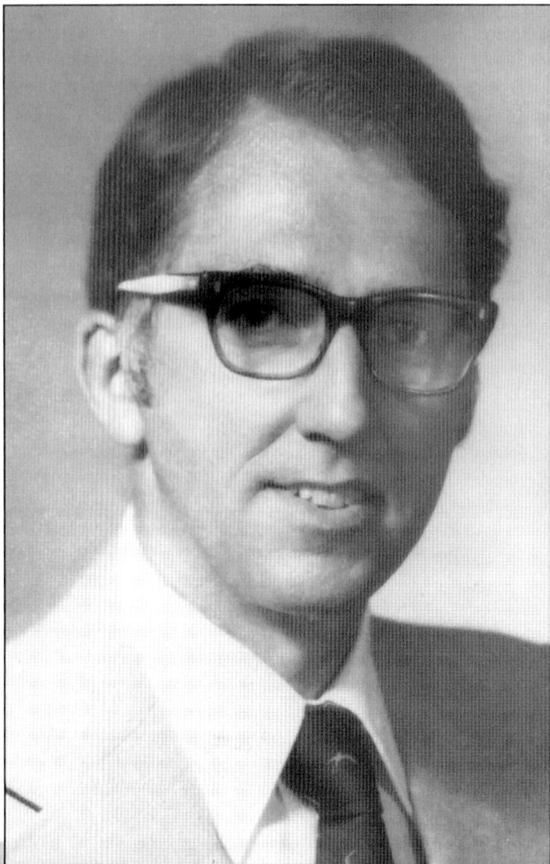

Allen Morgan (1925–1990)
Morgan was the driving force behind the founding of the Sudbury Valley Trustees (SVT), a public land conservancy. He and six naturalist friends, Richard Stackpole, George K. Lewis, B. Allen Benjamin, Robert P. Stokey, Willis B. Ryder, and Henry W. Parker, sought to preserve vital open lands threatened by development. In 1953, they began efforts to create a conservation fund. For the next three decades, they met in homes, fields, and canoes until Bertha Smith donated 8.25 acres of land and two houses on her property to establish a headquarters. Today, SVT occupies a large farmhouse (pictured below) on the 54-acre former Winterbrook Farm, donated by John Wolbach in 2000. SVT has helped to preserve 8,000 acres in the valley of the Concord, Sudbury, and Assabet Rivers. (Below, author's collection.)

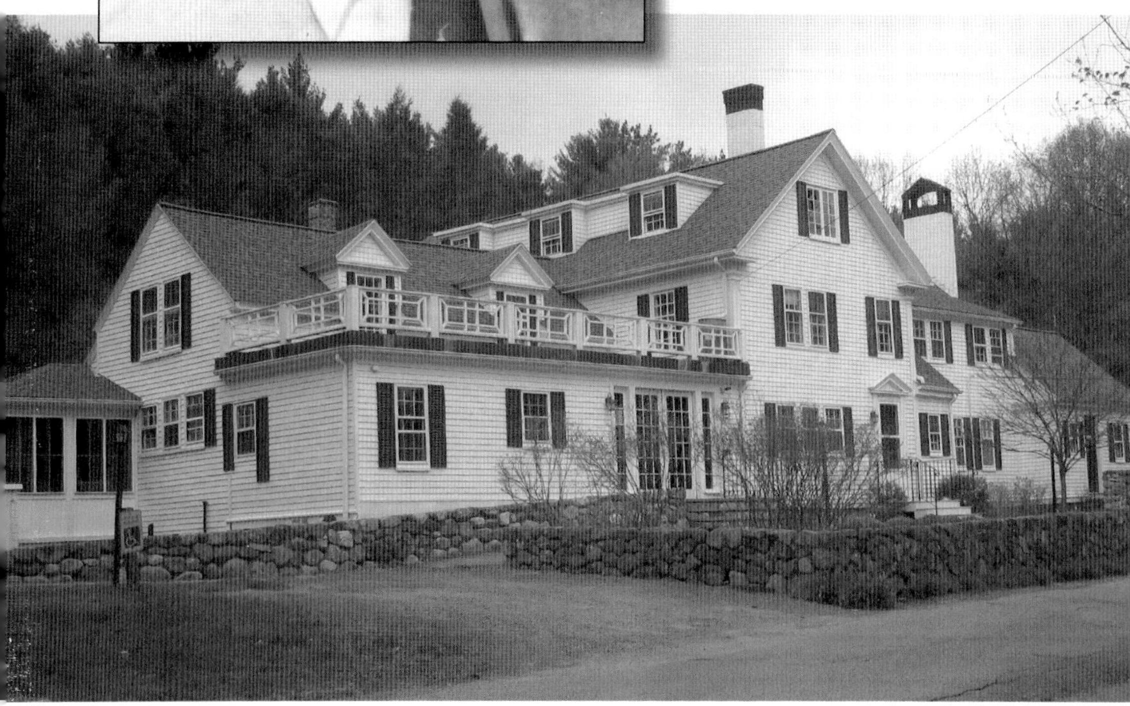

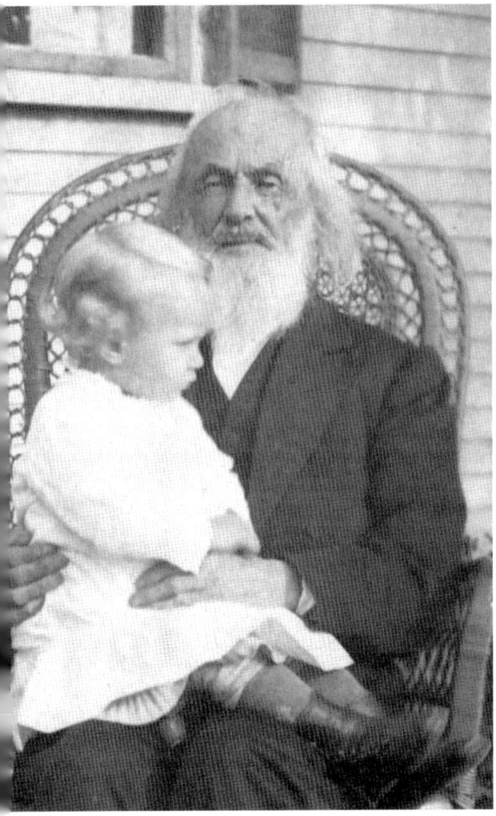

Reverend John Burt Wight (1790–1883)

Reverend Wight established the Sudbury Charitable Library in 1815 with a collection of 300 volumes kept in the church and supported by private contributions, but available to everyone. The collection was shared by six district schools and was later added to the Wayland library collection. While minister of First Parish Church, he oversaw the establishment of the Trinitarian Congregation Church in 1828 and the end of public money to support his church.

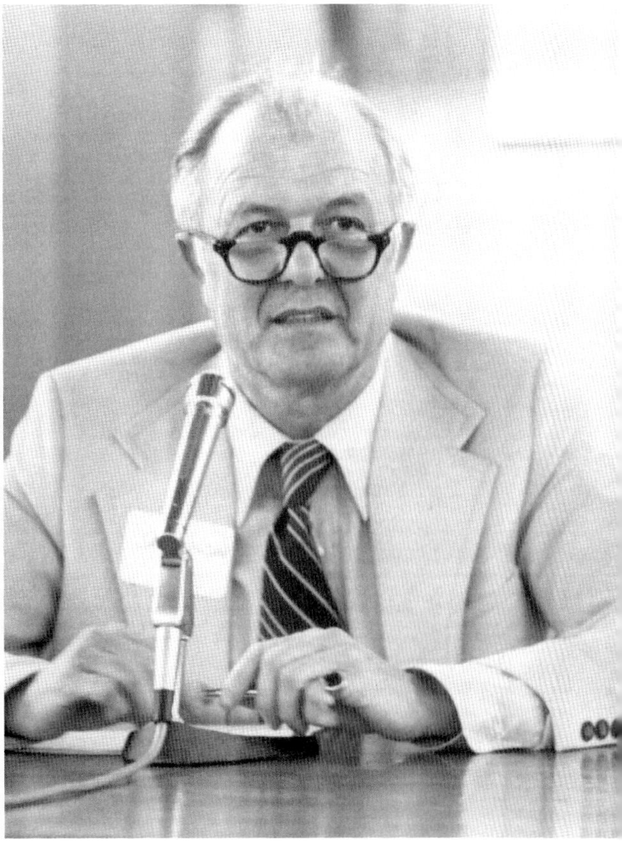

John "Jack" Wilson (1926–2011)

Jack was a warm, friendly, and devoted town servant. During his 59 years in town he served on more than a dozen boards and committees, including long stints as a selectman and member of the Wayland Historical Society. He was the go-to man when a cog in the wheels of government got stuck. His second home on Cayman Brac in the Cayman Islands was a refuge from the busy life he led as president of a large manufacturing company and his many commitments to the town.

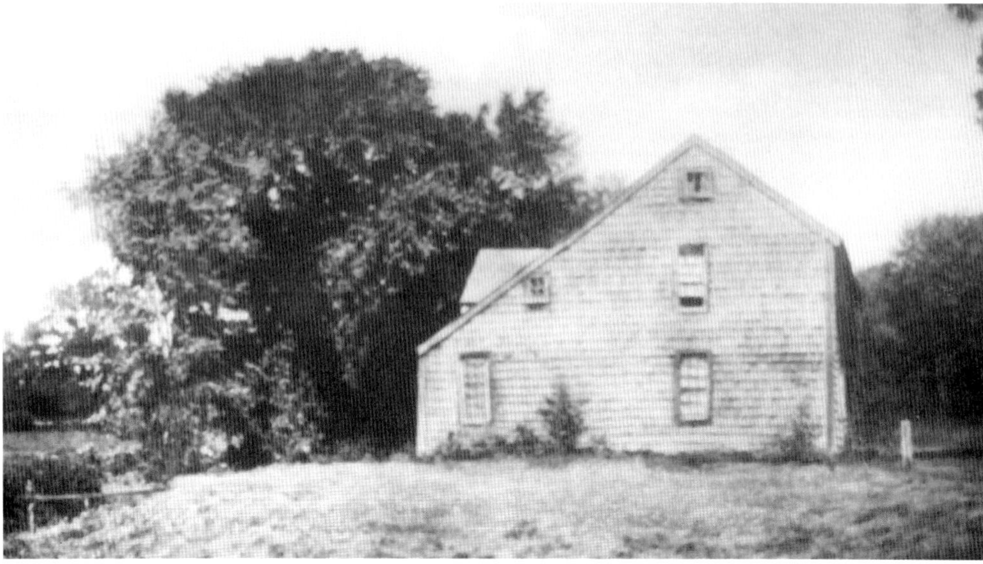

Edmund Rice (1594–1663)

Beginning in 1638, Rice served for many years as a leader in the community. He was a representative in the Massachusetts legislature for five years and a selectman for 11 years. He was granted four acres of land near the first meetinghouse, and 20 acres in southeastern Sudbury. He became the largest individual landowner in Sudbury, purchasing land granted by the colony to the Dunsters, Glovers, and Jennisons in southeastern Sudbury. Cochituate Village includes the bulk of these private grants. The Rice name is mentioned in both Sudbury and Wayland histories. Edmund married twice and had 12 children, some of whom were born in Marlborough, where he and several sons moved. Pictured above is the original Rice homestead. (Below, author's collection.)

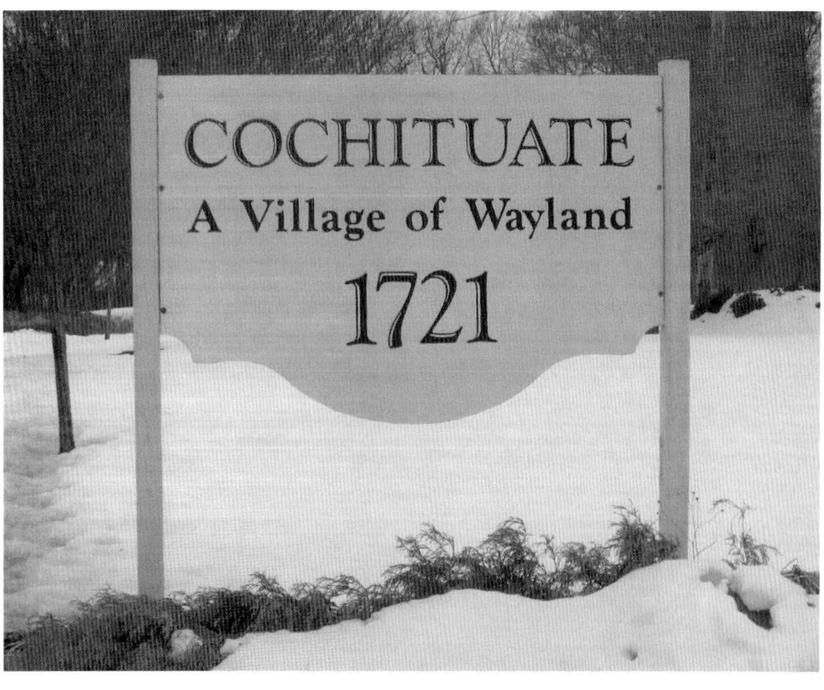

Anne P. Hale Jr. (1908–1968)

Anne Hale Jr. was a Radcliffe graduate who joined the Wayland school faculty in 1948. She was a popular teacher, member of the League of Women Voters, and congregant of First Parish Church. During the US Senate's McCarthy hearings in the 1950s, many citizens, including Hale, were accused of being Communists for their membership in the Communist party. After a series of public hearings, the school committee voted to dismiss her.

AMERICANS.....

DON'T PATRONIZE REDS!!!!

YOU CAN DRIVE THE REDS OUT OF TELEVISION, RADIO AND HOLLYWOOD.....

THIS TRACT WILL TELL YOU HOW.

WHY WE MUST DRIVE THEM OUT:

1) The REDS have made our Screen, Radio and TV Moscow's most effective Fifth Column in America . . . 2) The REDS of Hollywood and Broadway have always been the chief financial support of Communist propaganda in America . . . 3) OUR OWN FILMS, made by RED Producers, Directors, Writers and STARS, are being used by Moscow in ASIA, Africa, the Balkans and throughout Europe to create hatred of America . . . 4) RIGHT NOW films are being made to craftily glorify MARXISM, UNESCO and ONE-WORLDISM . . . **and via your TV Set** they are being piped into your Living Room—**and are poisoning the minds of your children under your very eyes ! ! !**

So REMEMBER — If you patronize a Film made by RED Producers, Writers, Stars and STUDIOS you are aiding and abetting COMMUNISM . . . every time you permit REDS to come into your Living Room VIA YOUR TV SET you are helping MOSCOW and the INTERNATIONALISTS to destroy America ! ! !

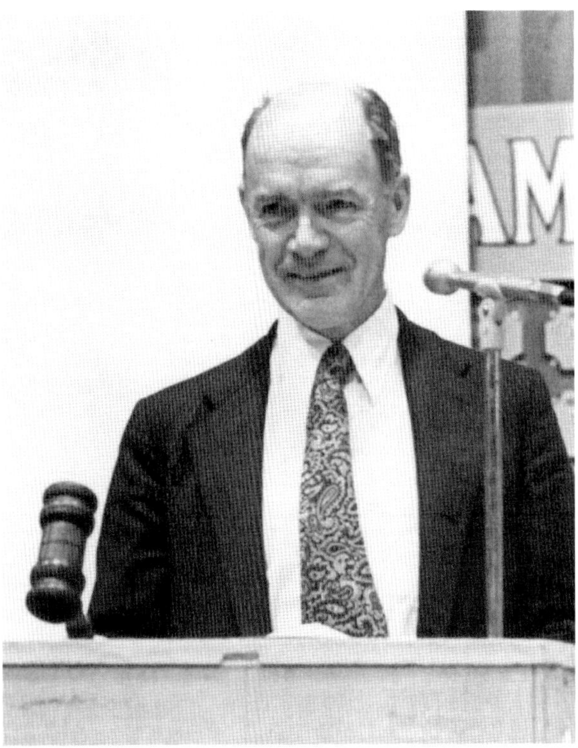

Roger Stokey (1921–1985)

Stokey is best known for his years as town moderator. As lead counselor, he was determined to give Anne Hale Jr. a fair trial during the 1950s school committee hearings on her membership in the Communist party. In the end, however, she was dismissed as a teacher. A founding member of SVT, Stokey did all of the organization's legal work in addition to scripting the bylaws, which remain virtually unchanged today.

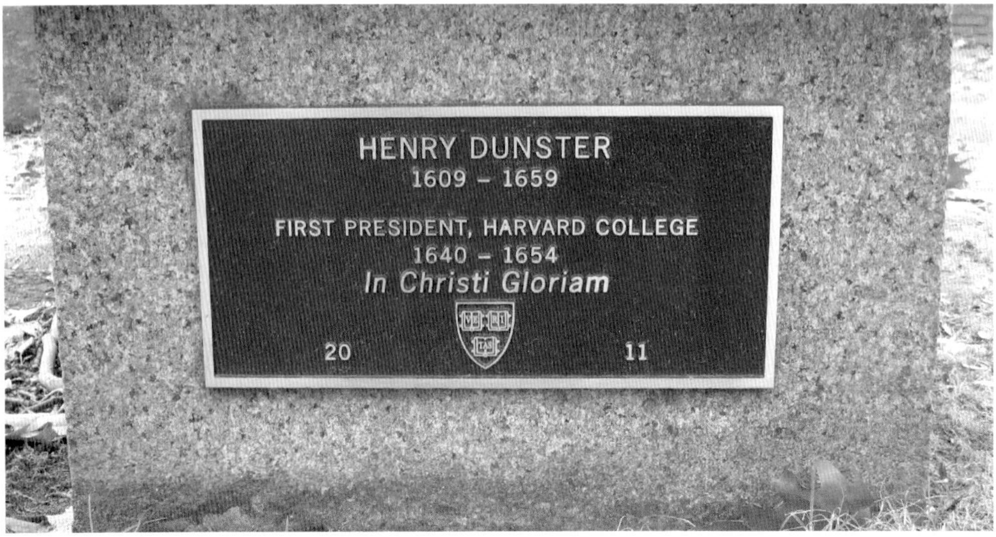

Henry Dunster (1609–1659)
Dunster was the first president of Harvard College, and the legislature granted him 600 acres of land adjacent to Sudbury Plantation's southern boundary. In 1641, he married the widow Elizabeth Glover, whose husband, Josse, had died on the voyage from England to Cambridge, Massachusetts. Josse had been granted 600 acres adjacent to Dunster's. Elizabeth died only two years after their marriage, leaving Dunster as guardian of her children and administrator of the Glover estate. (Author's collection.)

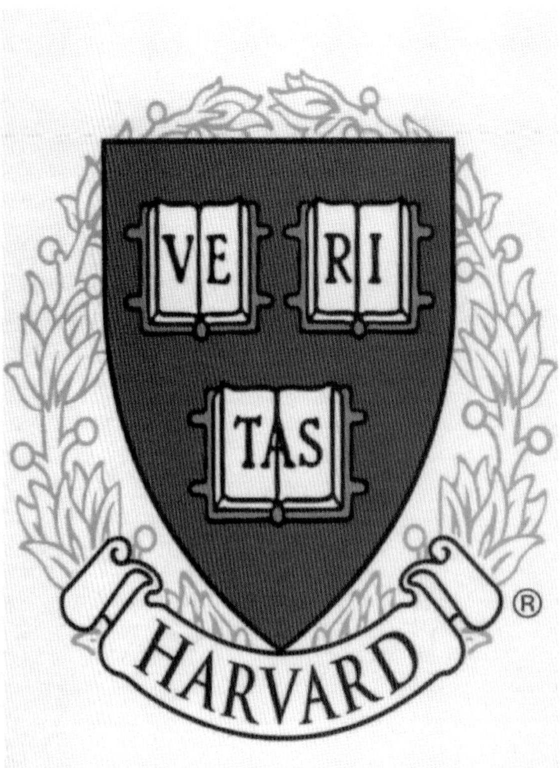

Herbert Pelham (1600–1673)
Pelham came to America with Gov. John Winthrop in 1635. He was the first treasurer of Harvard College and one of the commissioners of the United Colonies who arranged a treaty with the Narragansett and Niantic Indians in 1646. In exchange for his services to the colony, he was granted 400 acres of land adjacent to Sudbury Plantation (modern-day Pelham Island). Pelham's request to cast an absentee vote in town was turned down because he lived in Cambridge, Massachusetts. He returned to England and willed the land to his son Edward. (Author's collection.)

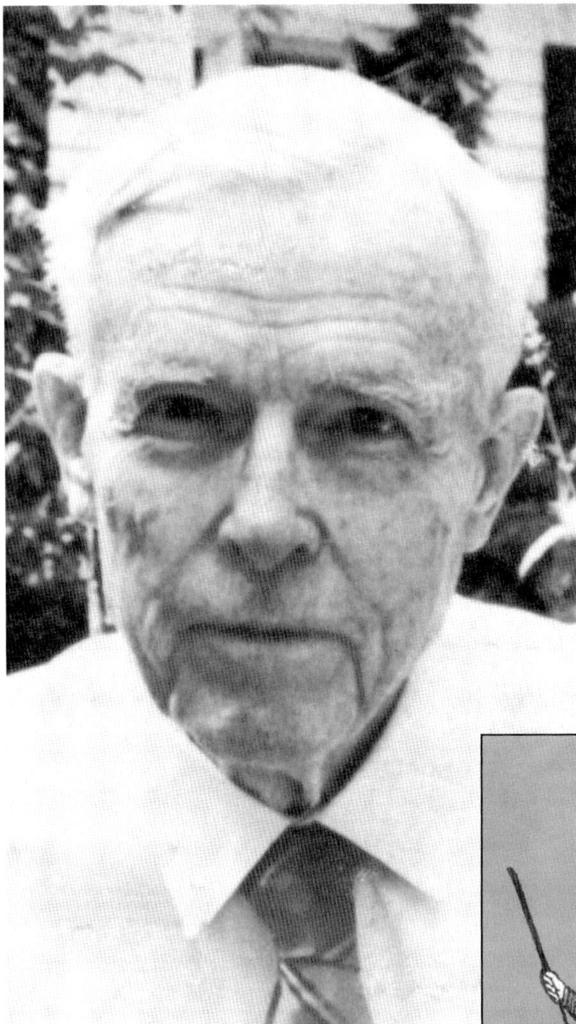

Howard Russell (1887–1980)
Russell came to town in the 1920s and campaigned to establish a planning board. By 1933, a five-member committee had completed an official town map, establishing uses for the town's 15.2 square miles. Russell continued his stewardship after World War II, when people began to flock to the suburbs. He served as town moderator for 20 years. His books, *A Long, Deep Furrow: Three Centuries of Farming in New England* and *Indian New England Before the Mayflower,* remain valuable resources for historians. (Below, Courtesy of University Press of New England.)

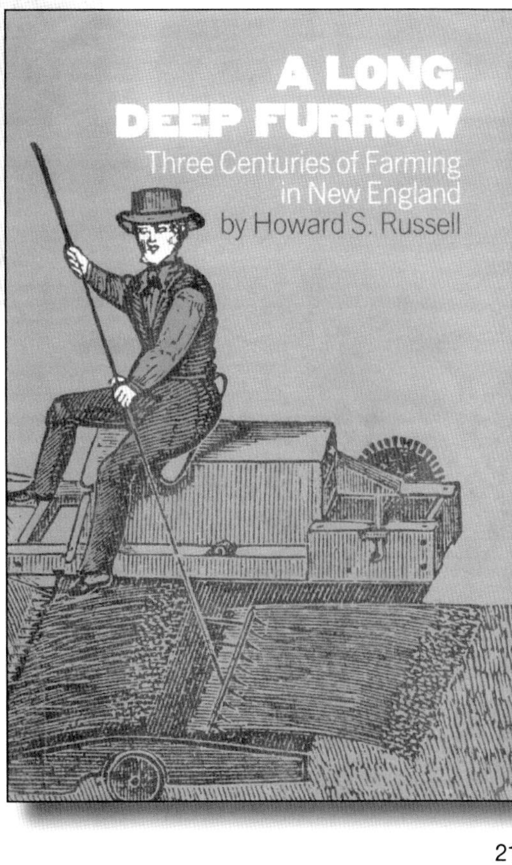

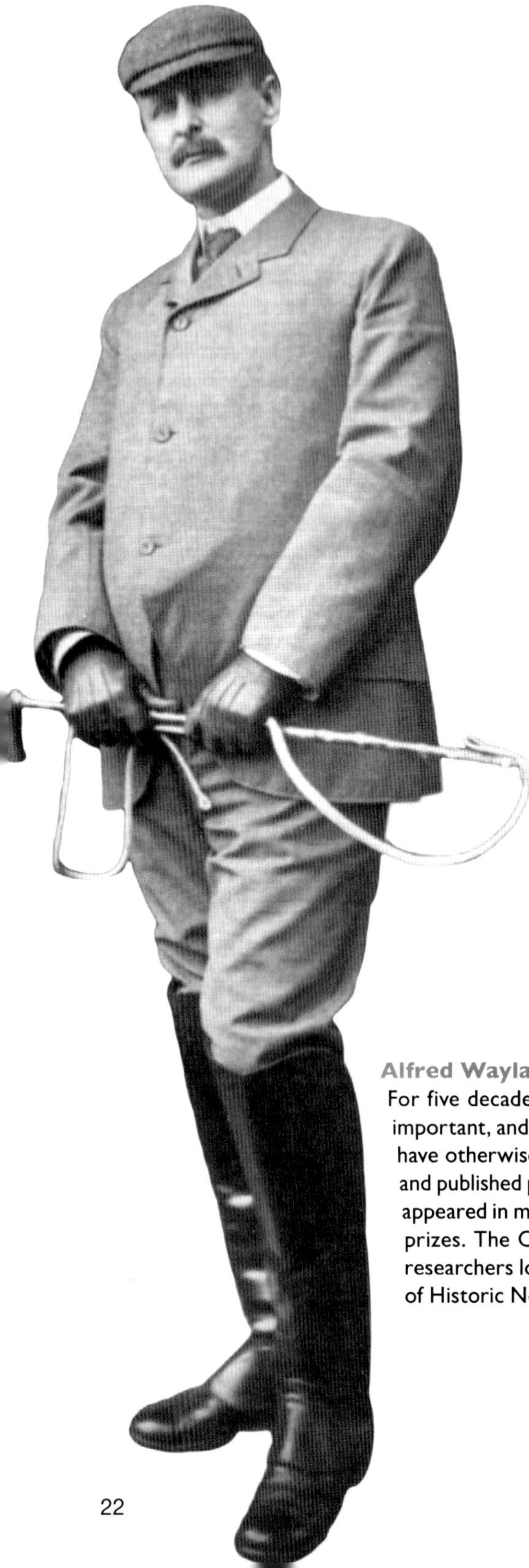

Alfred Wayland Cutting (1860–1935)
For five decades, Cutting kept his camera with him always, recording important, and not-so-important, events, people, and places that might have otherwise been lost in time. He was a history buff who lectured and published pamphlets and booklets on local history. His photographs appeared in major magazines, and he was the recipient of photography prizes. The Cutting Photography Collection is an essential tool for researchers locally and at Historic New England in Boston. (Courtesy of Historic New England.)

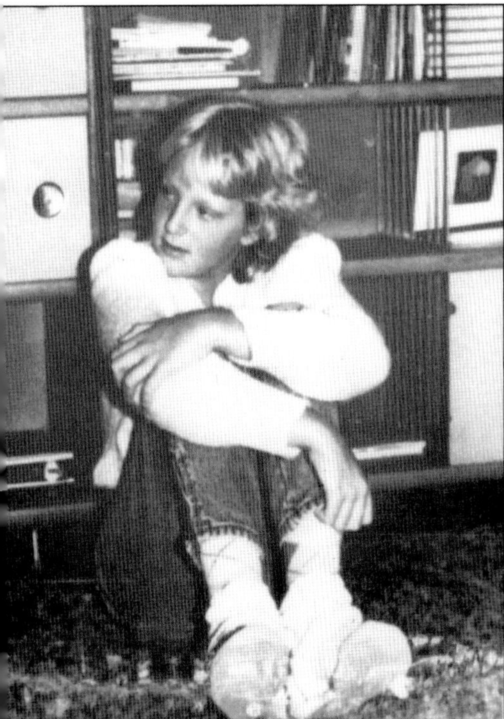

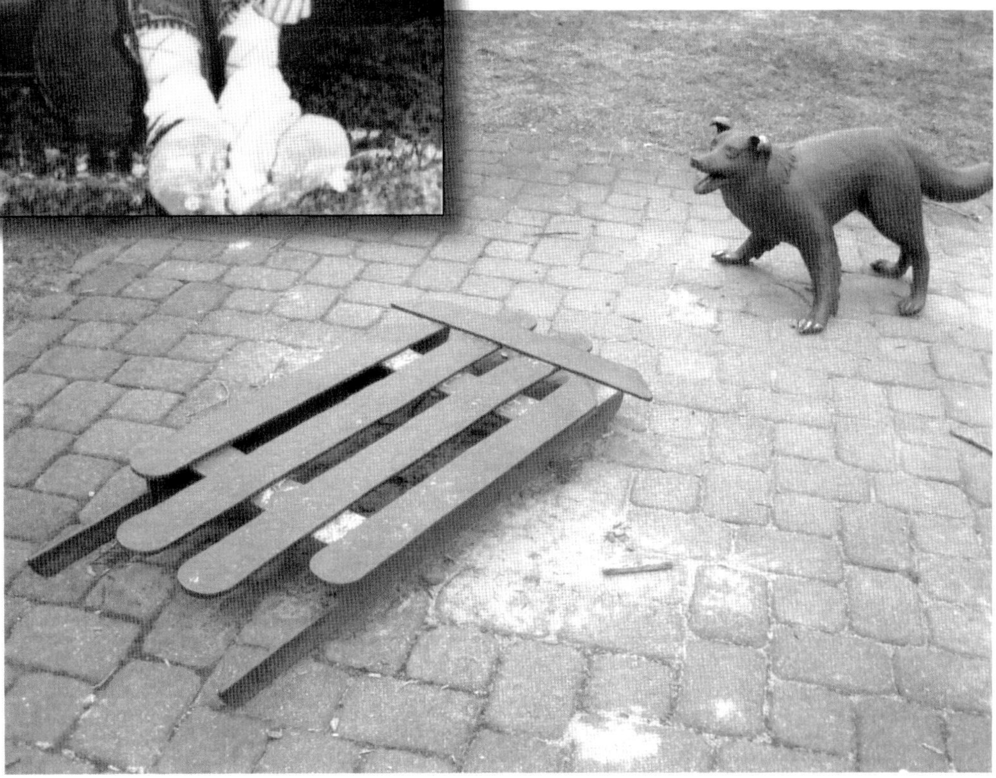

Sarah Pryor (1976–1998?)

Sarah disappeared while walking along a main road in Wayland in 1985. Many people continued to search for her for over two years. Her remains were found less than three miles from home, 12 years later. It is said that she became an emblem for parents' fears and a tool for a children's safety movement. Sarah's rescue efforts spawned the Search and Rescue Association, a nonprofit organization made up of volunteers throughout New England. Artist Nancy Schon created a bronze statue of Sarah's sled and her dog, Katie, for the Hannah Williams playground. The Middlesex Courthouse created Sarah's Place, a waiting area on the eighth floor for families of victims. (Bottom, author's collection.)

Willis Ryder (1919–1994)
Bill Ryder was one of the original founders of the SVT and an early advocate of land preservation. He was a skilled fisherman and hunter of game animals. His expertise on the woodcock made him a popular evening guide to witness their dramatic mating performances. He was a World War II veteran, served as a town assessor, and had a real estate office in the two-room Mellen law office on the town green.

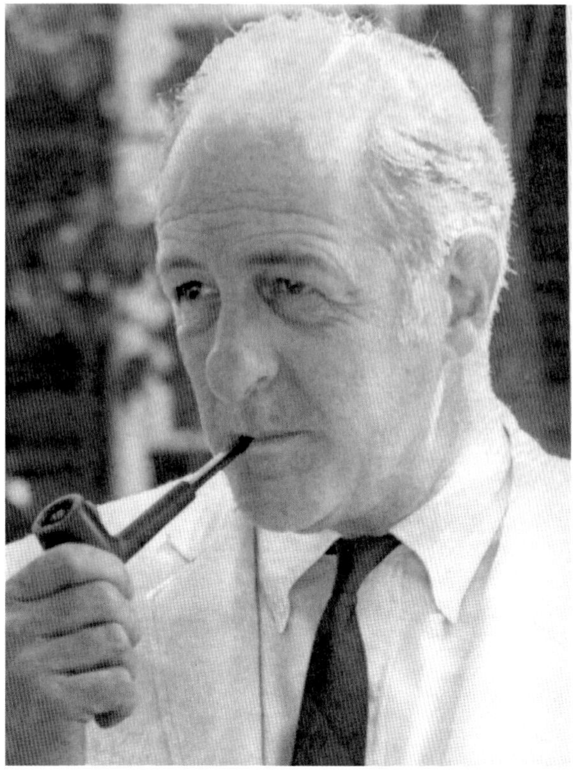

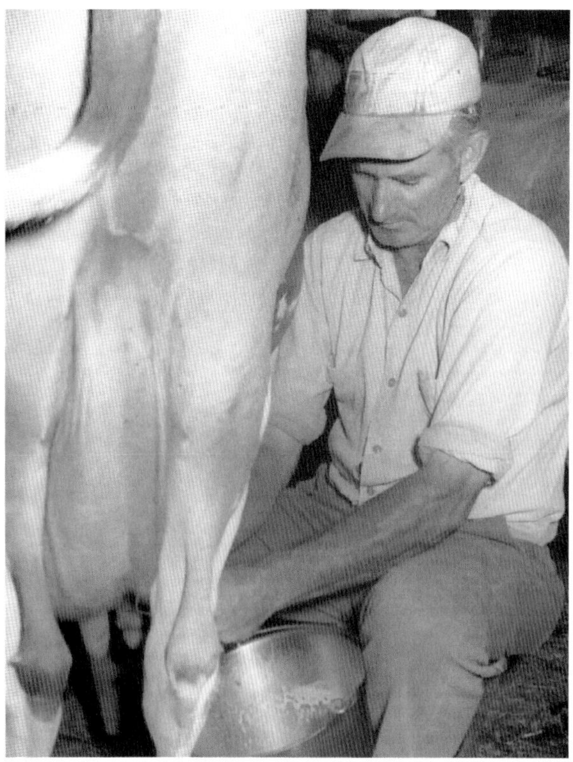

Walter Harrington (1913–1994)
Walter and his wife, Dorothy, maintained a herd of cows on their farm, Waldot, at Plain and Millbrook Roads until the late 1960s. Together they milked up to 85 cows daily, shipping their milk to Clarke's Dairy in Weston, Massachusetts, for processing and distribution. After the cows were gone, they raised hens and chickens. They adopted baby chicks hatched from eggs incubated in local classrooms, and let them roam free on their farm. (Courtesy of Clifford Wedlock.)

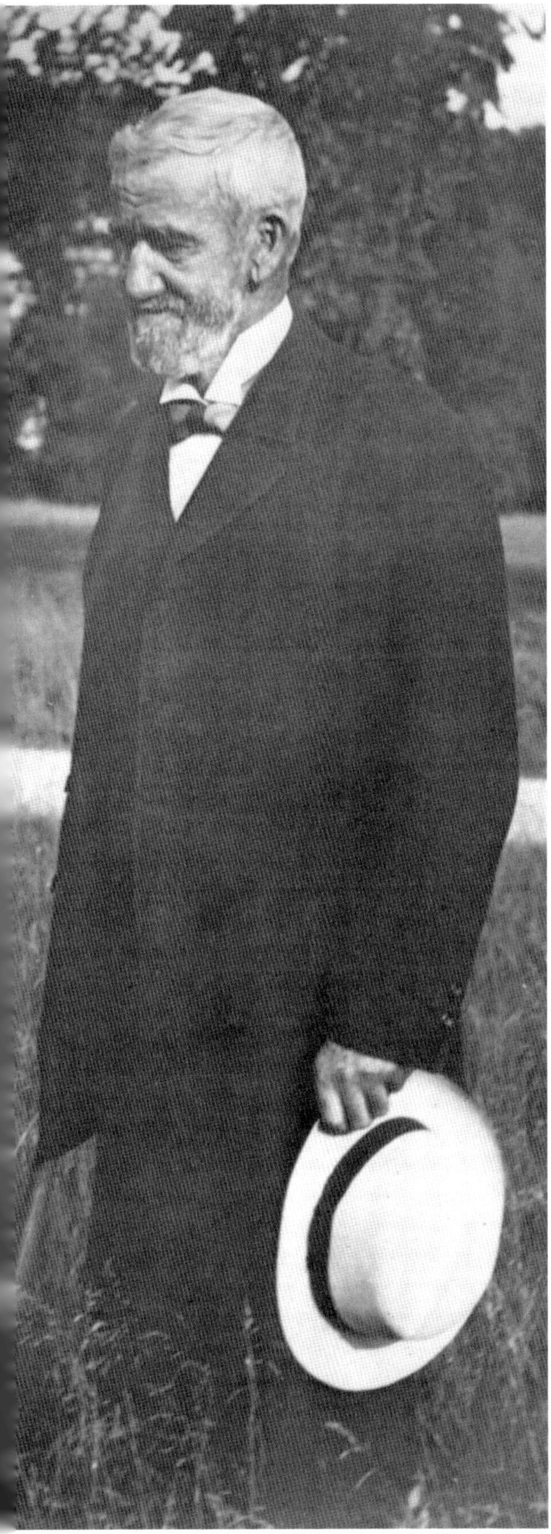

Jonathan Parmenter (1831–1921)

Jonathan and his brother Henry lived according to the traditions of New England farmers in a modest farmhouse on 160 acres of land not far from Wayland center. In 1883, they owned 67 head of cattle, the largest herd in town. Each spring, they drove the herd to Troy, New Hampshire, to graze. In fall, the plump herd was driven back to Wayland, with some sold along the way. The brothers would sell the rest of the cattle at the Brighton stockyards, then deposit the receipts with their friend, Willard Bullard, president of the First National Bank of Cambridge. Bullard summered in Wayland, living in the handsomely remodeled home he christened Kirkside, still standing next to First Parish Church. It was Bullard who suggested, in the mid-1880s, that the brothers invest in Wellington-Sears Company, which was launching mills in the South. Trusting their friend, they invested $10,000. When Henry died in 1907, Jonathan became sole heir to his brother's estate. Over the next 10 years, Jonathan grew concerned about what to do with all his money. He sought advice from Bullard's successor after Bullard died, and decided to dispose of his fortune for the benefit of Wayland and humanity in general. Before making public bequests, he willed sums of money to nine cousins and their children, to various Wayland men and women because of friendship or loyal service, and to the widow of Willard Bullard. To the town, he bequeathed $7,000 to First Parish Church, the income to be used for church expenses; $5,000 for upkeep of the Parmenter family cemetery and other cemeteries; $10,000 to be used by the library; $5,000 for needy Wayland students going to Radcliffe, in memory of his mother and sister; and $200,000 in securities to be held in trust, with the income used for scholarships for Harvard students. For the installation of a water supply system for the town, he left $225,000 to be held and expended by the Harvard Trust Company, originally the First National Bank, and $200,000 for a hospital, now Parmenter Visiting Nurse Association and Community Care Inc. To his neighbors, nothing seemed remarkable about J.M. Parmenter until they learned that his will had been filed for probate, listing the value of his estate at $1.5 million. Today, this amount would be close to $25 million.

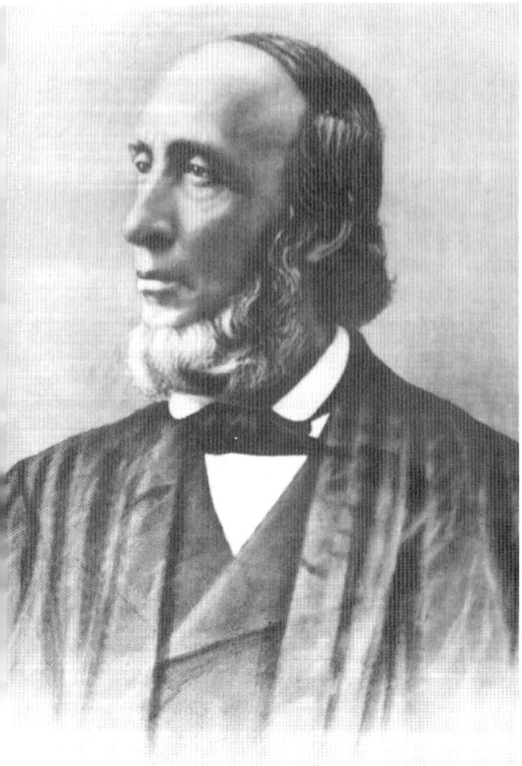

Reverend Edmund Hamilton Sears (1820–1876)

Reverend Sears, a graduate of Harvard Divinity School, served as minister of First Parish Church in Wayland for 17 years. A preacher, poet, and strict abolitionist, he was deeply religious. In 1849, at the request of a friend, he wrote the poem "It Came Upon a Midnight Clear." It was first sung at a First Parish Sunday school celebration that same year and later published in the Boston *Christian Register*. Generations continue to enjoy the song during the Christmas holidays.

Samuel Parris (1653–1720)

After the Salem Witch Trials, Parris was asked to leave his Salem parish for preaching against witches. His daughter had created hysteria in the town after their slave Tituba told stories of sorcery, conjuring, and the appearance of specters. His first wife, Elizabeth, later died in Salem. The rest of the family eventually settled in Sudbury after Samuel married Dorothy Noyes. They moved into the original 1690s Noyes homestead (pictured), where Parris taught school part time. Today, it is the oldest private home in town.

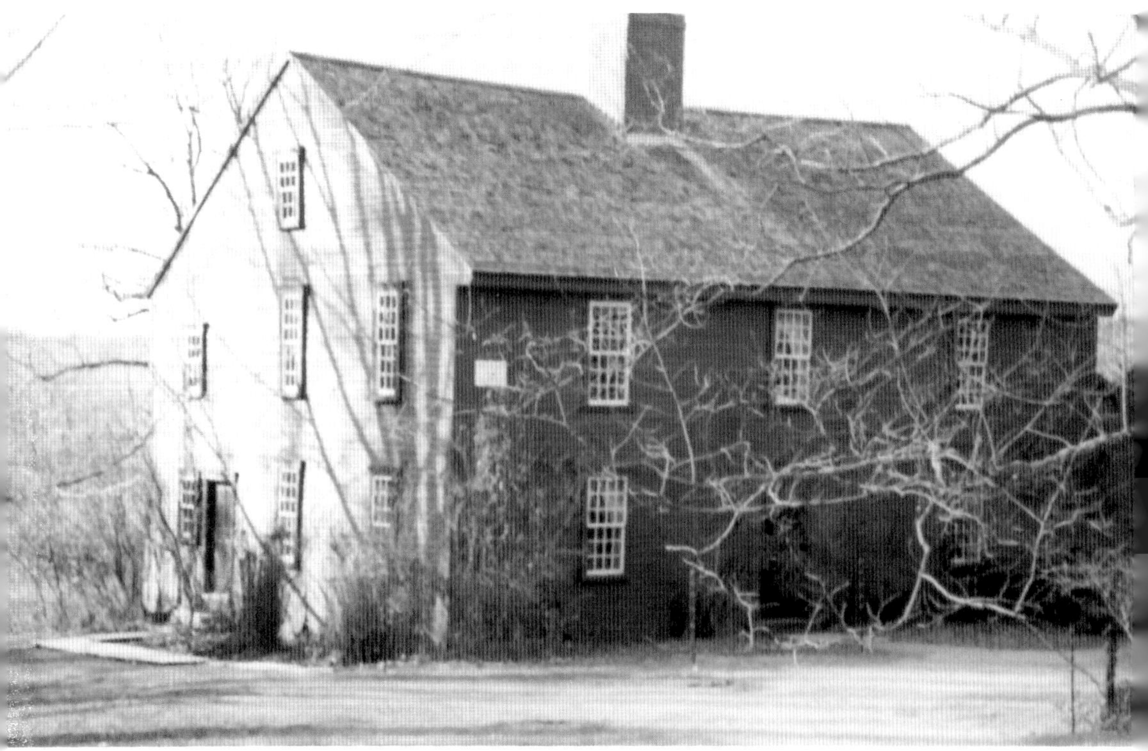

Mabel Draper (1887–1970)

Mabel Draper, first curator of the Wayland Historical Society, oversaw restoration of the Grout-Heard House after Raytheon Company donated it to the town in 1955. She arranged to have Charles Malcolm Campbell, a friend, move into the house and serve as the society's first resident custodian. As curator, she spent almost a decade acquiring many of the artifacts, records, and documents preserved today. She was a founder of the Wayland Junior Town House and a much-loved teacher who taught for 32 years at the Center School. Draper continued to uphold the family legacy of service to the town.

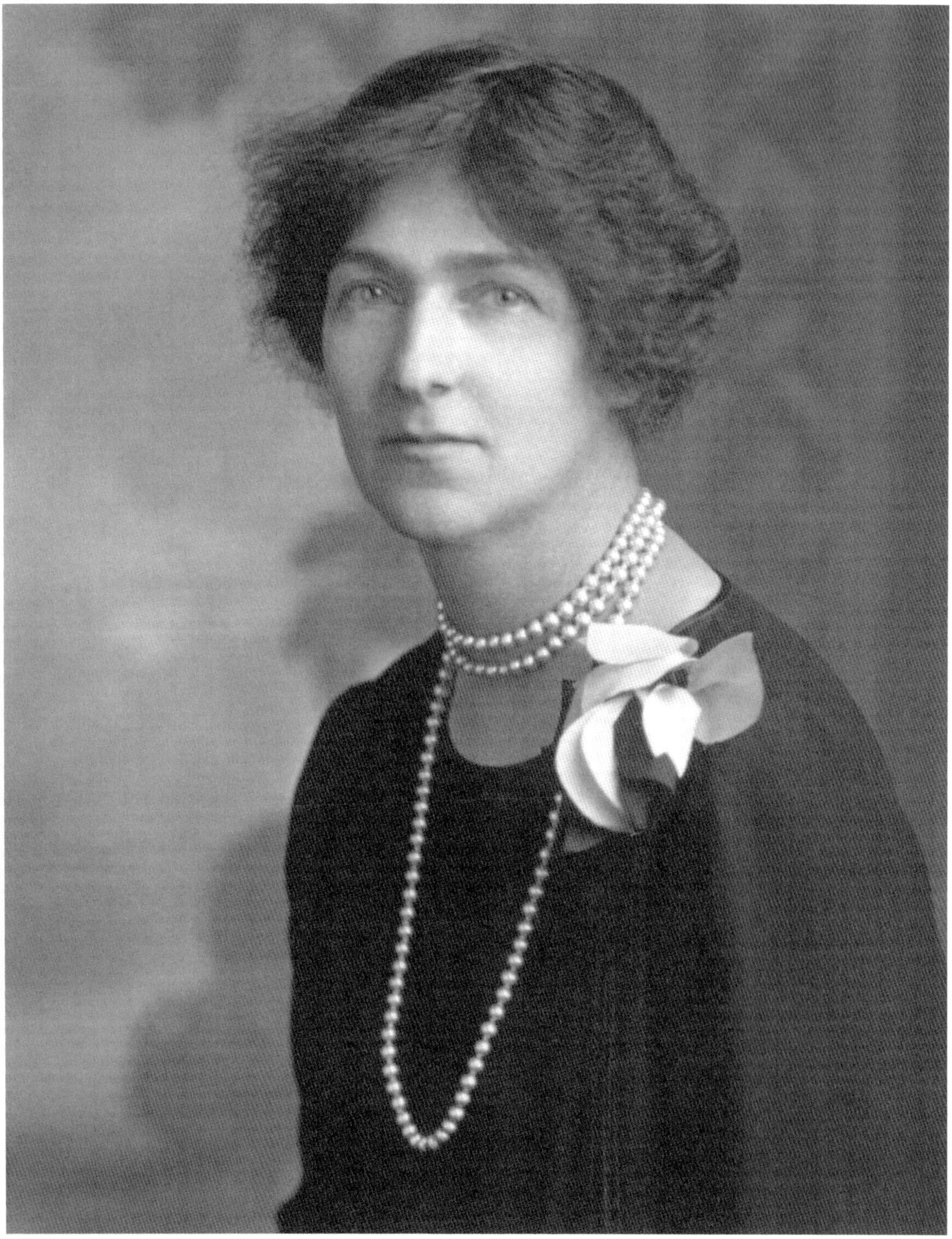

Helen Fitch Emery (1912–2003)

After moving to Wayland in 1946, Helen Fitch Emery chose to stay home with her two sons and volunteer her talents, declining an invitation to teach economics at Wellesley College. It was a fortunate decision for Wayland. She was a founding member of the Wayland Historical Commission and wrote *The Puritan Village Evolves*, the definitive history of Wayland, which was published in 1981. Her book continues to serve as a major resource for residents and officials. (Below, courtesy of Town of Wayland.)

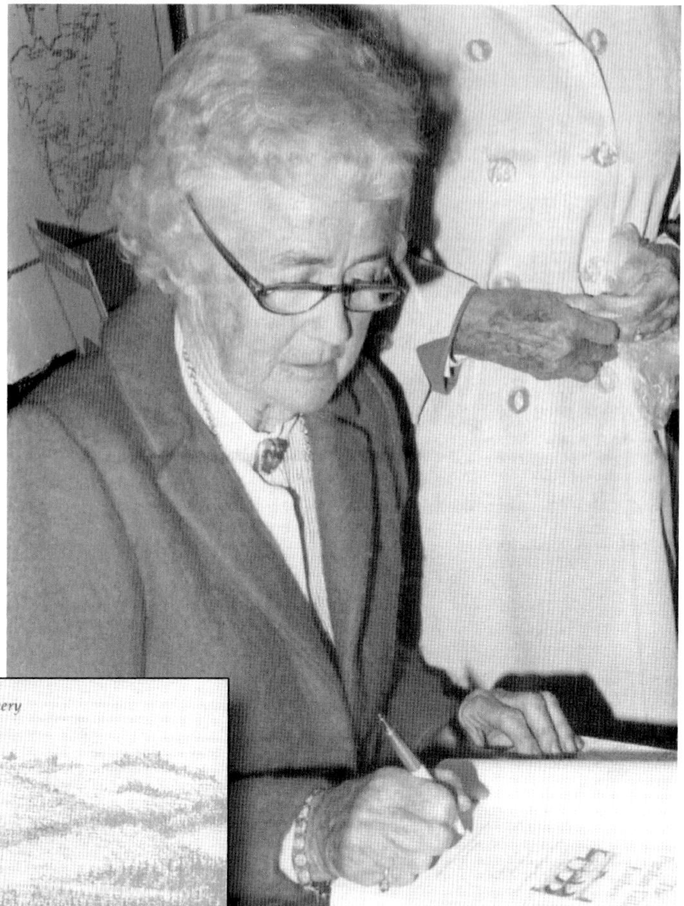

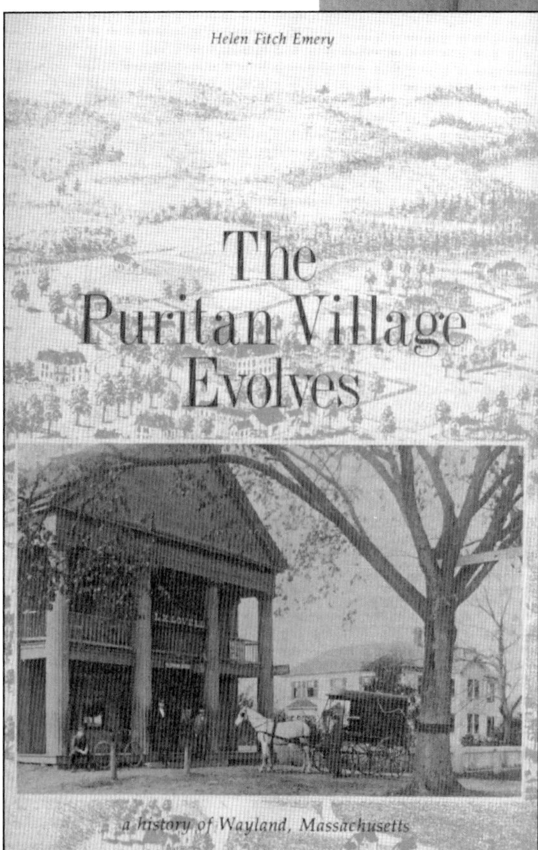

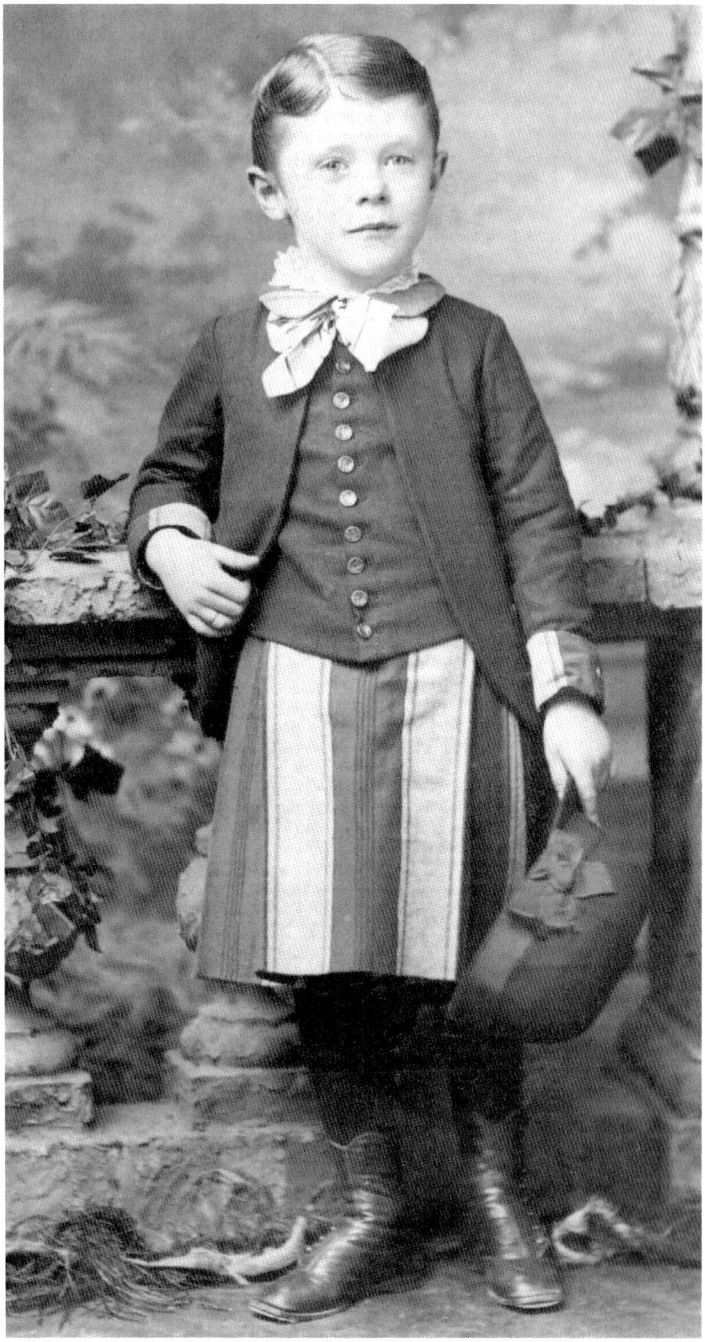

Wallace Draper Folsom (1884–1954)
A lifelong resident of Wayland, Wallace Draper Folsom worked at a publishing house in Boston and was known as an excellent penman. He enjoyed photographing daily life in Wayland and made it a point to chronicle the installation of the 1926–1928 Water Department. Later, he captured on film much of the March 1936 flood that inundated the town. Folsom maintained membership in First Parish Church and was an officer of the Odd Fellows Club. The Wayland Historical Society houses over 750 of his negatives.

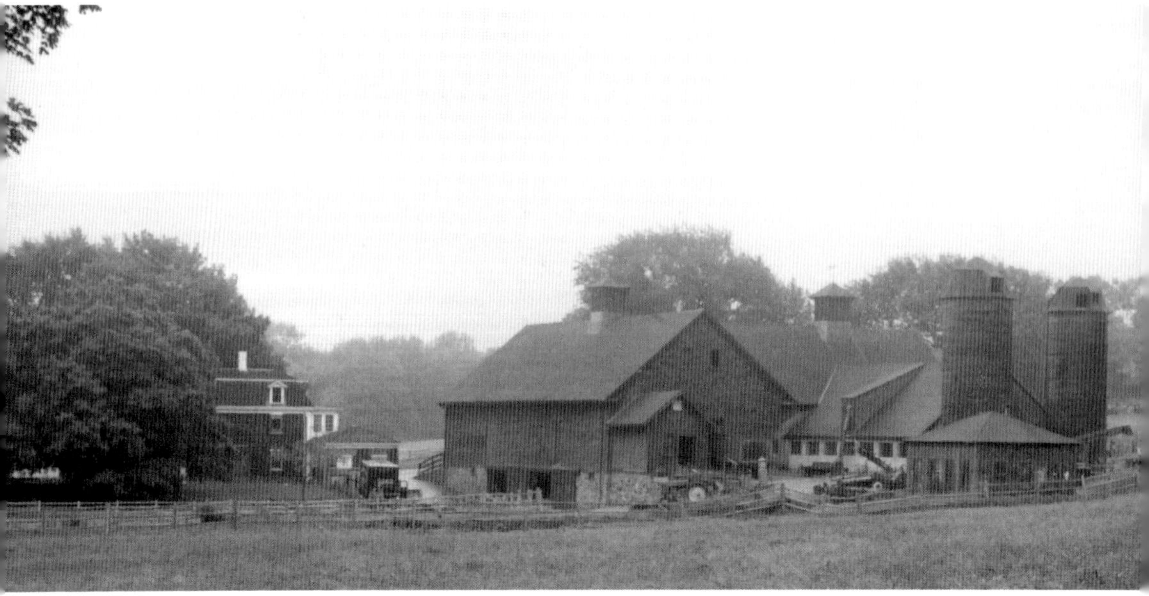

William Powell Perkins (1807–1891)

In 1868, Perkins bought Mainstone Farm in Wayland (pictured) for $10,000, intending to develop it. After a financial disaster in 1872, he had to sell his Brookline estate and move to Wayland. He established the first Guernsey herd in Massachusetts, the second in the United States, when he purchased four Guernsey cows and one bull from the Isle of Jersey. He liked the rich golden color of the cream and butter of these cows. A confirmed bachelor, Perkins left the farm in trust to his many nieces and nephews, whose descendants continue to maintain Guernsey cows on the land. Mainstone Farm is the last of Wayland's large farms remaining in private hands.

James Sumner Draper (1811–1896) (OPPOSITE)

James Sumner Draper dedicated his life to the community, eager to carry on his father, Deacon Draper's, long tradition of public service. James Sumner was a teacher, farmer, cartographer, amateur poet, and town librarian from 1865 to 1885. He worked tirelessly to improve local schools, and helped to establish rail service from Boston to Hudson. The money he raised for the town's first library became a lasting legacy. When the Rev. Francis Wayland offered to donate $500 for the establishment of a free library, provided townsfolk donate an equal amount, Draper took on the task of raising the money. He collected donations between $5 and $20, and in the end, the gift was matched with a small amount in excess. His father and his uncle Ira Draper each gave $500 to the library in 1863. When the town needed a new town hall, James Sumner joined the committee that chose the site where the Grout-Heard House was located. The house was then moved up to Old Sudbury Road, and a Gothic-style town hall was built on the land. For the 1878 dedication of the new town hall, he summarized town history in a 79-page booklet. His map, *A Plan of the Town of Wayland in 1775*, was drawn presumably in time for the 1875 Centennial celebration of the beginning of the American Revolution. It is a reconstruction of how he believed the town appeared based on his research. The map remains a valuable tool for researchers studying old homes and land ownership. Equally important is the memorial volume he prepared of the history of the town's service in the Civil War, which includes letters, diaries, and records of the experiences of Wayland's servicemen. Portraits of James Sumner and his wife, Emilene A. Reeves Draper, hang in the Wayland Historical Society's Draper Room.

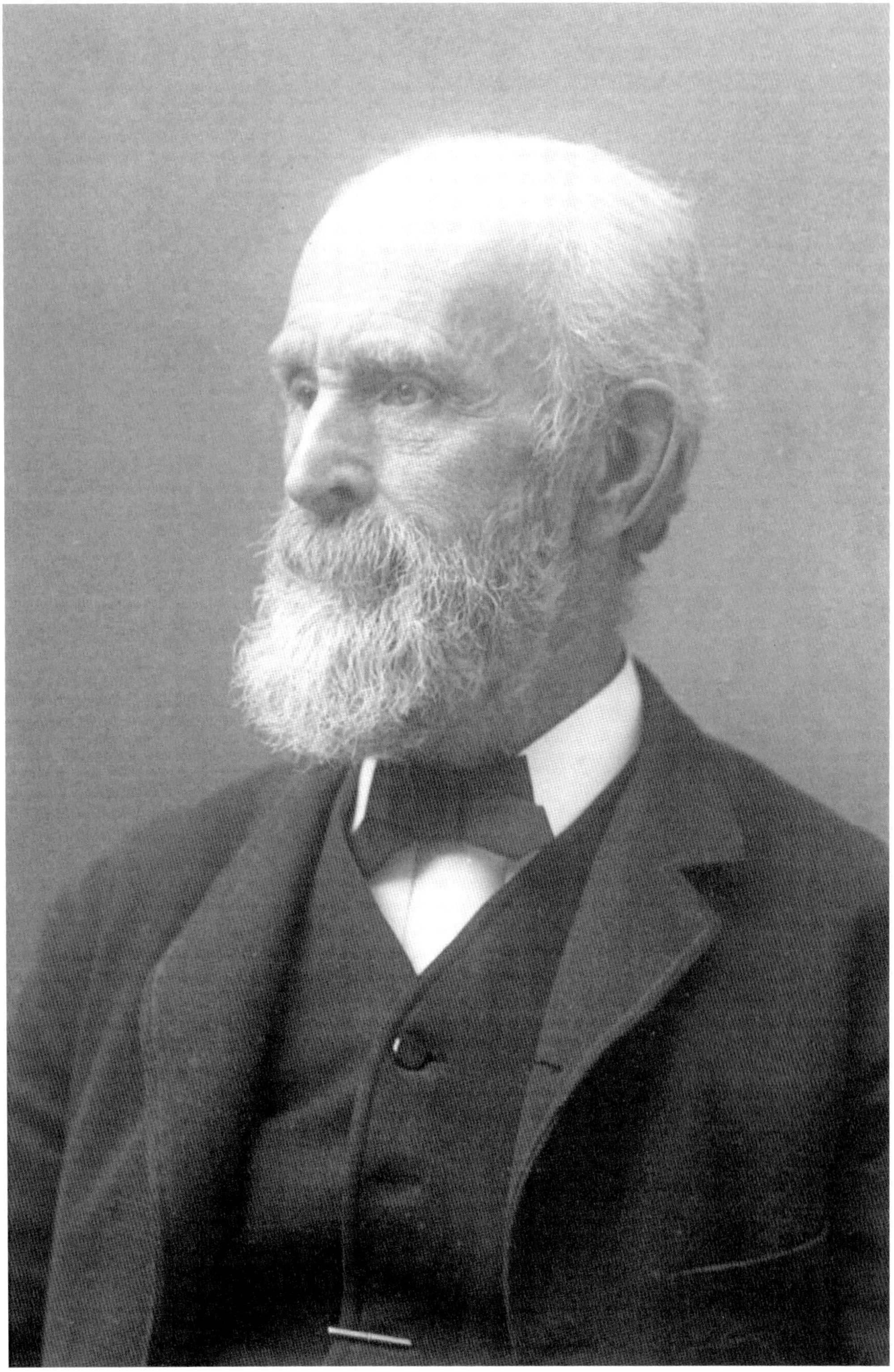

Francis Shaw (1854–1935)

Shaw, a wealthy Bostonian, had a longtime interest in farming. He owned a large farm in New Braintree in western Worcester County before purchasing land closer to Boston. Slowly, he acquired land in Wayland and had assembled a large estate at the junction of Cochituate Road and Old Connecticut Path by 1892. Employing the architectural firm of Little and Browne, Shaw had a 22-room mansion built on top of the hill. Design features were taken from the James Barrell Mansion in Charlestown, Massachusetts, and flagstones were taken from the old state house in Boston. Shaw called his estate Five Paths, and he housed farm workers and gardeners on the property. He continued to maintain a home in Boston and property in Maine while a resident and voter in Wayland, paying taxes for 849 acres of land. In 1896, Shaw offered to contribute $3,000 to build a new Center School in town, and in 1920, he joined a group of private citizens interested in improving town center. Together, they purchased the long-neglected Pequod Inn, had it torn down, and donated the land to the town. He and his friend Edmund Sears also bought and tore down other unsightly buildings in the town center, again donating the land to the town. After Shaw died, his heirs decided to sell the estate, and in 1942, a proposed subdivision plan with 10,000-square-foot lots, a community of stores, a motion-picture house, and other facilities came to the attention of the planning board. A private group of Wayland citizens, concerned that loss of the estate would adversely affect the town, formed a real estate company and purchased all but a small piece of the land that had already been sold. Today, this area includes Woodridge and Happy Hollow. The original Shaw estate is pictured here.

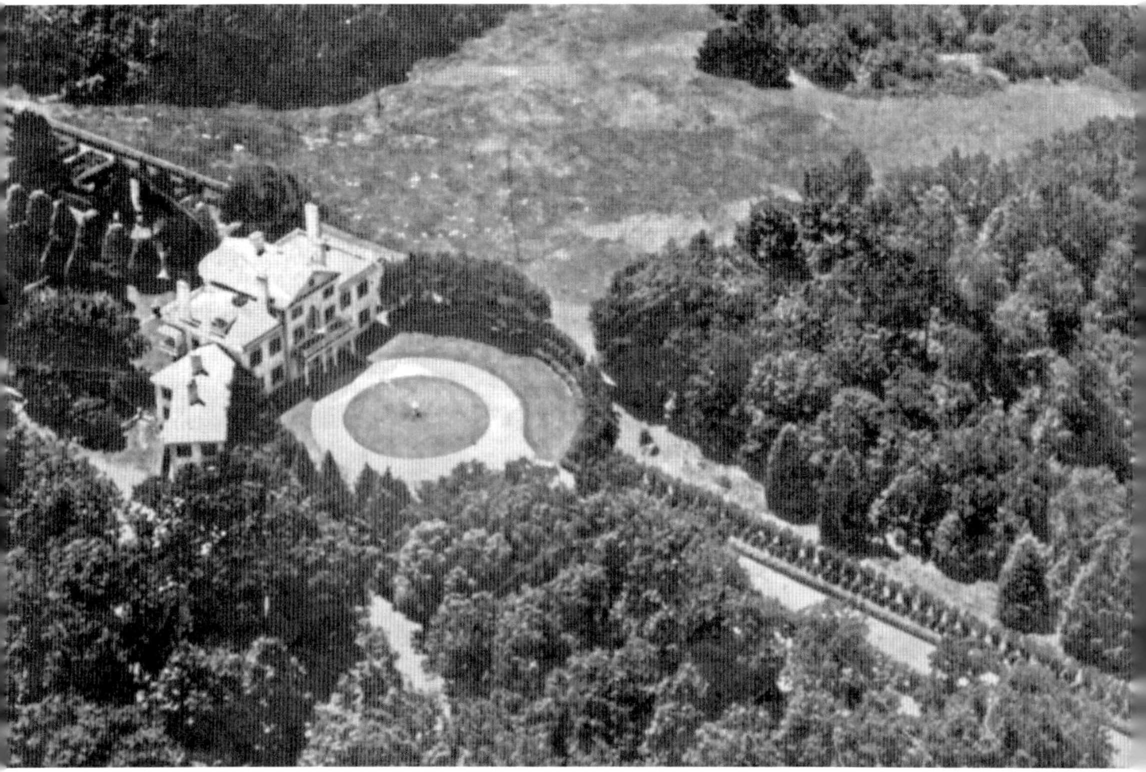

CHAPTER TWO

Artists and Entertainers

O great creator of being grant us one more hour to perform our art and perfect our lives.

—James Morrison

For a small town, Wayland has produced more than its share of artists and entertainers. As early as the 1850s, the writer Lydia Maria Child was penning papers and protests, speaking out against slavery and in support of American Indians and a woman's right to vote. She left behind numerous books on a variety of subjects. Other authors such as Alfred S. Hudson and Sumner Chilton Powell chronicled the town's history in volumes that remain valuable resources. Powell won a Pulitzer Prize for his book *Puritan Village: The Formation of a New England Town*, and more recently, David Hackett Fischer won a Pulitzer for his book *Washington's Crossing*. Future generations may have caught the entertainment bug from Beatrice Herford, who built a miniature model of a real theater in her backyard in 1904. She entertained friends by private invitation in her little theater for almost two decades. Later, Herford gave a group of amateur players, the Vokes Players, permission to use the theater. It has been gently remodeled, and the tradition of live theater has continued for almost seven decades.

Musical traditions continue throughout town for both adults and children. Alan Barker founded the Little Theater Series 50 years ago, which features a wide variety of musicians and dancers who perform free to the public. Maddie Sifantus organized a group of retired men and women to sing and dance to lift spirits and promote good health. After three decades, the group is still performing and conducts more than 60 concerts a year at senior centers, schools, and public events. Joanne Hammil established a children's choral program in town, the Choral Connection, which ran for 30 years. She has produced award-winning records of her original children's and adult songs.

The many young men and women who have graduated from Wayland High School and become professional writers and entertainers show the strong commitment to the arts by Wayland educators. Students who graduated during the 1980s continue to achieve success: Gerard Cosloy co-owns a record label, Juliet Lambert Pratt performs on and off Broadway, and Alex Taub and Gregg Kavet write and produce for television and the movies. In the decades since, Eric Poydar has produced three original movies, and Taylor Schilling has starred in a number of popular television series, including the Netflix series *Orange Is the New Black*.

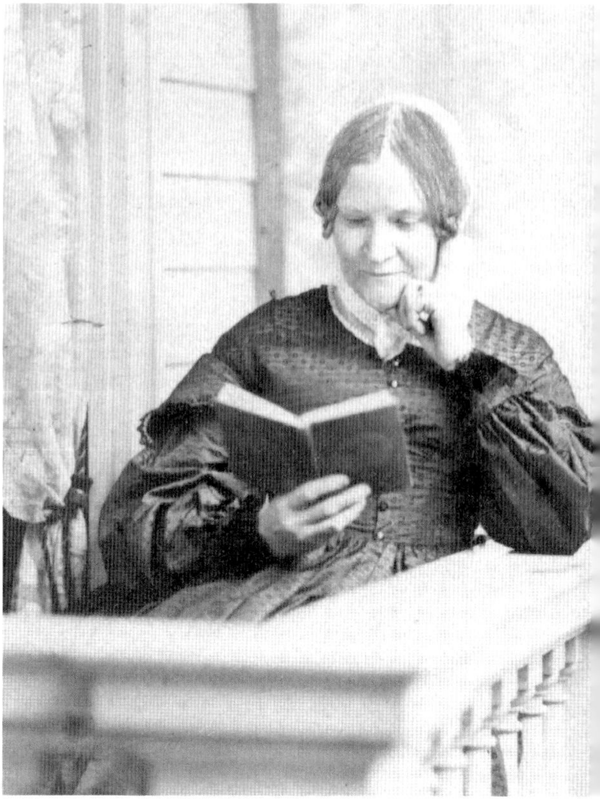

Lydia Maria Child (1802–1880)
Lydia Maria Child wrote novels, cookbooks, and books of poetry. She spent her life crusading against slavery and supporting the rights of American Indians and a woman's right to vote. She came to town in 1853 to care for her elderly father, calling Wayland "this little drowsy village." Then she fell in love with the village and its people, spending most of her time in Wayland. She is often remembered for her poem, "Over the River and through the Woods," which has been a popular song for generations. Pictured below is the Child family homestead, which is still standing.

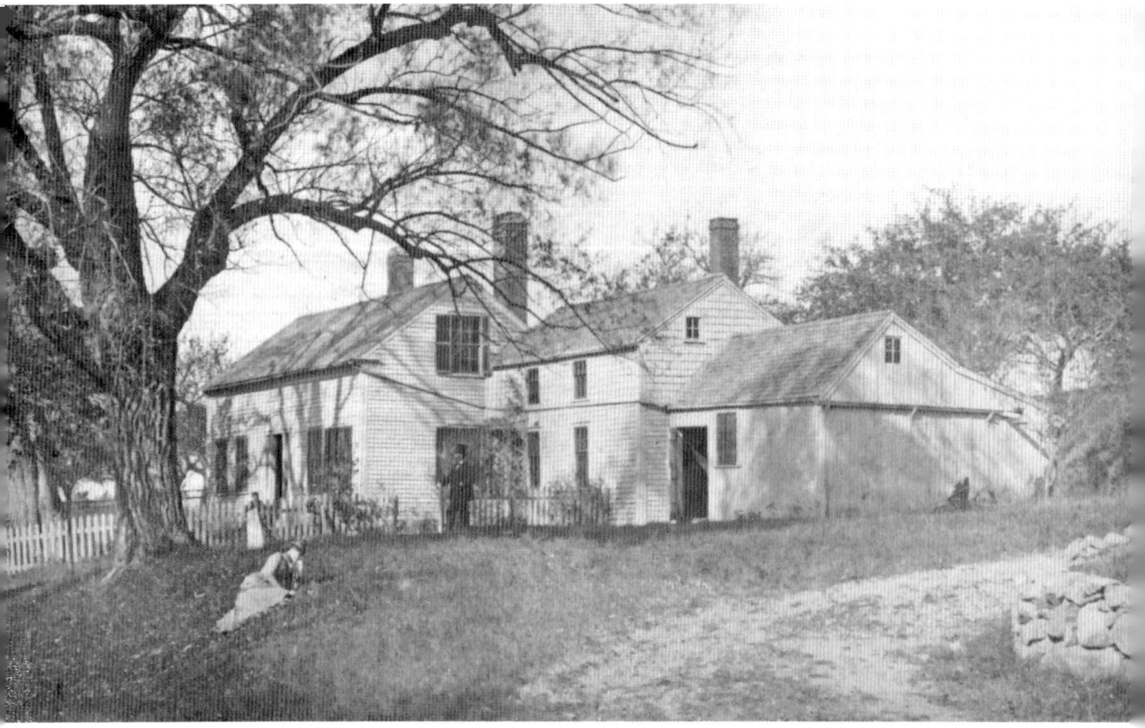

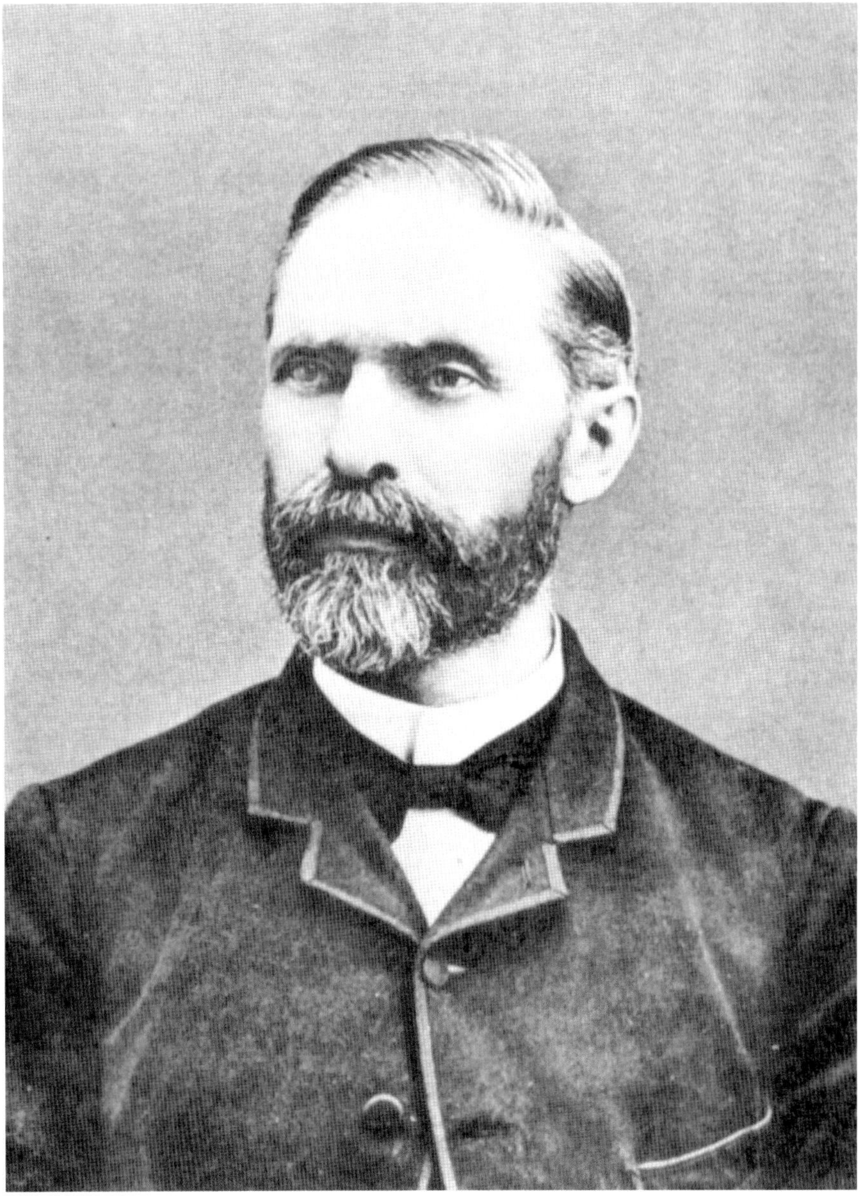

Alfred Sereno Hudson (1839–1907)
Hudson, a Protestant minister, was commissioned by the town of Sudbury to write the annals or general history of Sudbury—the age of the town, its importance and prominence in the past, and the fullness of its records. The town required that the book be readable by a wide audience. Hudson had been raised in the town and was eager to comply. Blaine E. Taylor, in his introduction to *The History of Sudbury Massachusetts, 1638–1889,* says, "He had a job to do and wrote on page by page without creativity or an awareness of great themes. Yet this is the excitement of the book. The reader is forced to be his own detective and this is raw material . . . At the same time the book has the flavor of authenticity and cannot be ignored." While some debated whether or not Hudson ever reached a wide audience, many agree it remains the primary source of Sudbury and Wayland history during that period, as does his second book, *The Annals of Sudbury, Wayland, and Maynard, Middlesex County, Massachusetts*, published two years later.

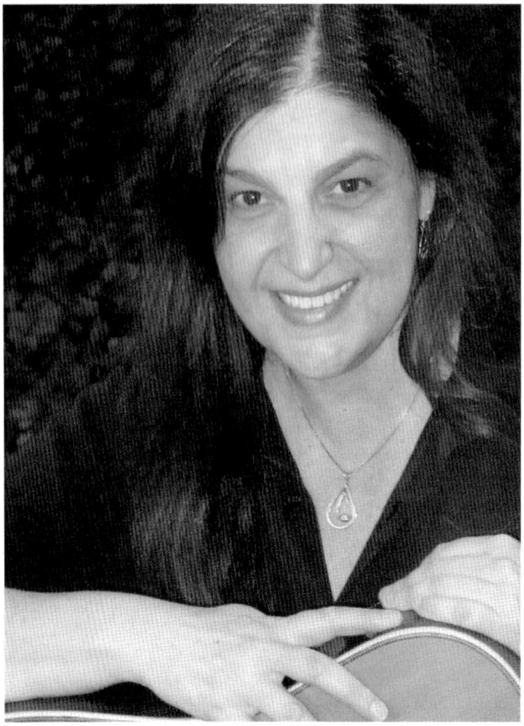

Joanne Hammil
Hammil, a nationally renowned composer, performer, choral director, and teacher, created a children's choral program in Wayland, the Choral Connection, which she ran for 30 years. She performed with Pete Seeger, was president of the Children's Music Network, won the prestigious Magic Penny Award in 2011, and produced award-winning recordings of her original children's and adult songs. She directs the Greater Boston Intergenerational Chorus and presents at many national conferences and music institutions. (Courtesy of Joanne Hammil.)

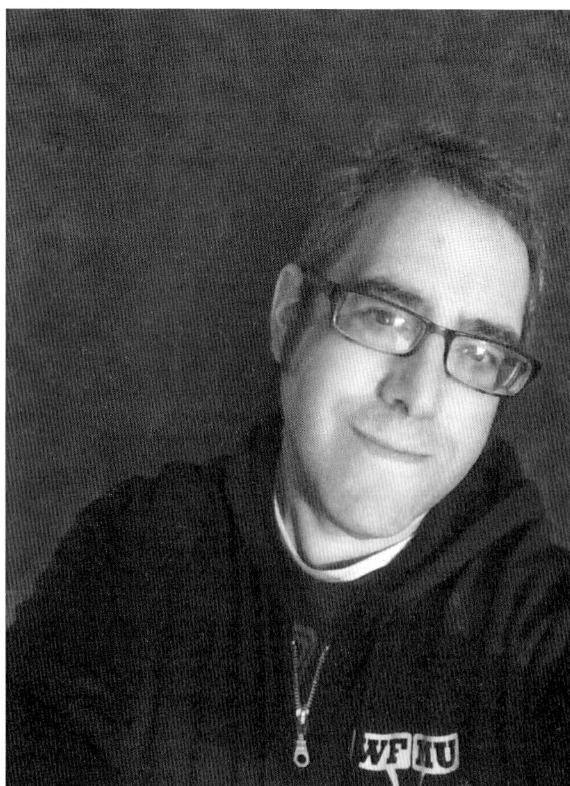

Gerard Cosloy
Growing up in Wayland, Cosloy began his music career before going to college. At age 15, he began writing and publishing *Conflict* and writing reviews for the *Village Voice*. He released independent records, disc jockeyed, booked shows, and hosted a college radio station. At 19, he was managing Homestead Records in New York, and in the early 1980s, he joined Chris Lombardi as partner in Matador Records. In the alternative-rock world, Matador has been a huge success. (Courtesy of Gene and Lois Cosloy.)

Marilyn Wallin

Marilyn Wallin has made 200 violins, violas, and cellos over the past 30 years for prestigious organizations such as the New York Philharmonic, Juilliard School, Boston Symphony Orchestra, New England Conservatory, Kennedy Center Opera Orchestra, Peabody Conservatory, Cleveland Institute of Music, and many other learning and performing institutions. She taught dozens of violin-making apprentices at the North Bennet Street School in Boston. In international violin-making competitions, she has been awarded three medals and eight Certificates of Excellence for Craftsmanship and Tone. She is an active participant in the Oberlin violin-making workshops. Her studios were both at home and at Emerson Umbrella in Concord. She credits John, Hollie, and Julia Emery for their support. (Both, courtesy of Pierre Chiha.)

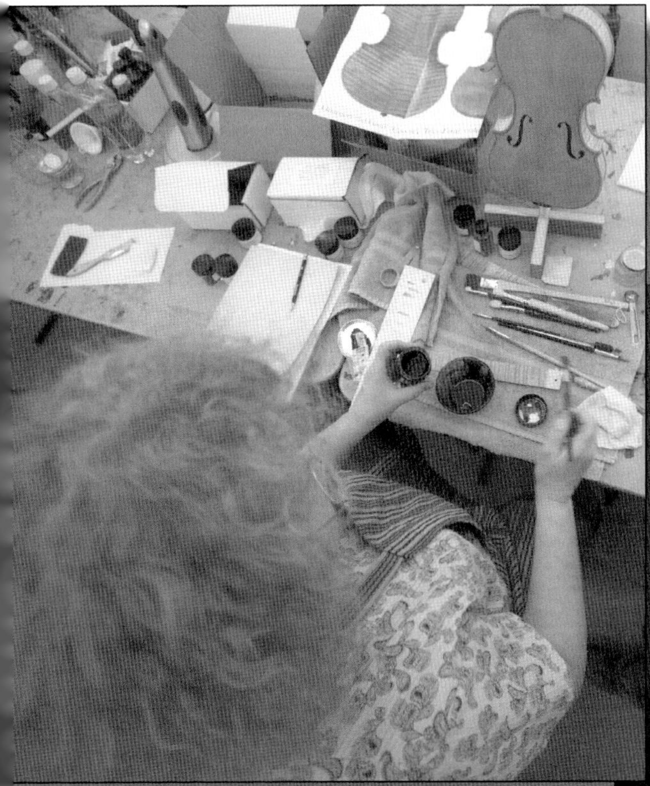

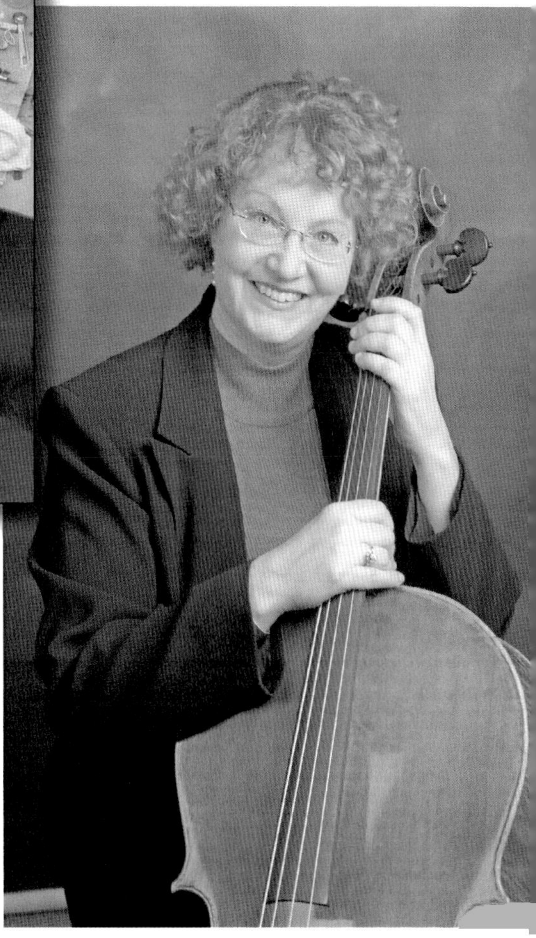

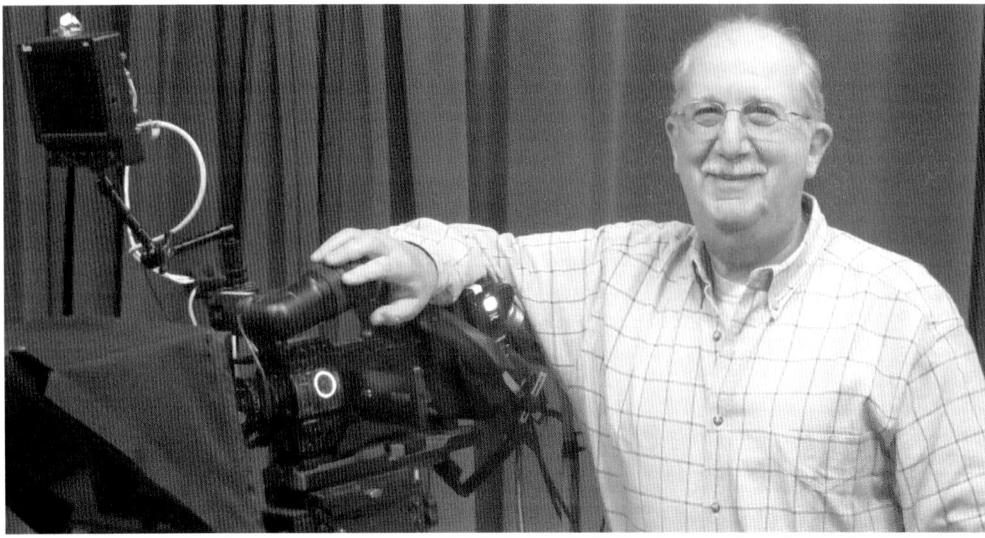

Kenneth Isaacson

For 40 years, Ken Isaacson was owner of a Boston-area advertising agency before retiring to do more sailing and traveling. An avid devotee of open communications, Isaacson was elected in 2008 as chair of WayCAM, Wayland's nonprofit public access cable television and online media provider. He helped negotiate new provider contracts from Comcast and Verizon, and, in 2011, successfully led the funding and construction of WayCAM's state-of-the-art Community Media Center adjacent to the high school. (Courtesy of Kenneth Isaacson.)

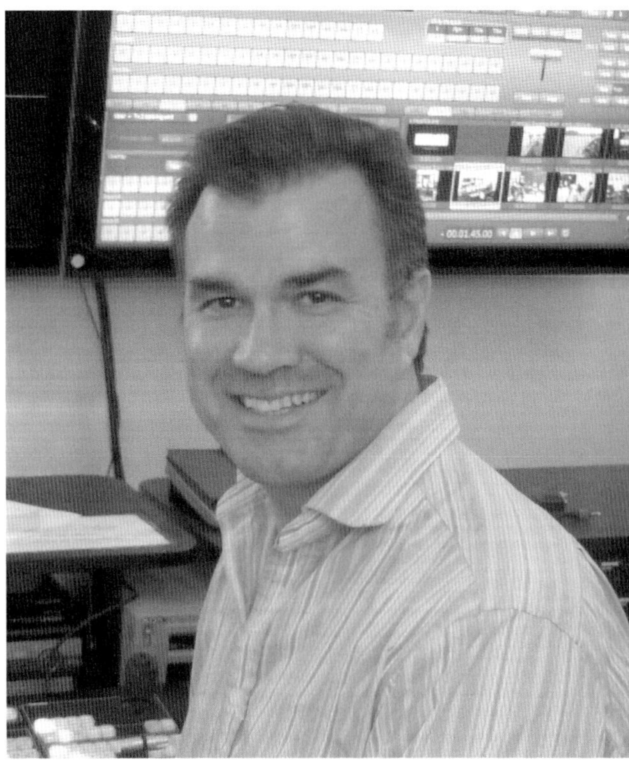

James Mullane

Jim Mullane graduated from Emerson College and started a career in acting and modeling. He became writer, producer, and director of theater and cable programs. He has been the executive director of WayCAM since 1998. Mullane is a natural mentor to the volunteers he trains, and the center's educational programs provide a valuable service to the town. His vision for the studio and community has been a major part of WayCAM's success. (Courtesy of James Mullane.)

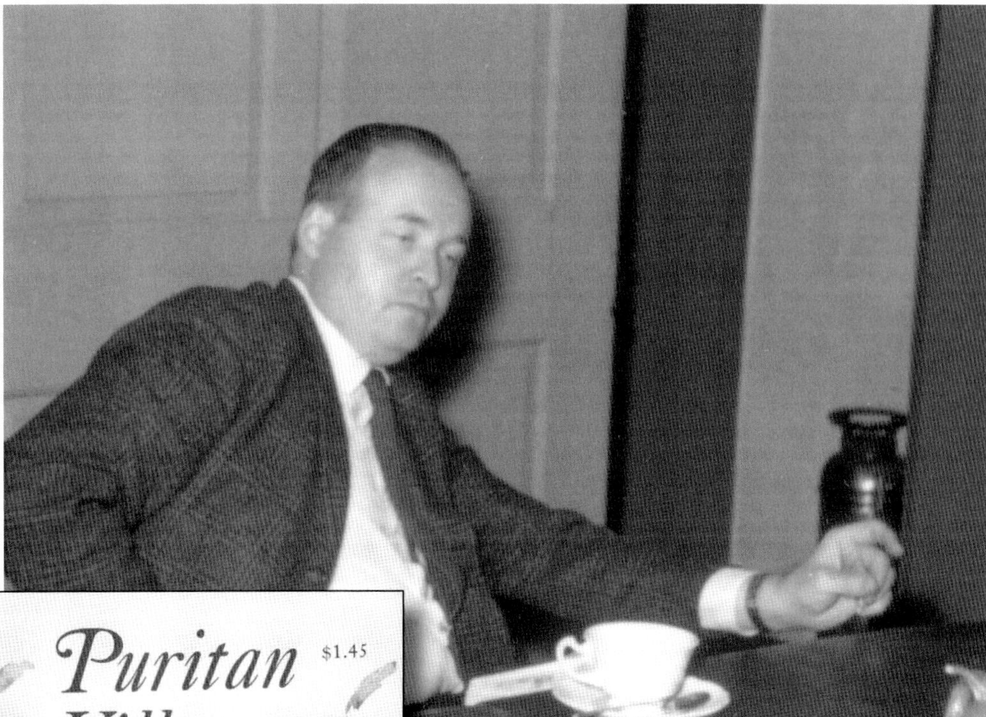

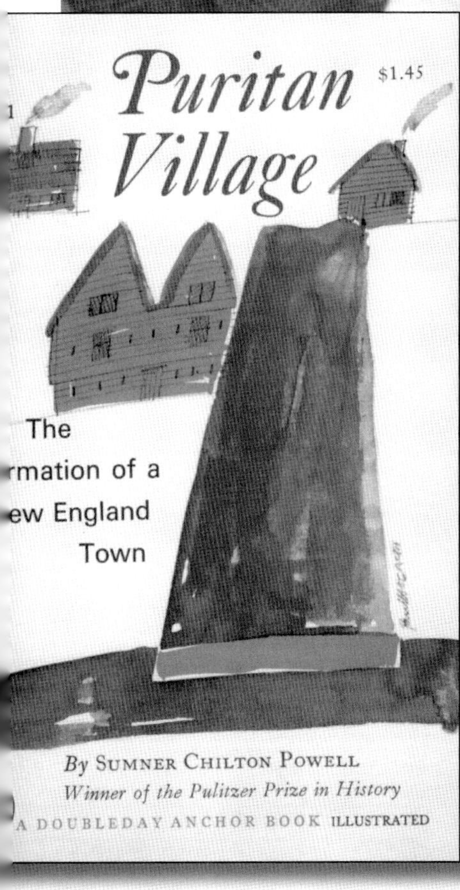

Sumner Chilton Powell (1924–1993)
Powell spent 10 years tracing the genealogical origins and antecedents of four-fifths of Sudbury's first settlers. He walked every acre of town and interviewed dozens of residents. His book *Puritan Village: The Formation of a New England Town* is a remarkably detailed account of the early government and social organization of Sudbury Plantation. In 1964, Powell won a Pulitzer Prize for the book. It remains one of the town's must valuable research tools. (Left, courtesy of Wesleyan University Press, 1963.)

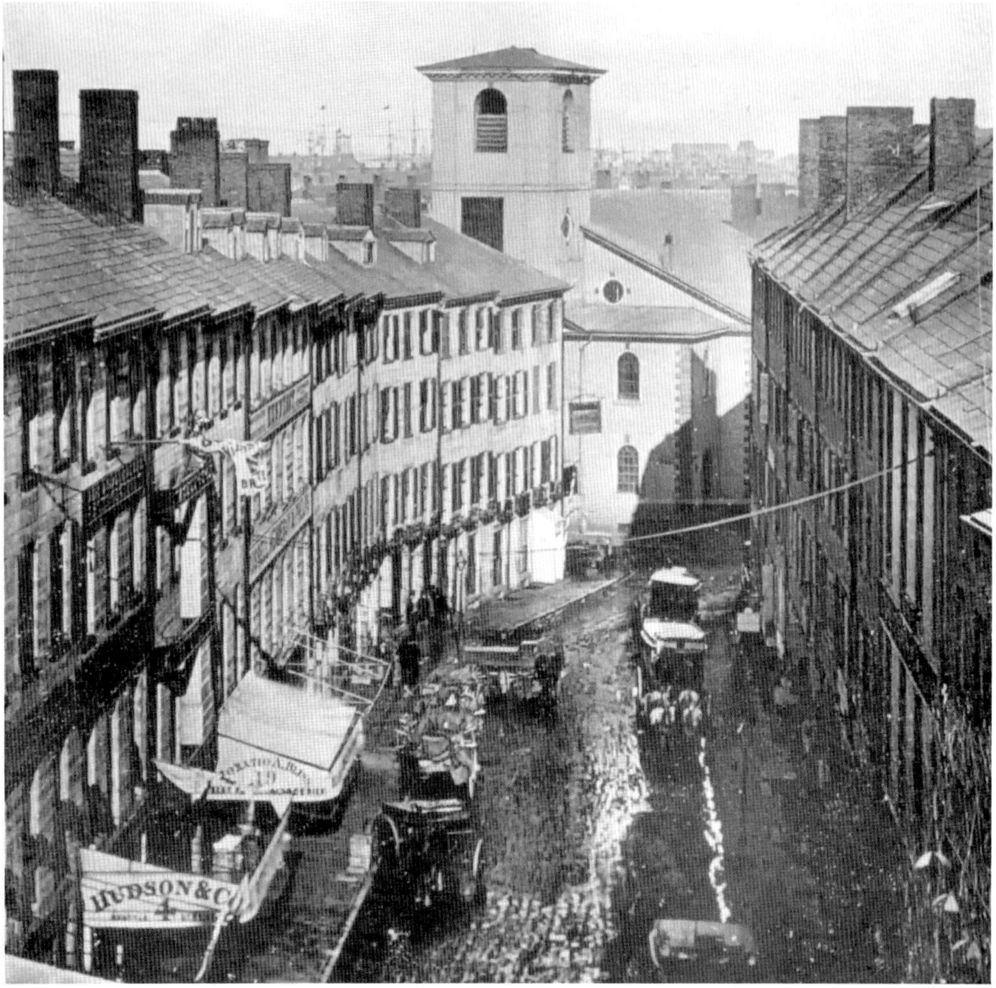

Josiah Johnson Hawes (1808–1901)

Josiah Johnson Hawes was born in Wayland and began a career in portrait painting before studying photography with Frances Fauvel-Gouraud. He formed a partnership with Albert Sands Southworth in 1843, and they opened a studio overlooking Boston's Scollay Square. Their studio produced daguerreotype portraits of many notables, including Henry Wadsworth Longfellow and Daniel Webster. After the partnership dissolved in 1863, Hawes continued to work and became known as the "oldest working photographer in this country." Pictured above is a 19th century view of Scollay Square from Hawes's studio. At right is a Hawes photograph of a child in a chair. (Both, courtesy of Josiah J. Hawes.)

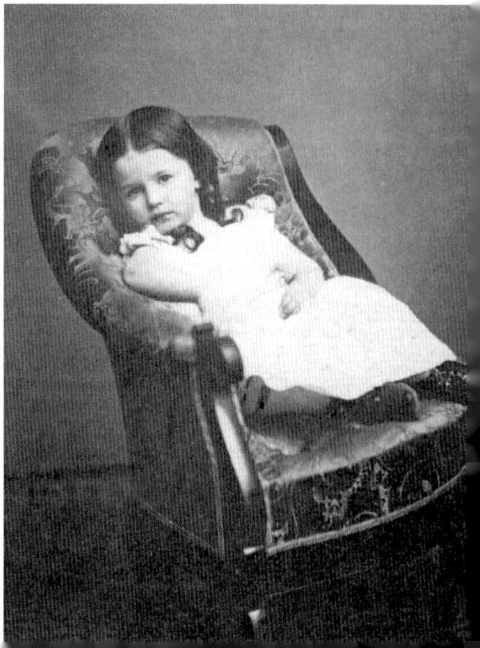

Alan Barker (1923–2008)

Barker was a concert pianist, mentor, and teacher who taught in his home. He founded the Little Theater Series in 1965, featuring local and emerging artists and student ensembles, including orchestras, bands, choruses, drama, and dance troupes. For almost five decades, these free performances have been financed by contributions from residents of Wayland and surrounding towns, the Wayland Cultural Council, and the Creative Arts Parents Association. One famous student, Frederick Moyer, often returns to perform in the series.

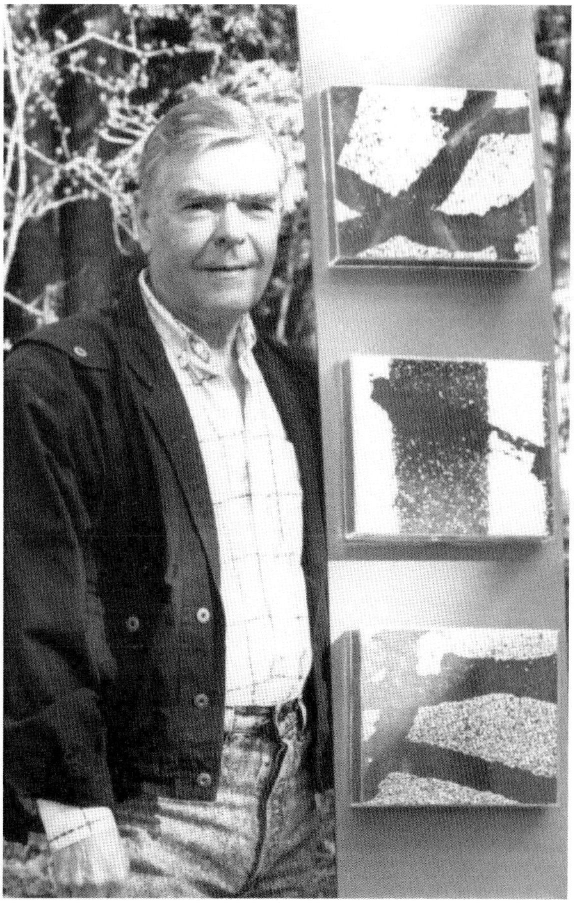

Frederick "Fred" Moyer

Fred Moyer performed as a teenager with the Boston Symphony and the Boston Pops, and made his Carnegie Recital Hall debut in 1982. He has appeared as piano soloist with 24 orchestras throughout the world and has recorded 22 albums with works by 30 composers. Moyer returns to Wayland regularly to honor his mentor, Alan Barker, and perform in the Little Theater concerts held at Wayland High School.

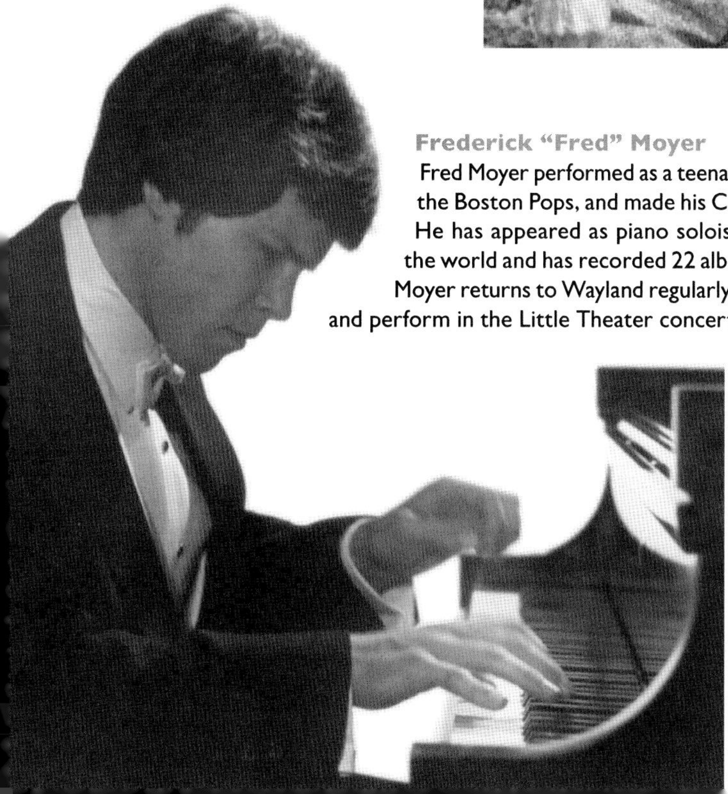

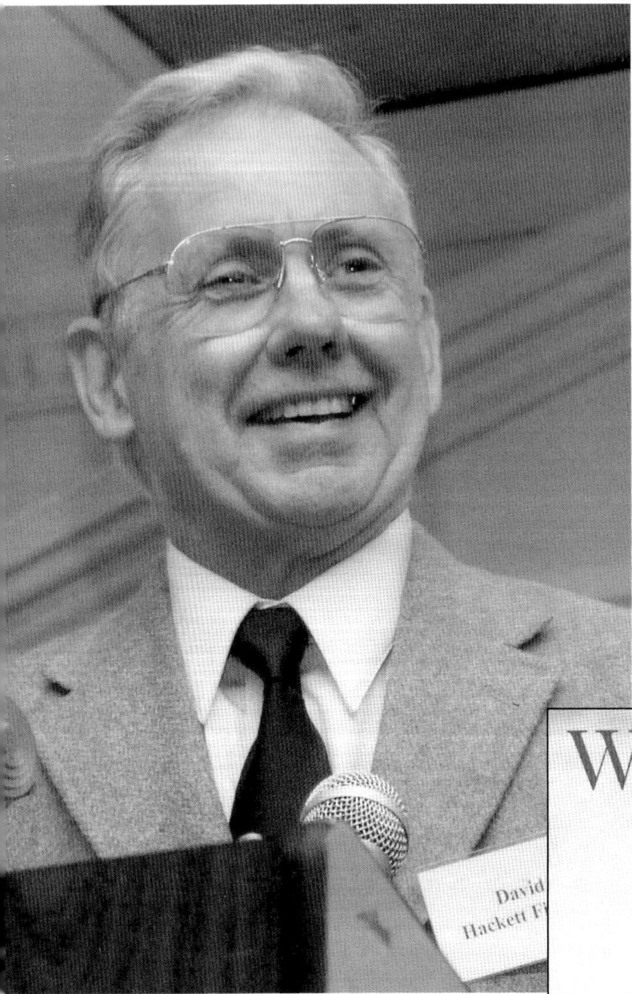

Dr. David Hackett Fischer
University and Earl Warren Professor at Brandeis University, Dr. Fischer is a longtime resident of Wayland and the author of 10 books. He is best known for two major works, *Albion's Seed* and *Washington's Crossing*. For the latter, he won a Pulitzer Prize in 2005. He is well respected for his meticulous and methodologically rigorous reconstruction of famous events. Dr. Fischer is a popular speaker who gives generously of his time to local organizations. (Left, courtesy of David H. Fischer; below, courtesy of Oxford University Press.)

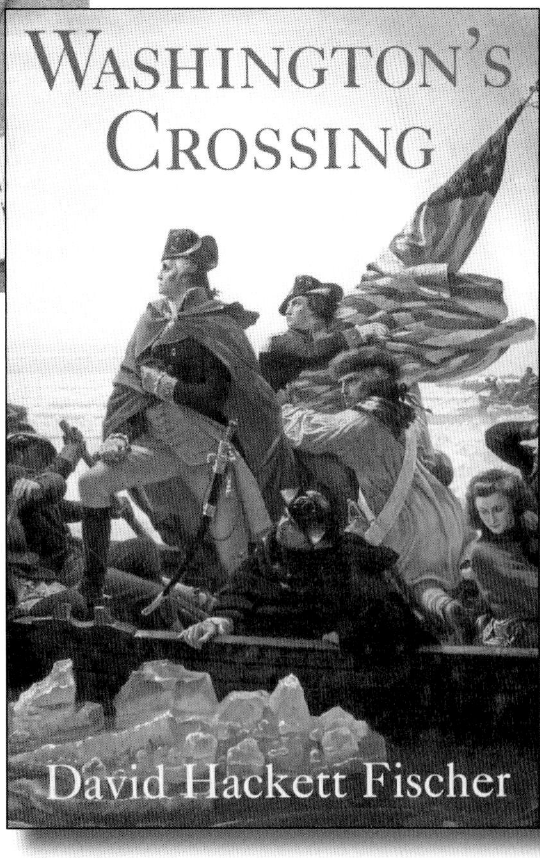

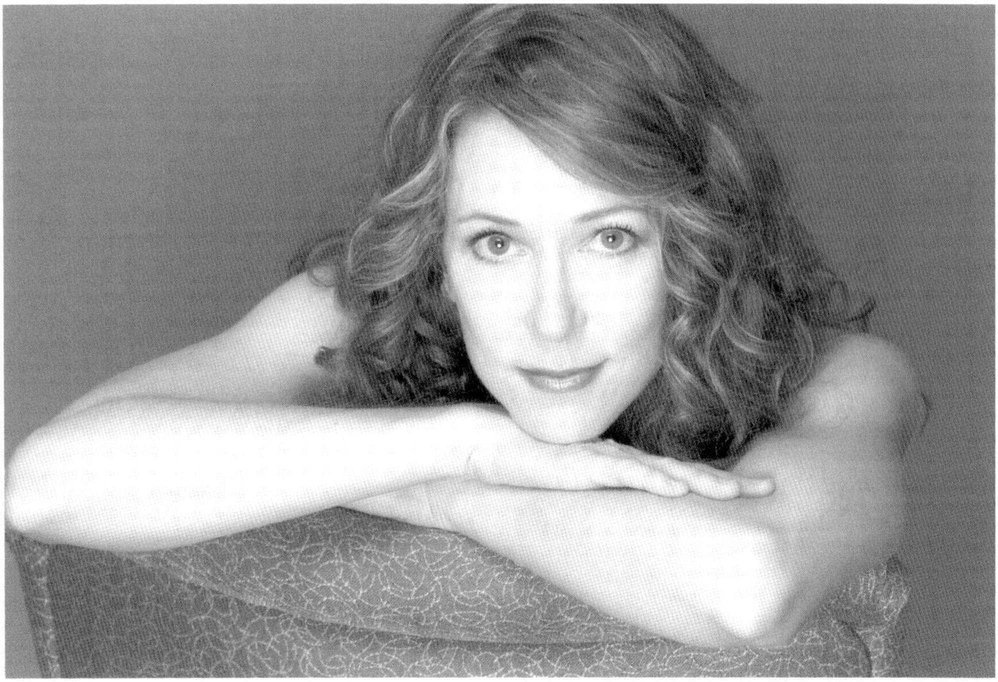

Juliet Lambert Pratt

Juliet Lambert Pratt's star performances at Wayland High School were only the beginning of a long and successful career on stage. She has appeared on Broadway in *Les Misérables*, *Passion*, and *Meet Me in St. Louis*, has performed in regional theaters across the United States, and toured internationally with several productions. She resides in Connecticut with her husband, four children, dogs, cats, and chickens. (Courtesy of Juliet L. Pratt.)

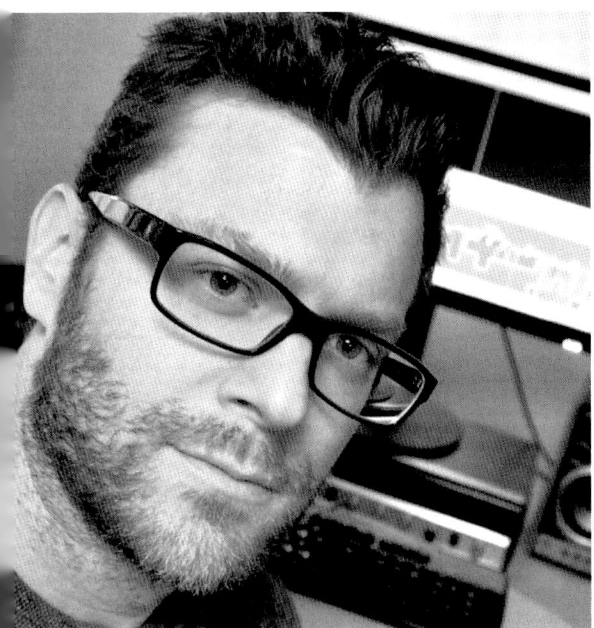

Eric Poydar

Poydar is a filmmaker, known for *Safety First*, *Larry (the Actor)*, and *About Barbers*. He studied film at the Museum of Fine Arts in Boston after graduating from Tufts University in 1996 and worked at the Boston Film Factory as postproduction supervisor for their digital editing suites. In addition to his freelancing, Poydar produces media with his father, Henry, at the family firm, Axyz Inc., and coaches basketball at Wayland High School. (Courtesy of Henry R. Poydar.)

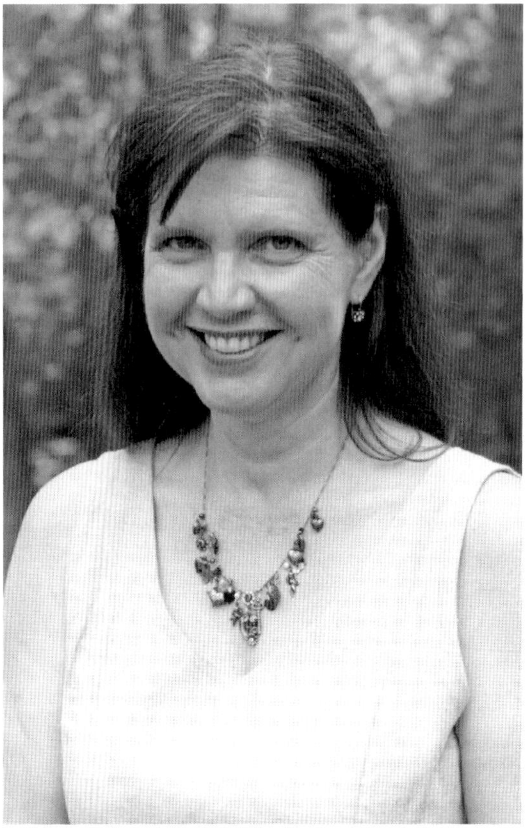

Madeleine "Maddie" Sifantus
Maddie Sifantus is a professional singer and Unitarian Universalist minister. In 1988, she founded the Golden Tones, an elder chorus that brings together the aging, school, arts, and faith communities. They create joyful music and engagement to senior facilities, schools, faith communities, and public events. During her tenure, the group performed more than 60 concerts a year and was made a "best practices" of the Creative Aging program of the National Endowment for the Arts. She is a recipient of awards from Arts Wayland Foundation and Bolli Lifelong Learning Institute. (Both, courtesy of Madeleine Sifantus.)

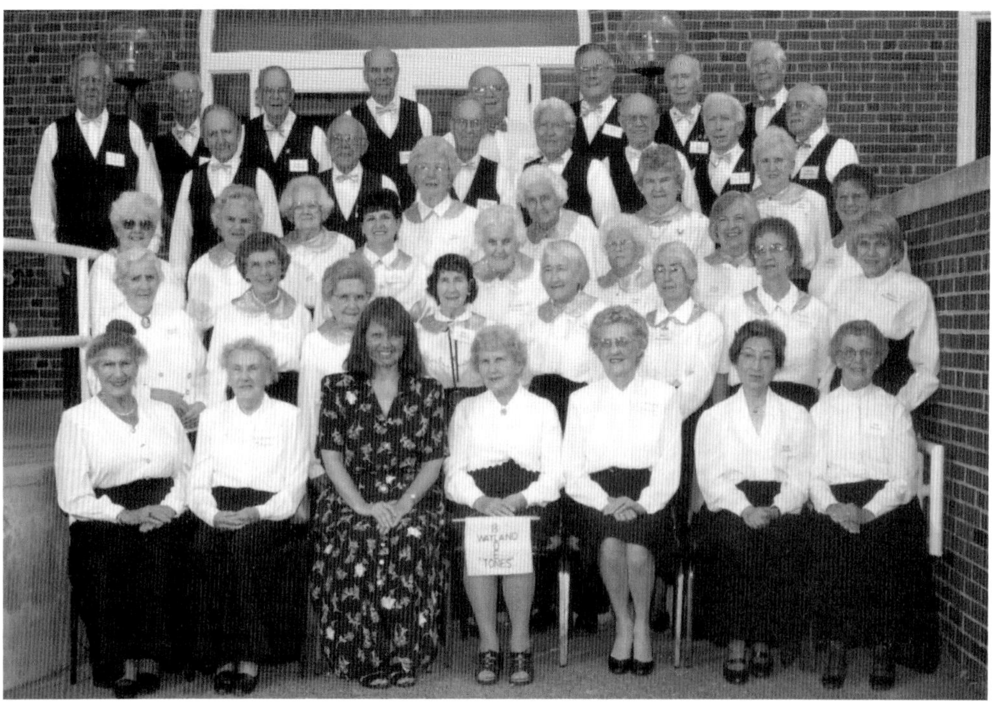

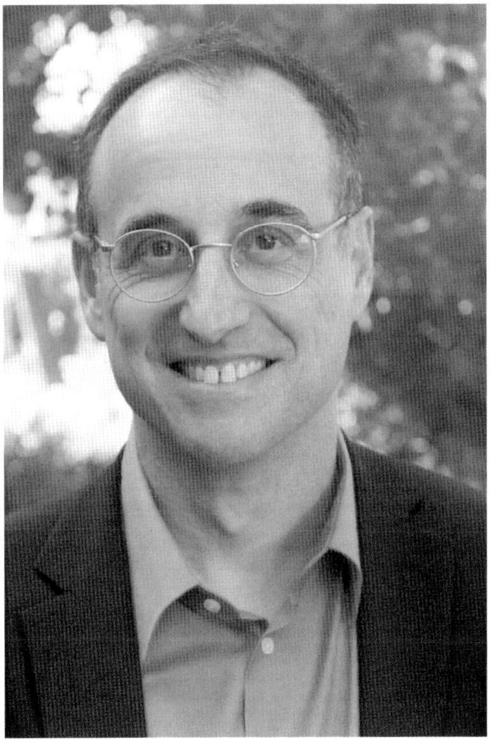

Alexander J. Taub
Since graduating from Wayland High in 1983, Alex Taub has written for and produced television shows including *Revenge, Heart of Dixie, Drop Dead Diva, Eli Stone, Judging Amy, Kevin Hill, Felicity, Early Edition,* and *Life with Louie,* for which he won the Humanitas Prize in the children's animation category (1996 and 1997). He also spent some time writing for the beloved Norwegian sitcom *Mot I Brøstet.* (Courtesy of Elisa Taub.)

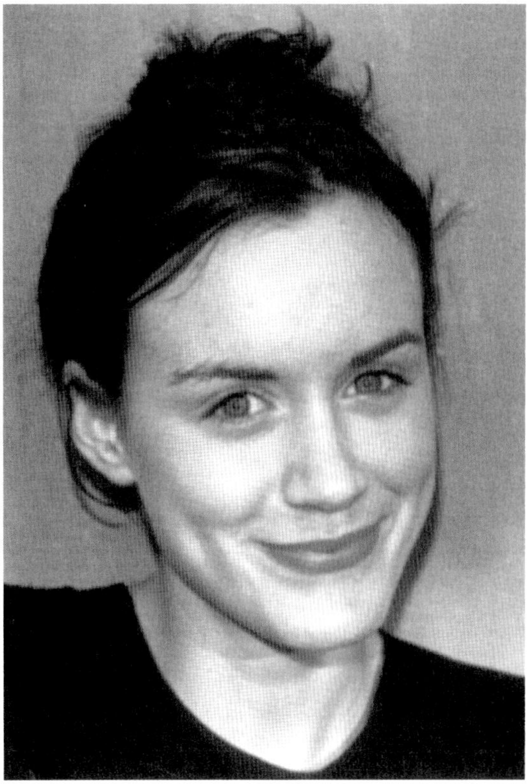

Taylor Schilling
As a Wayland High School student, Schilling appeared in *Fiddler on the Roof* before graduating in 2002. She went on to study at Fordham and New York Universities, taking part in stage productions while earning her degrees. She has since appeared in the films *The Lucky One, Atlas Shrugged: Part I,* and *Dark Matter.* Since 2013, she has been appearing in the Netflix series *Orange Is the New Black.* (Courtesy of Jostens Publishing.)

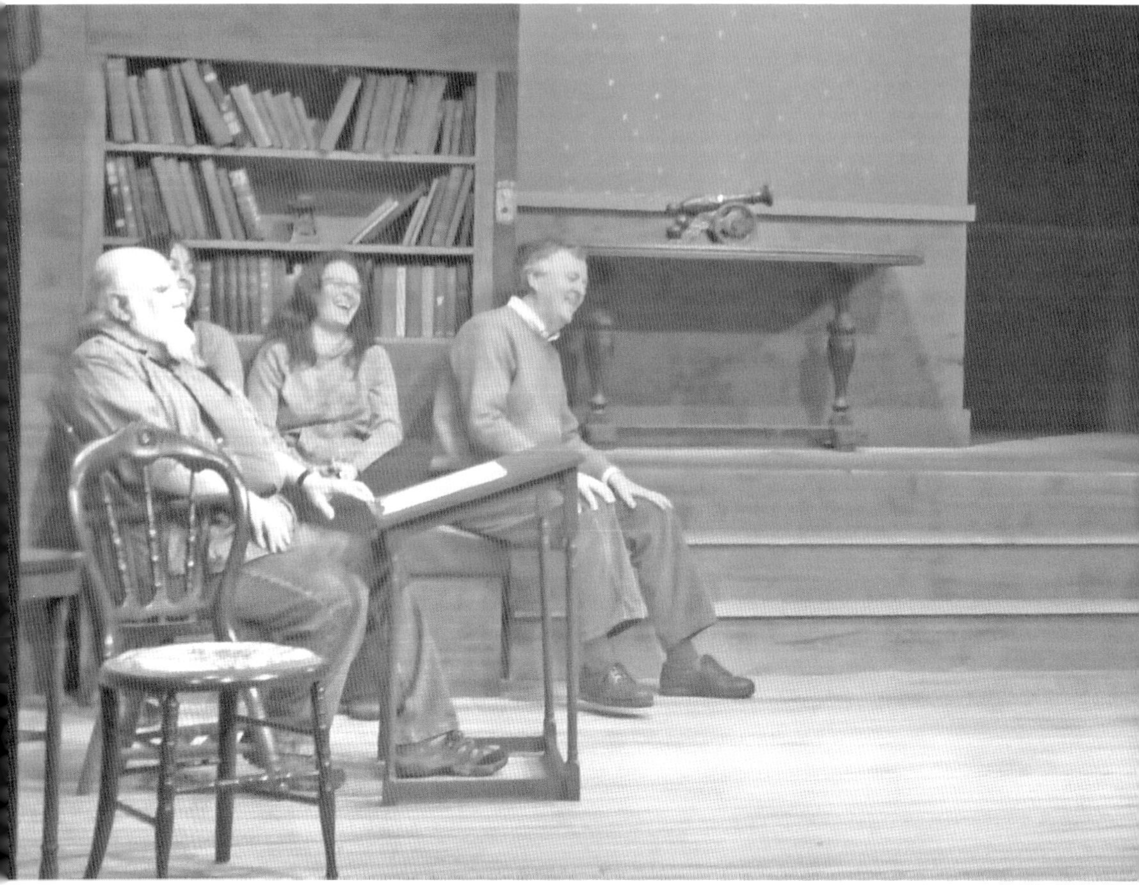

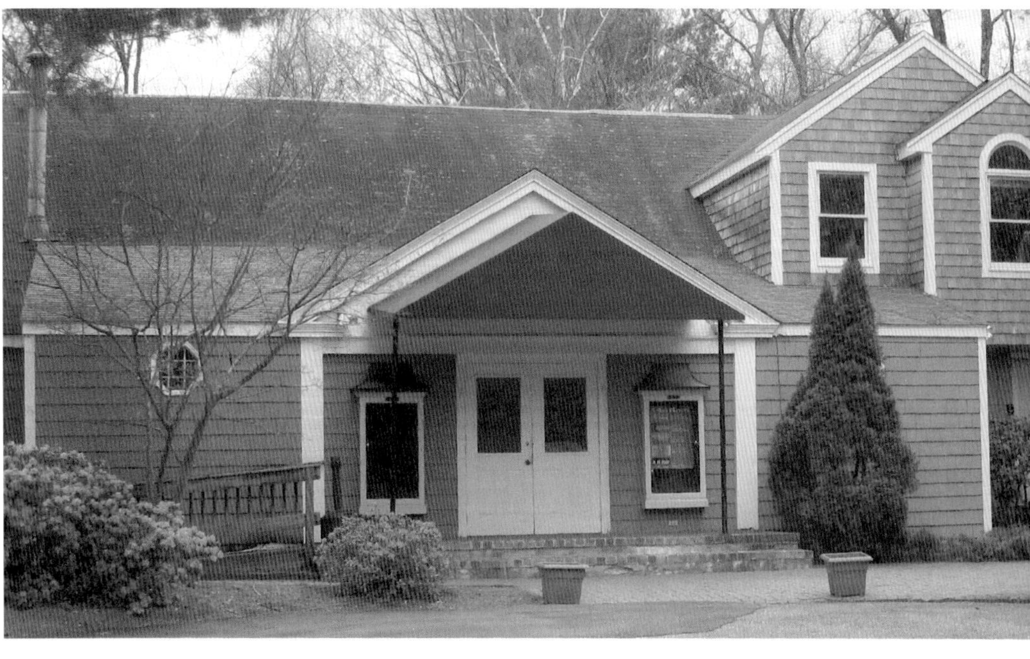

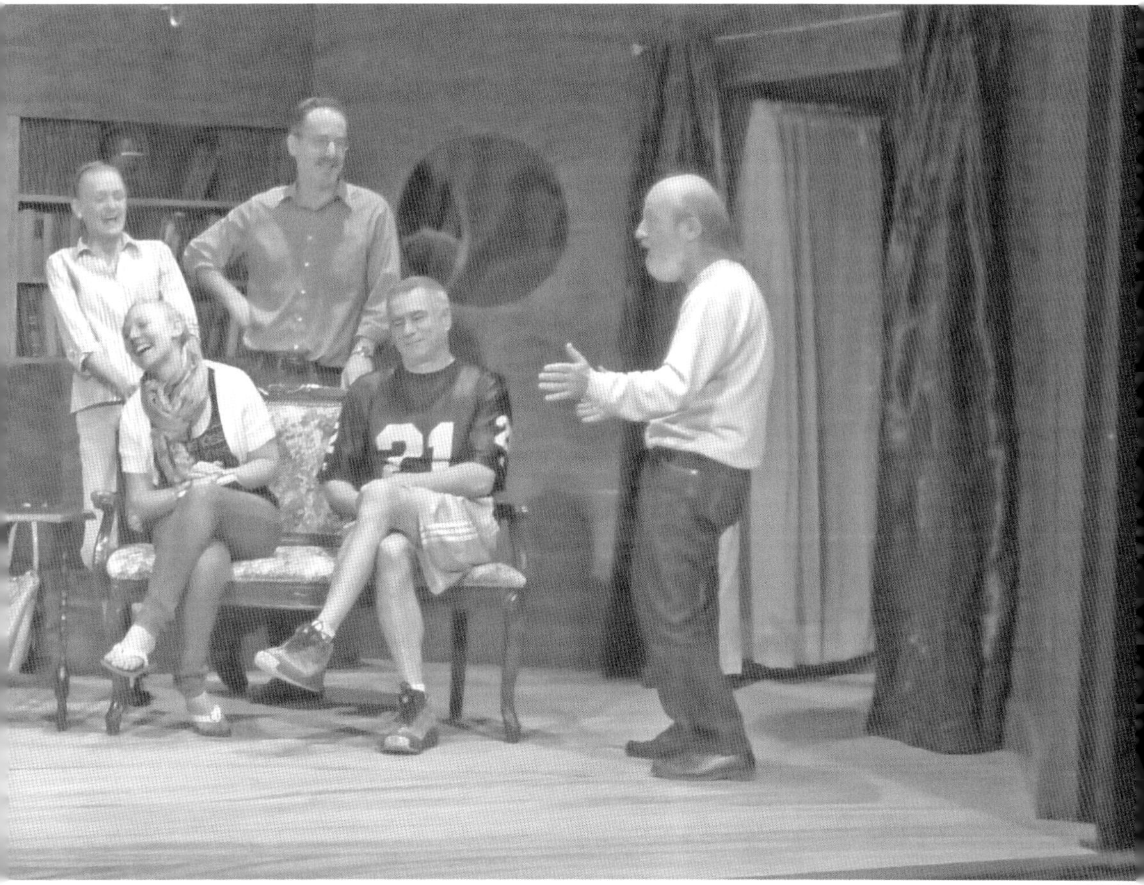

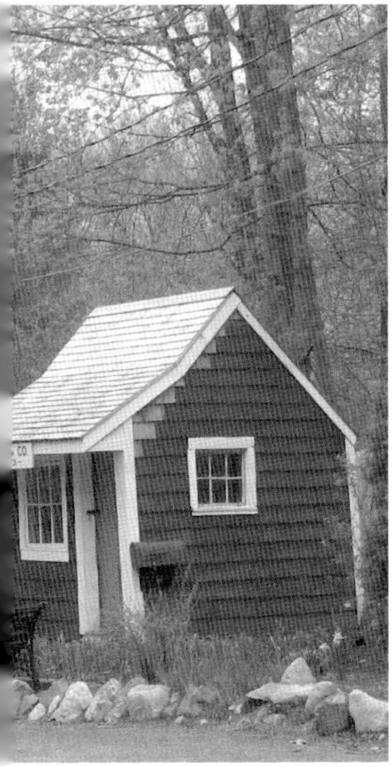

John Barrett

John Barrett is technical director at Curry College Theater in Milton, Massachusetts, and has been directing the Vokes Players for the past 33 years. Vokes Theater, built by Beatrice Herford Hayward to entertain her friends more than a century ago, has been remodeled, but it remains virtually unchanged. When Beatrice died at the age of 94, the company created a permanent memorial for their generous mentor by hanging a portrait in the box she had reserved for herself. Few towns in America can boast as rare and precious a possession as Beatrice Herford's Vokes Theater, which has continued the tradition of amateur theater for almost seven decades. From left to right above are Robert Zawistowski, (partially obscured) Daphne Nayer, Kim Anton Myatt, Jonathan Ashford, Deanna Swan (standing), Richard Schieferdecker (standing), Madeline Merenda (seated), John Murtagh (seated), and John Barrett. (Above, courtesy of John Schlafer; left, author's collection.)

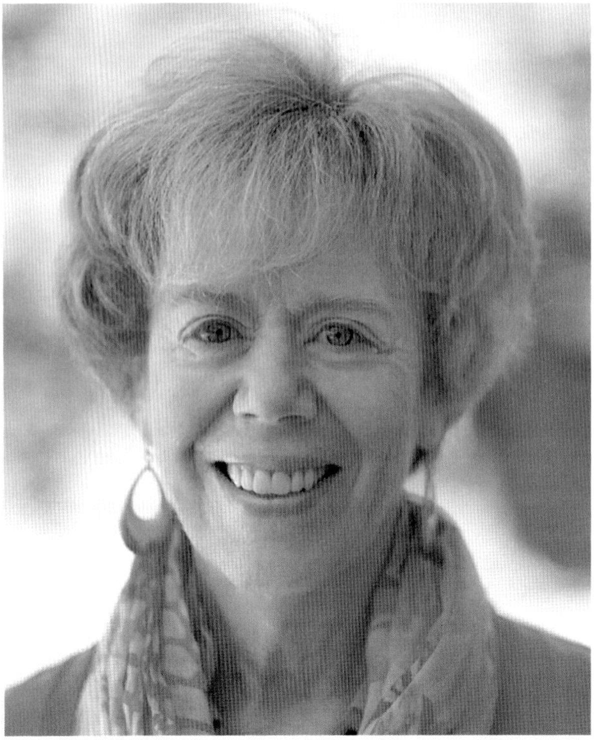

Nancy Poydar

While teaching, Nancy Poydar illustrated a trails book for the Conservation Commission and taught art classes in her home. She left teaching in 1988 to illustrate, and eventually write, children's books full time. Her first picture book job was published in 1992. She went on to illustrate 24 picture and chapter books. The first picture book she both wrote and illustrated was *Busy Bea* in 1994. Since then, Nancy has written and illustrated 16 highly acclaimed children's books. (Courtesy of Henry R. Poydar.)

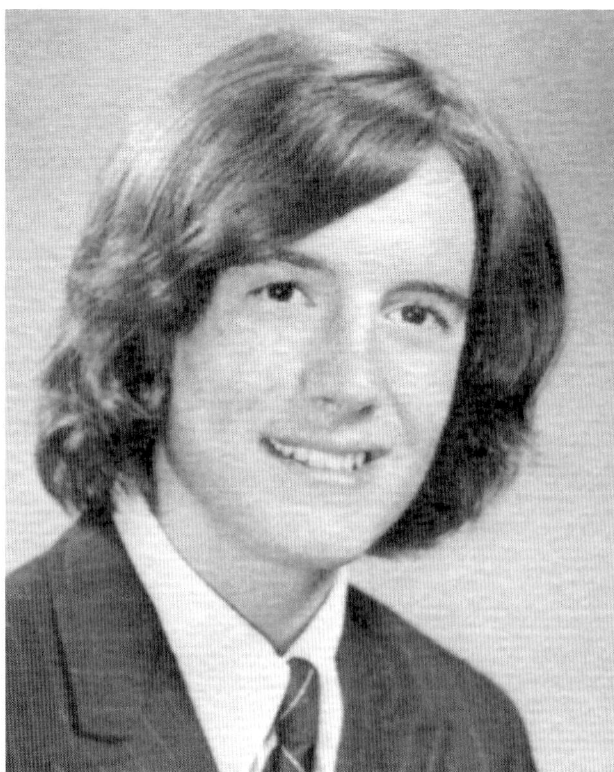

Lorin Rowan

Lorin and his brother Chris graduated from Wayland High and became part of the music scene in San Francisco in the 1970s. They performed with the Grateful Dead's Jerry Garcia, Phil Lesh, and drummer Bill Kreutzmann. The brothers returned in 2001 to perform in the Center for Arts in Natick, Massachusetts. They have been called two guys with sweet voices who can play. Their album *Now & Then* includes tunes from the 1970s. (Courtesy of Jostens Publishing.)

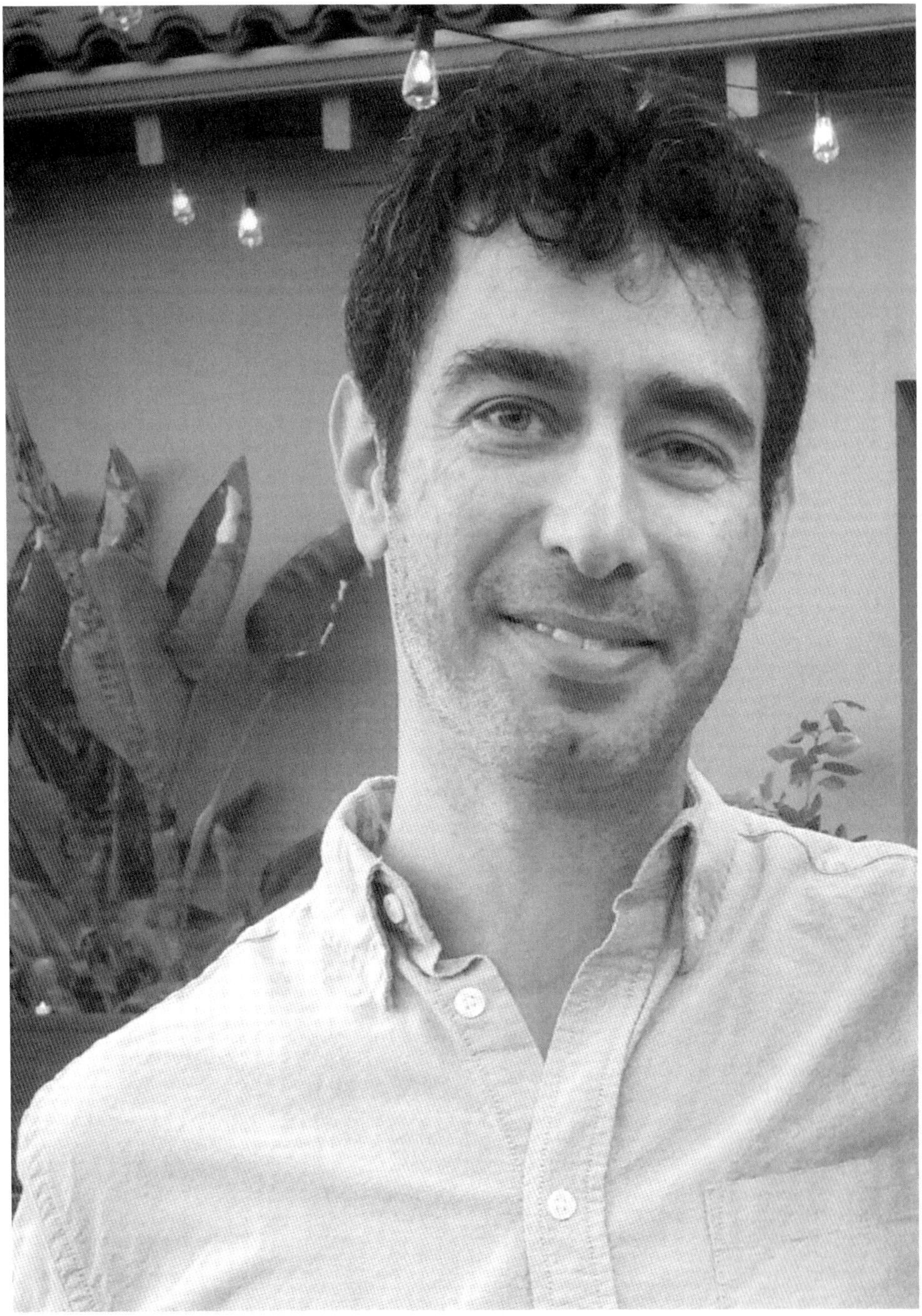

Gregg Kavet

Gregg Kavet met his partner, Andy Robin, at Harvard. Upon graduation, the two set out for Hollywood and have since written and directed for a number of television series, including episodes of the *Michaels Show* and *Seinfeld*. Their *Seinfeld* episode, *Fatigues*, won the 1997 Writers Guild of America Award for best television comedy. Their movie *Live Free or Die* won the competition award at the 2006 SXSW Film Festival and the New American Cinema Award later that year at Seattle Fest. (Courtesy of Lindsay Kavet.)

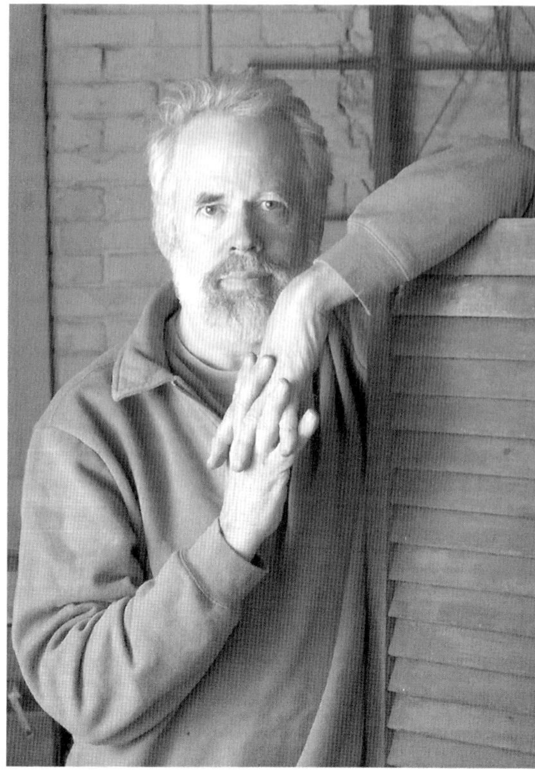

David Lang

David Lang's sculptural work has become largely kinetic and interactive. It is often witty, profound, and provocative. He works in the last remaining pre–Civil War shoe factory in Natick, Massachusetts, in a studio packed with junk and finely crafted old things, all with stories. He began his career at Harvard as founder and head of Scientific & Graphic Arts in the Department of Chemistry and went on to head the Art Department at Middlesex School in Concord for 30 years. He taught at the DeCordova Museum School in Lincoln, Massachusetts. Lang was one of the founding members of the Danforth Museum in Framingham, Massachusetts. Additionally, he was one of the founding members of Arts Wayland and has taught numerous art workshops in photography, painting, and sculpture in Wayland and surrounding towns since the mid-1970s. One of his sculptures is pictured below. (Both, courtesy of David Lang.)

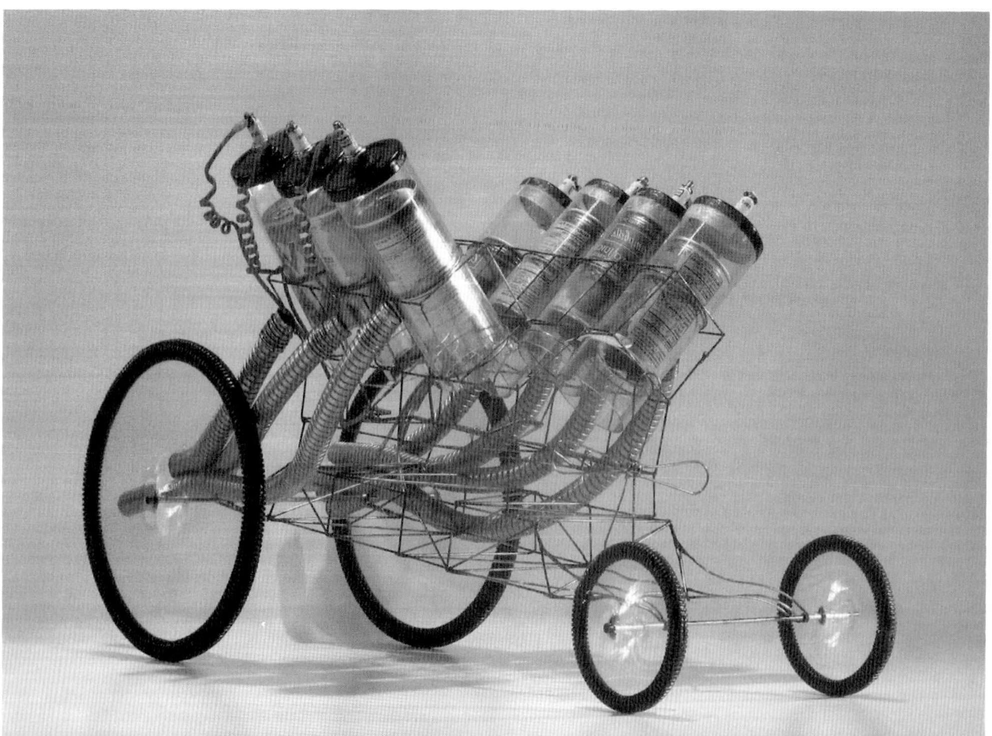

Judith S. Pratt

Judith Pratt was born in California but grew up in Wayland, where she attended high school before going on to major in drama at Tufts University. Later, she earned a master's degree from the University of Iowa and a doctorate at the University of Nebraska at Lincoln. Pratt is a freelance writer, playwright, college professor, and acting coach. Her plays have been produced in New York City, Boston, Philadelphia, Austin, and Cape Town, South Africa. Her full-length play *Spiraling* was workshopped by the Metropolitan Ensemble Theatre in Kansas City. Recently she presented *The Wright Place* at Wayland's Vokes Theatre as a birthday present to her mother, Jean. The story is about her grandmother's house in Cohasset, Massachusetts, where she spent many happy summers. (Courtesy of Judith Pratt.)

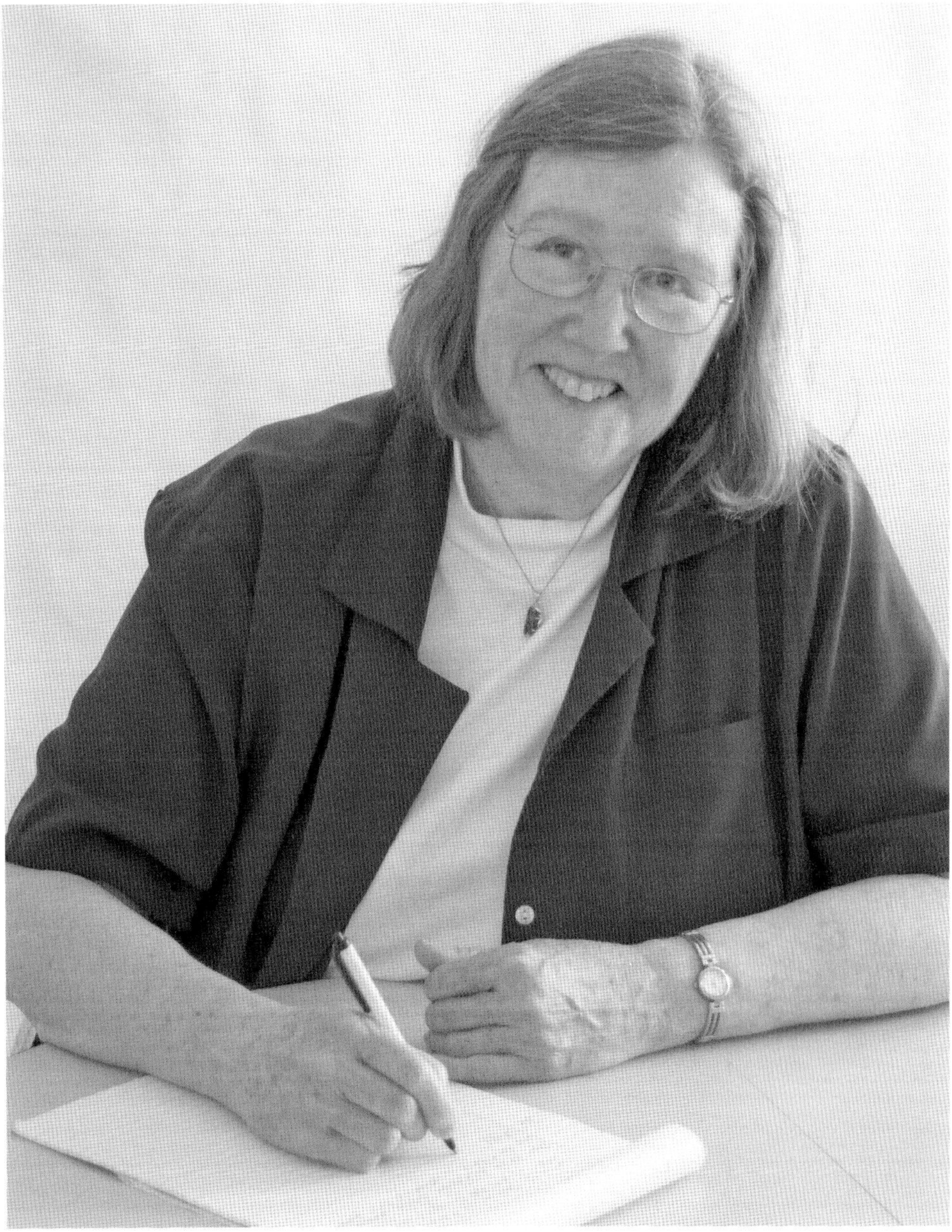

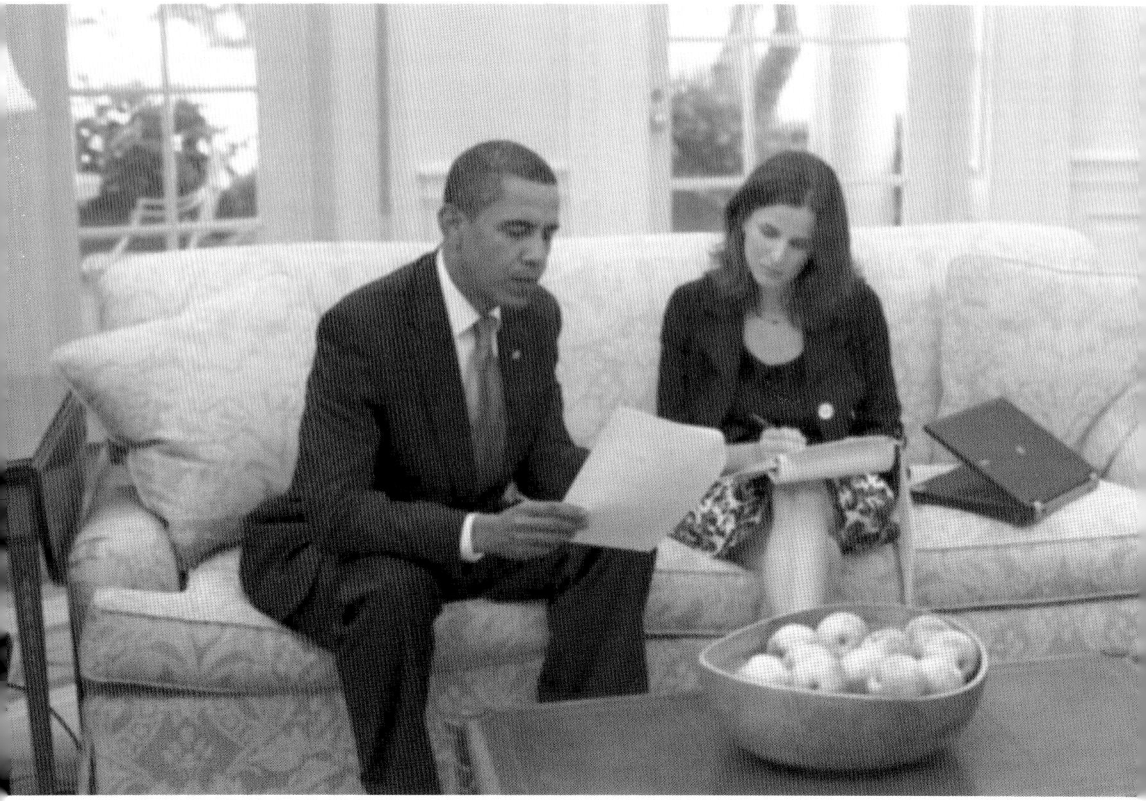

Sarah Hurwitz

Sarah Hurwitz is currently a speechwriter for Pres. Barack Obama. She graduated from Wayland High in 1995 and went on to graduate from Harvard College and Harvard Law School. Before working at the White House, Hurwitz was a senior speechwriter on President Obama's presidential campaign, chief speechwriter for Sen. Hillary Clinton's presidential campaign, deputy chief speechwriter on the presidential campaigns of Gen. Wesley Clark and Sen. John Kerry, and a speechwriter for Sen. Tom Harkin. She was also an attorney at the Washington, DC, office of Wilmer Hale. Recently, she wrote President Obama's speech on education. (Courtesy of Pete Souza/White House.)

CHAPTER THREE

Entrepreneurs

Good business leaders create a vision, articulate the vision, and relentlessly drive it to completion.

—Thomas Hardy

The first settlement of Sudbury Plantation on the Boston Post Road became the locus of a route from east to west for over a century. The Pequod House, built in 1771, was well situated on this main road on the northeast corner of Boston Post and Cochituate Roads, where the new Public Safety Building now stands. The inn was a favorite stagecoach stop offering food, drink, and comfortable overnight accommodations for travelers. Local people also gathered at the inn to discuss politics, religion, crops, and livestock. The inn was torn down in 1928.

During the 19th century, Lovells store, still standing as of this writing on Cochituate Road in the center of town, provided farmers and their families with fresh meat and vegetables, dry goods, and whatever commodities were needed. The building's tall Doric columns and porches on two levels have not lost their elegance and charm, although the interior has been altered to accommodate 21st-century office space.

During the middle part of the 19th century, in the southern part of town, Bent Shoe Factory grew to become one of Cochituate Village's largest employers. It was located on the corner of Commonwealth Road and Main Street, where a Starbucks coffee shop is now. Smaller shoe factories scattered throughout the village also thrived until early in the 20th century when newer, more efficient factories were built in the South and West. There is little doubt that the shoe industry left a lasting imprint on the town.

In recent decades, Wayland has been fortunate to have the longtime commitment of many family-owned businesses. Mel's restaurant, Bryant Funeral Home, and Community Nursery have been in operation for five decades and more; the Villa restaurant has been operating for four decades; Wayland Creative Preschool, Dr. Leonard Carapezza's office, Lavins, and Liberty Pizza for three decades; Longfellow Tennis and Sports Center for two and half decades; and the longest serving family-owned business of all, Russell's Garden Center, has been in operation for 138 years.

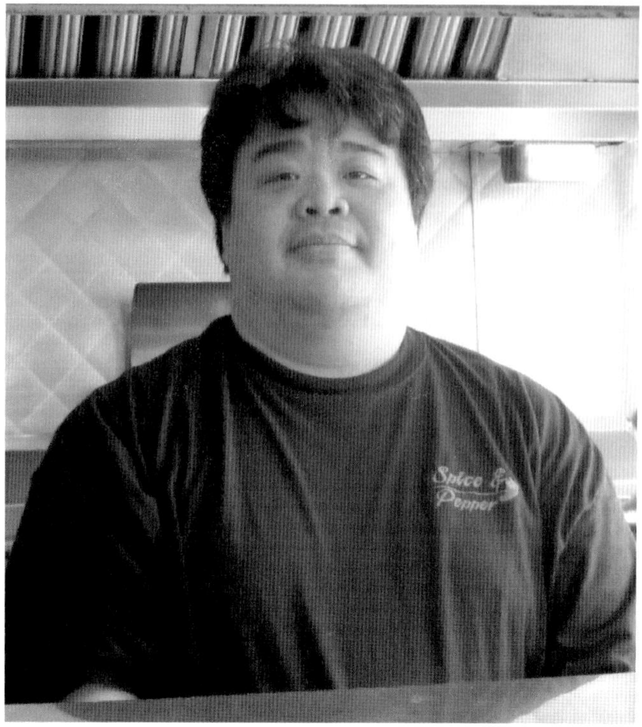

Tom Kaewsprasert

In 1993, Tom Kaewsprasert came to the United States from Bangkok and began his study of Thai cuisine. His first job taught him the basics, and he read lots of cookbooks and interviewed Thai chefs to learn their secrets. Still, he had to do his own experimenting to get the tastes he liked and to satisfy his customers. He can be seen most days in Spice & Pepper's open-style kitchen. The building has housed eateries for almost a century, including Benson's Store, a popular local luncheonette and gathering place opened in 1957. John Santamaria bought the business, along with the name, and his son-in-law Joe Doucette ran it for 37 years until he retired in 2003. (Right, author's collection.)

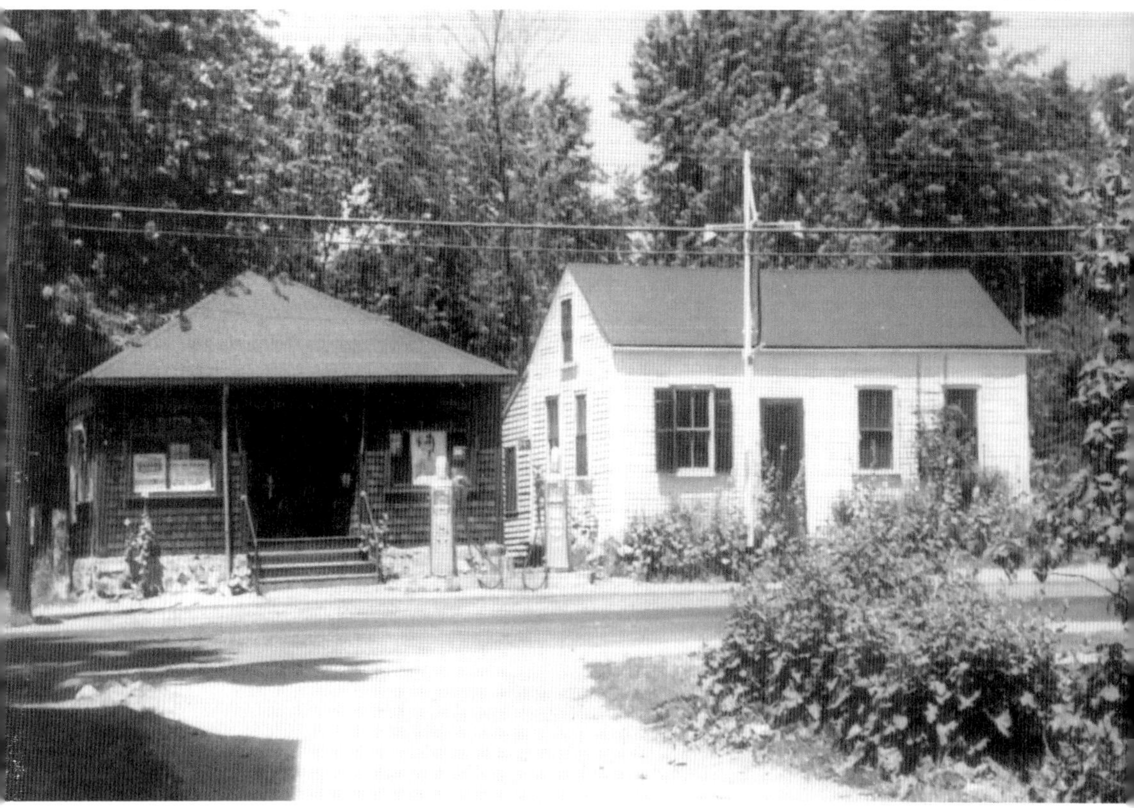

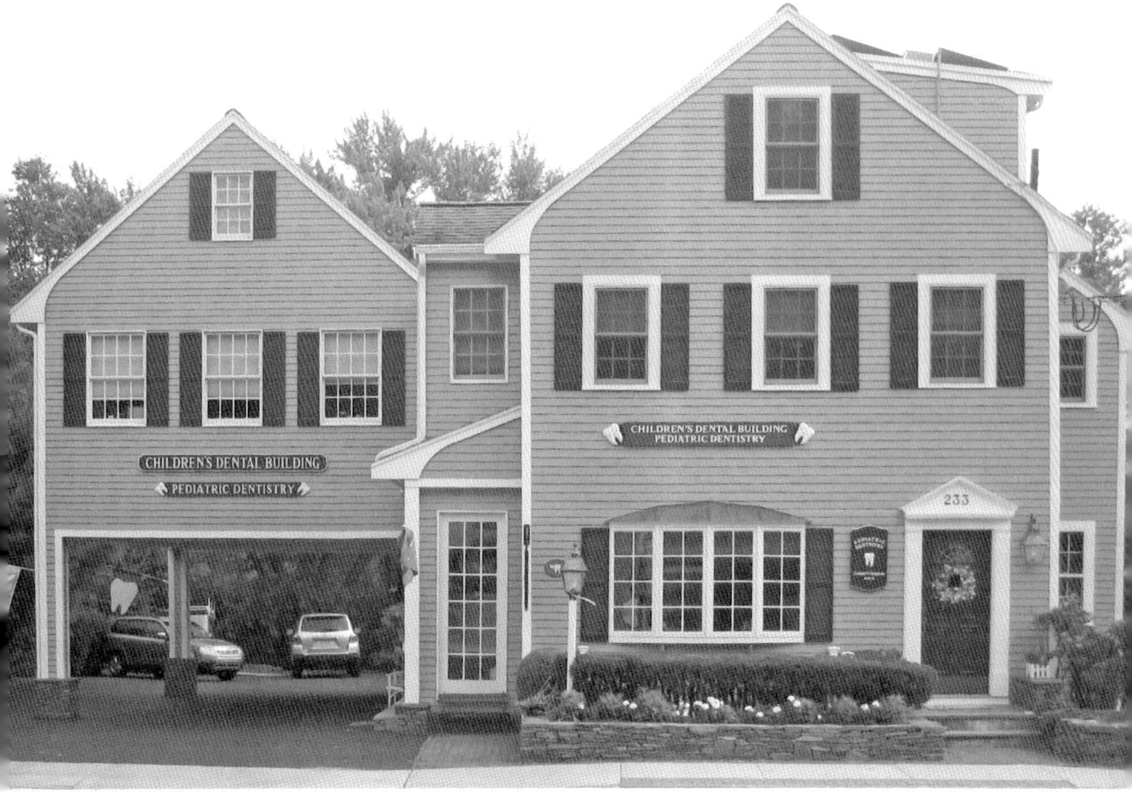

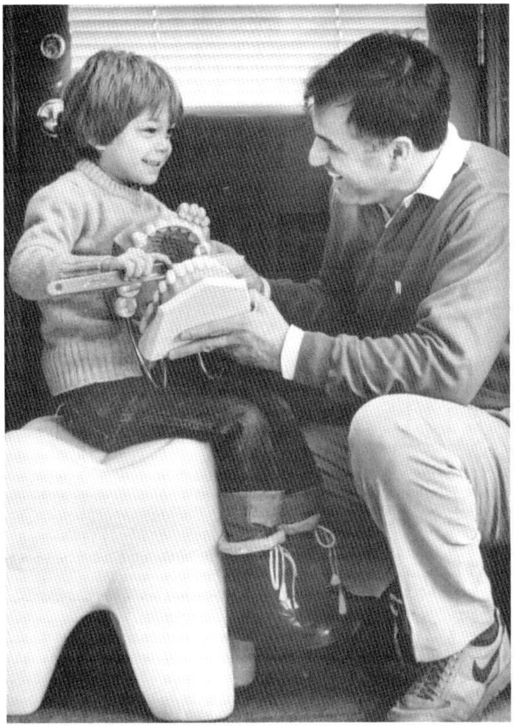

Dr. Leonard Carapezza

Dr. Carapezza has been practicing pediatric orthodontics in an antique three-story building in town center for the past three decades. The Children's Dental Building is an up-to-date facility occupying all three floors. A pioneer of early orthodontics, Dr. Carapezza specializes in early treatment of malocclusion (misalignment). He teaches and lectures on the subject at Tufts University School of Dental Medicine, New England Medical Center, and the University of Tennessee Department of Pediatric Dentistry. (Above, author's collection; left, courtesy of Leonard Carapezza.)

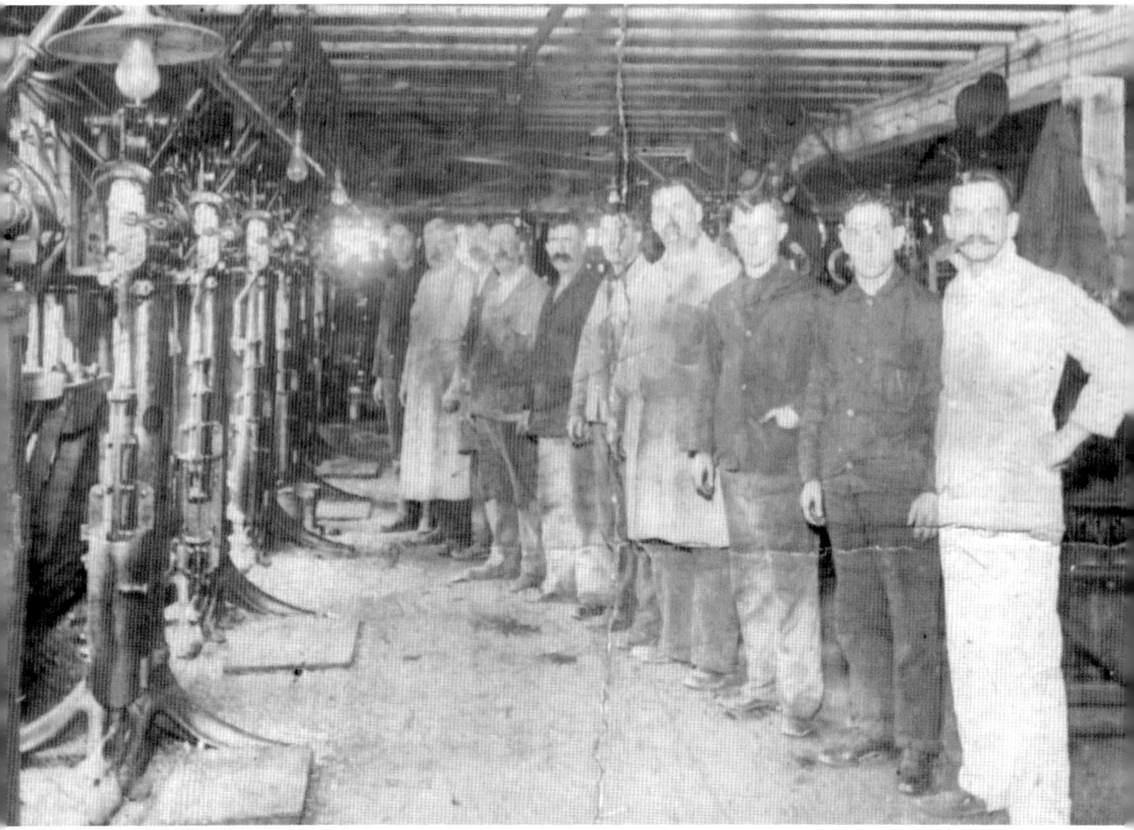

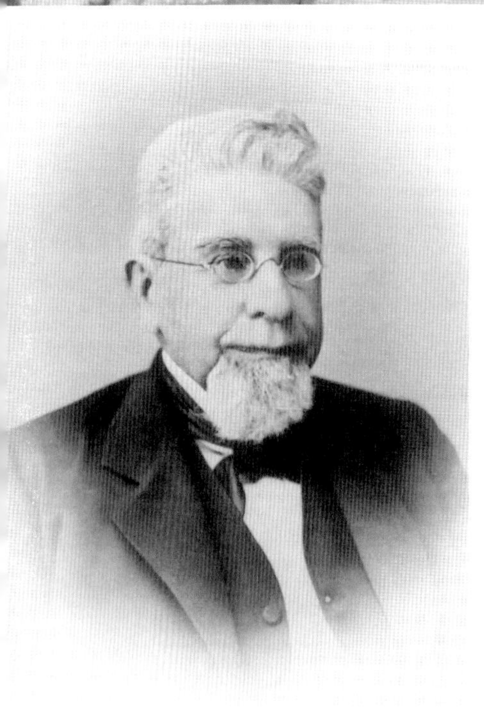

William Bent (1808–1863) and James Madison Bent (1812–1888)

The Bent brothers established the Bent Shoe Factory in 1830. The factory grew rapidly over the next 50 years, eventually occupying a large site on the corner of what is now Commonwealth Road and Main Street. William became an apprentice in 1827 to a Natick shoemaker and James (pictured at left) to a cabinetmaker in Framingham, Massachusetts. William set himself up in business and required his brother to learn the trade for five years before becoming a partner. James designed one of the first high shoemaker's benches and a head block to which lasts were strapped. He was reputed to be something of a mechanical genius and was quick to acquire advanced equipment for their factory. By 1880, the Bent factory employed 330 workers. James Madison Bent became a prominent leader in the region and is credited with turning the village of Cochituate into a bustling industrial and political center.

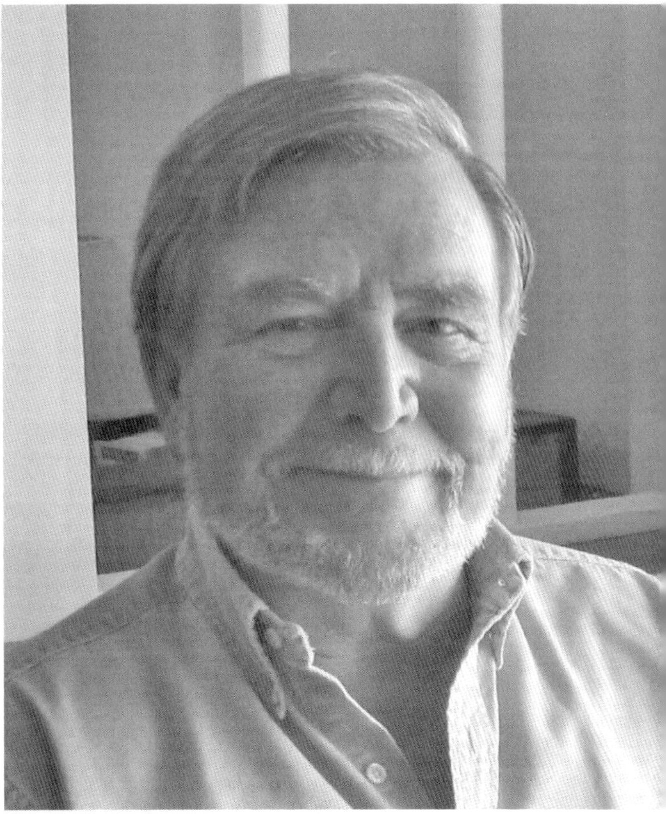

Richard Schnetke
Schnetke has owned the Villa restaurant since 1973 and attributes its great success to loyal employees and customers. He believes strongly in community service and has supported Parmenter Hospice, American Cancer Society, and the Humane Society, to name a few. Recently, the dining room featured an art sale with proceeds benefitting the Lymphoma Research Foundation. Customer birthdays are celebrated with a special discount to the entire party. (Both author's collection.)

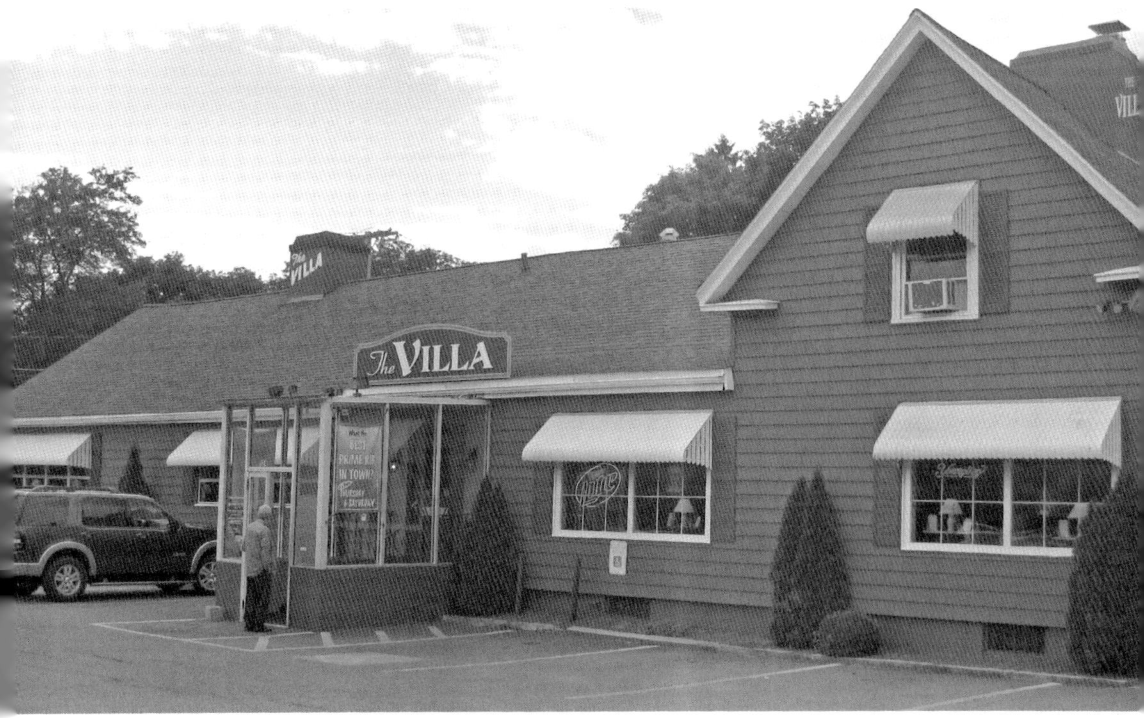

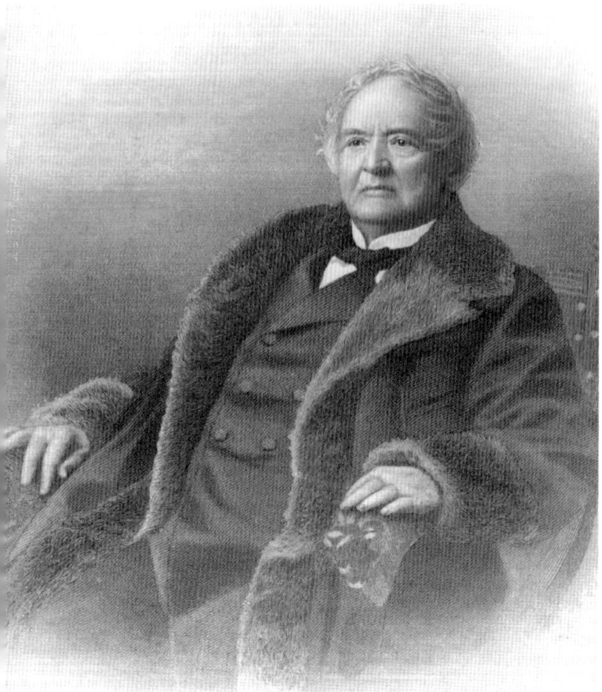

Michael Simpson (1809–1884)

Simpson owned Roxbury Mill in Saxonville, Massachusetts, less than a mile from his Wayland home. He was a kind and generous employer who paid his mill workers more than the going rate and contributed funds for the betterment of the village of Saxonville. A 72-year-old widower, Simpson married 27-year-old Evangeline Marrs in 1882. At a cost of $150,000, he built her a mansion on the corner of West Plain Street and Old Connecticut Path. Unfortunately, Simpson died two years after moving into their new home. After the house was sold, it became a popular, and often lawless, eating and entertaining establishment called Mansion Inn. Later, new owners converted it into an elegant dining and dancing facility. In 1956, the inn was ravaged by fire and all that remained were the walls on the first floor, which were built of stone, and part of the wood-framed second story. The rest was ash. (Both courtesy of Framingham Historical Center.)

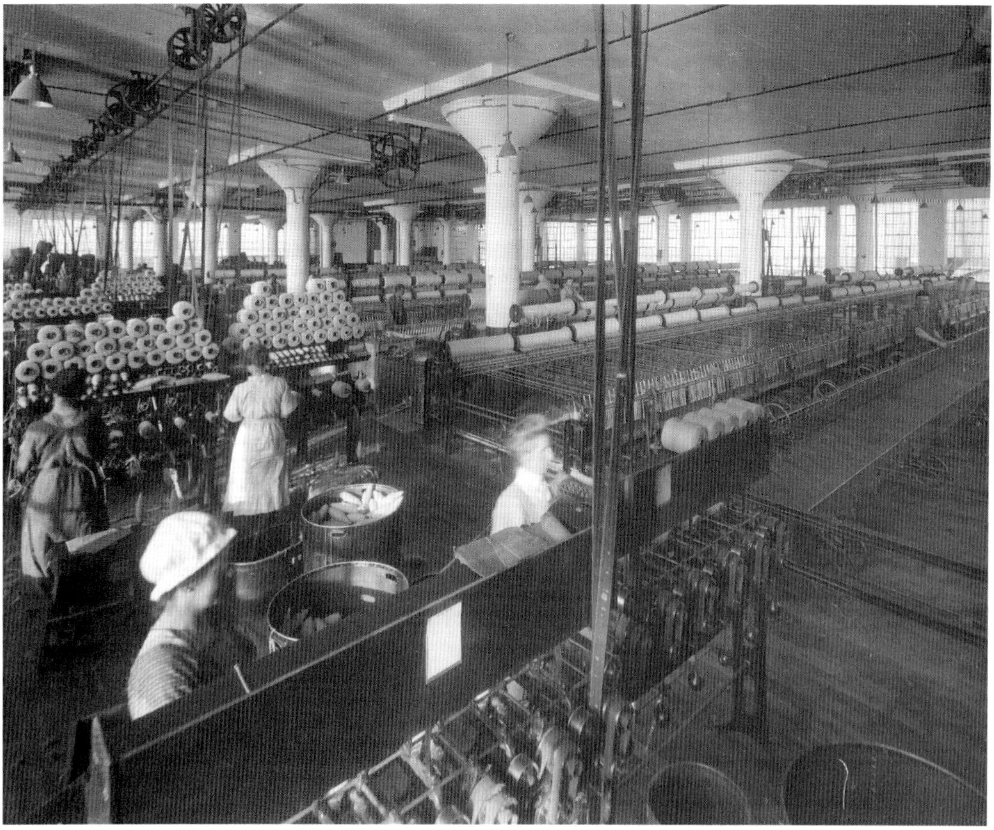

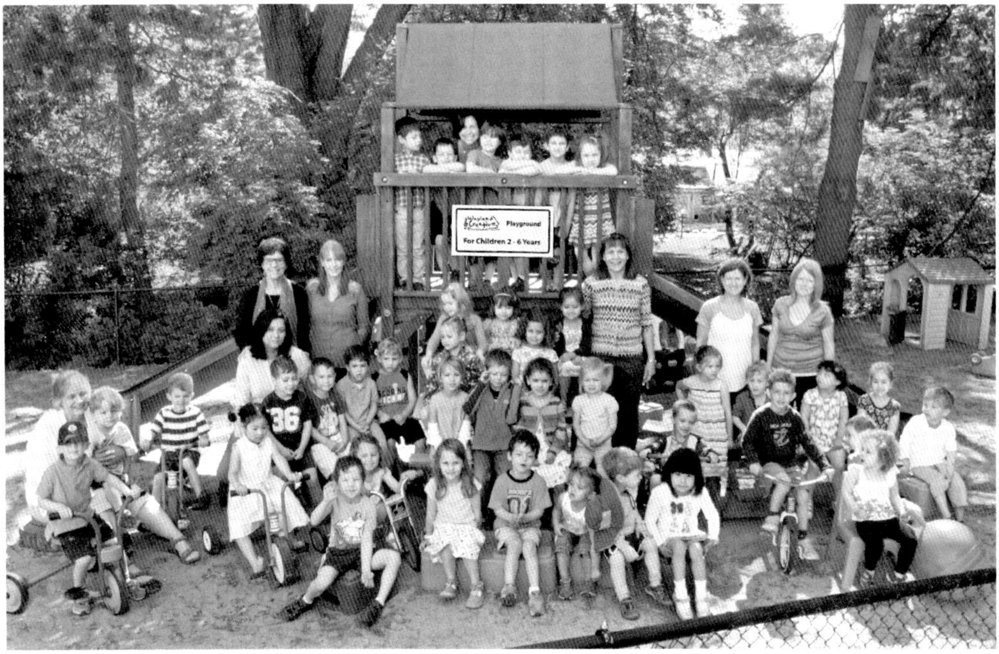

Sharon Engler and Susanne Geiger

Sharon Engler took over an existing preschool and soon partnered with Judy Prymak to create the nonprofit Wayland Creative Preschool in 1980. The school is popular for its creative and science-based programs and highly professional staff. A unique attraction is an environmentally based Indian program where children collect natural materials out-of-doors and create artifacts of their own. Now in its 34th year, the school is under the directorship of Susanne Geiger, a certified preschool teacher and director. She lives in town with her husband, a Wayland native, and two sons who attended the school. Engler stayed on as consulting director and currently teaches music in the preschool program. (Both courtesy of Stephen Engler.)

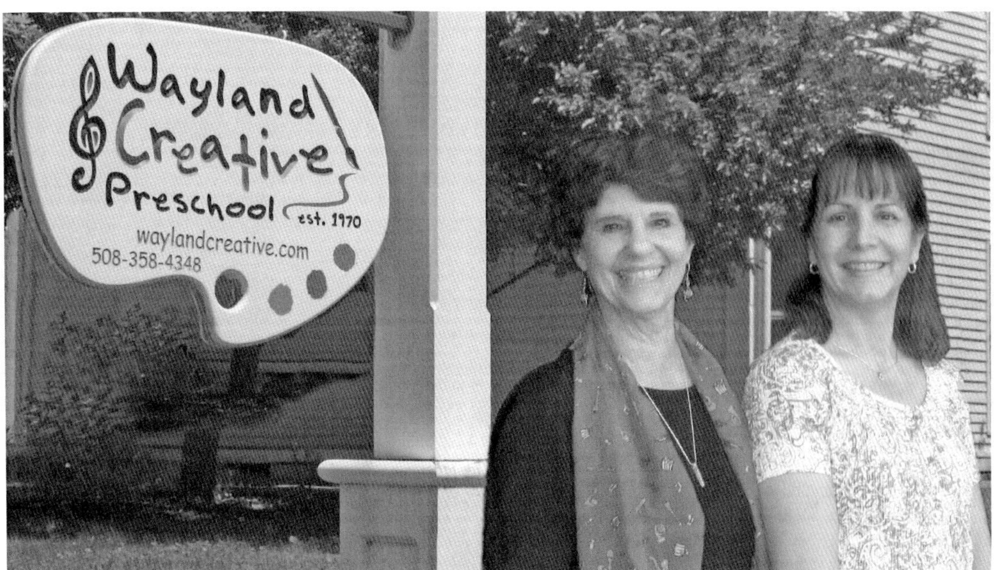

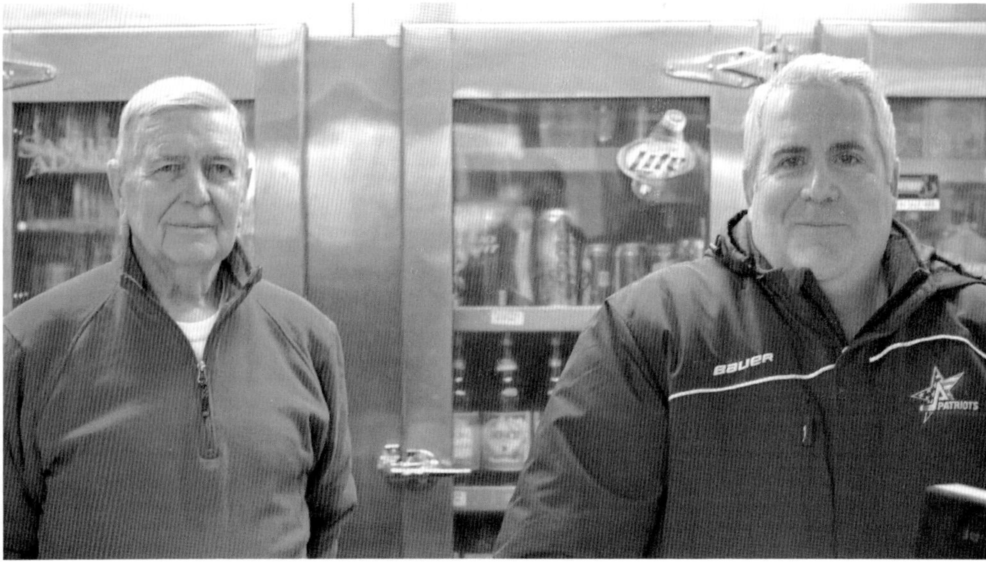

Robert Lavin Sr. and Robert Lavin Jr.

Father and son have been in business for 30 years on the site of the 1730 Caleb Moulton's tavern on Old Connecticut Path. The Havana Inn, a restaurant and nightclub, occupied the site until Frances J. Lavin converted it to a general/package store in 1945. The Lavin family has generously contributed to local organizations and schools, lending large punch bowls and cups, along with expert planning advice. (Courtesy of Dorothea Callen.)

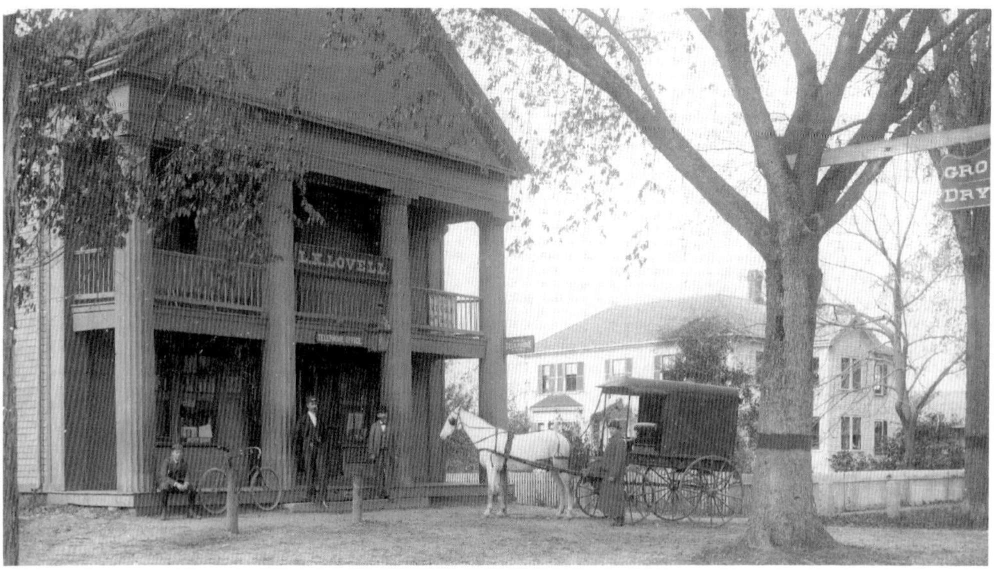

Lorenzo K. Lovell (1837–1909)

Lovell bought the old, Doric-columned town hall in 1878 after the town contracted to build a new one across the street. For four decades the building held town meetings, a schoolroom, and a library. Lorenzo sold groceries and dry goods there for 37 years before the Collins family leased and later purchased the building in 1922. The Collinses sold meat and groceries until 1962. Today, the building houses business offices.

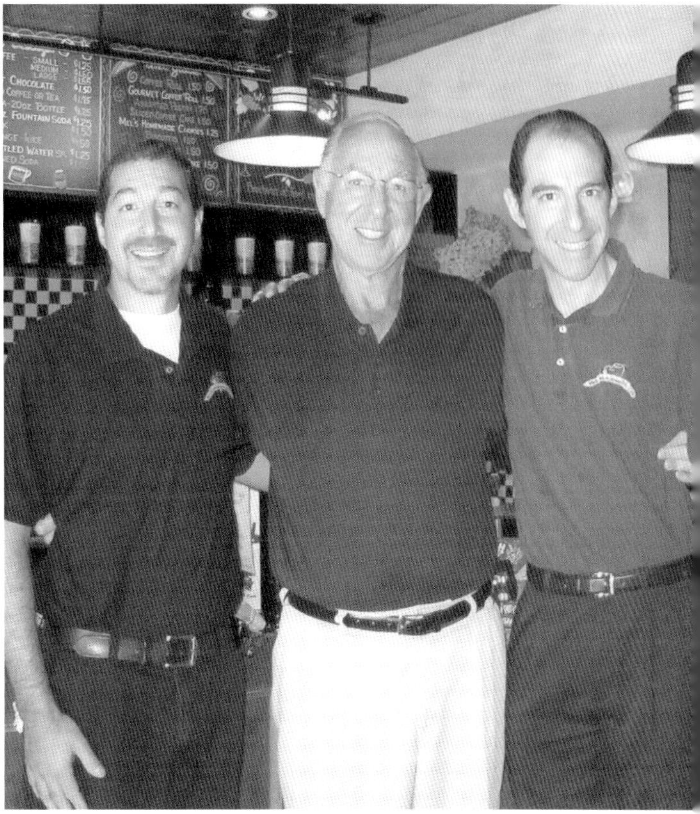

Melvyn Bloomstein, Paul Bloomstein, and Stewart Bloomstein
Mel Bloomstein was co-owner of the Elmwood Donut Shop at age 19. In 1958, he added a grill and started to cook hamburgers and hot dogs. Soon, customers wanted bacon and eggs, so breakfast was added. Then they wanted sandwiches and salads, so lunch was added. Years later, Mel's two grown sons, Paul and Stewart, joined the business, and today, Mel's Commonwealth Cafe is one of the oldest restaurants in town run by the same family. The brothers boast that a family member is on duty at all times. Paul and Stewart bought out their father after he retired to Florida in 2003. (Right, courtesy of the Bloomstein family; below, author's collection.)

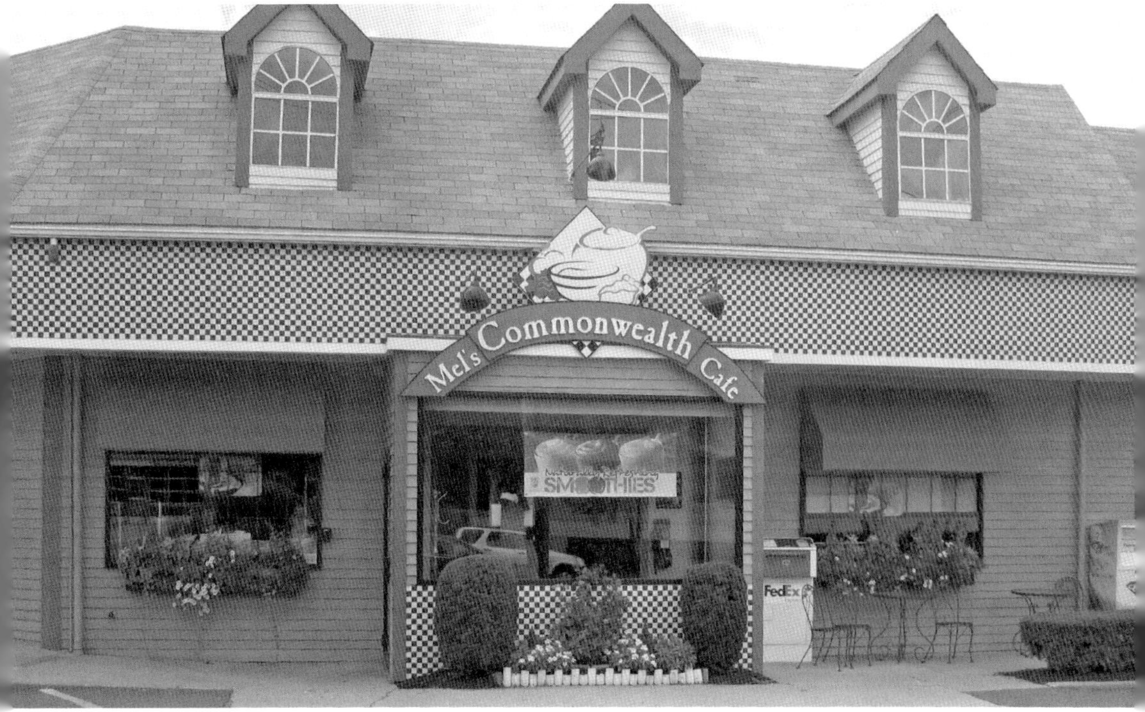

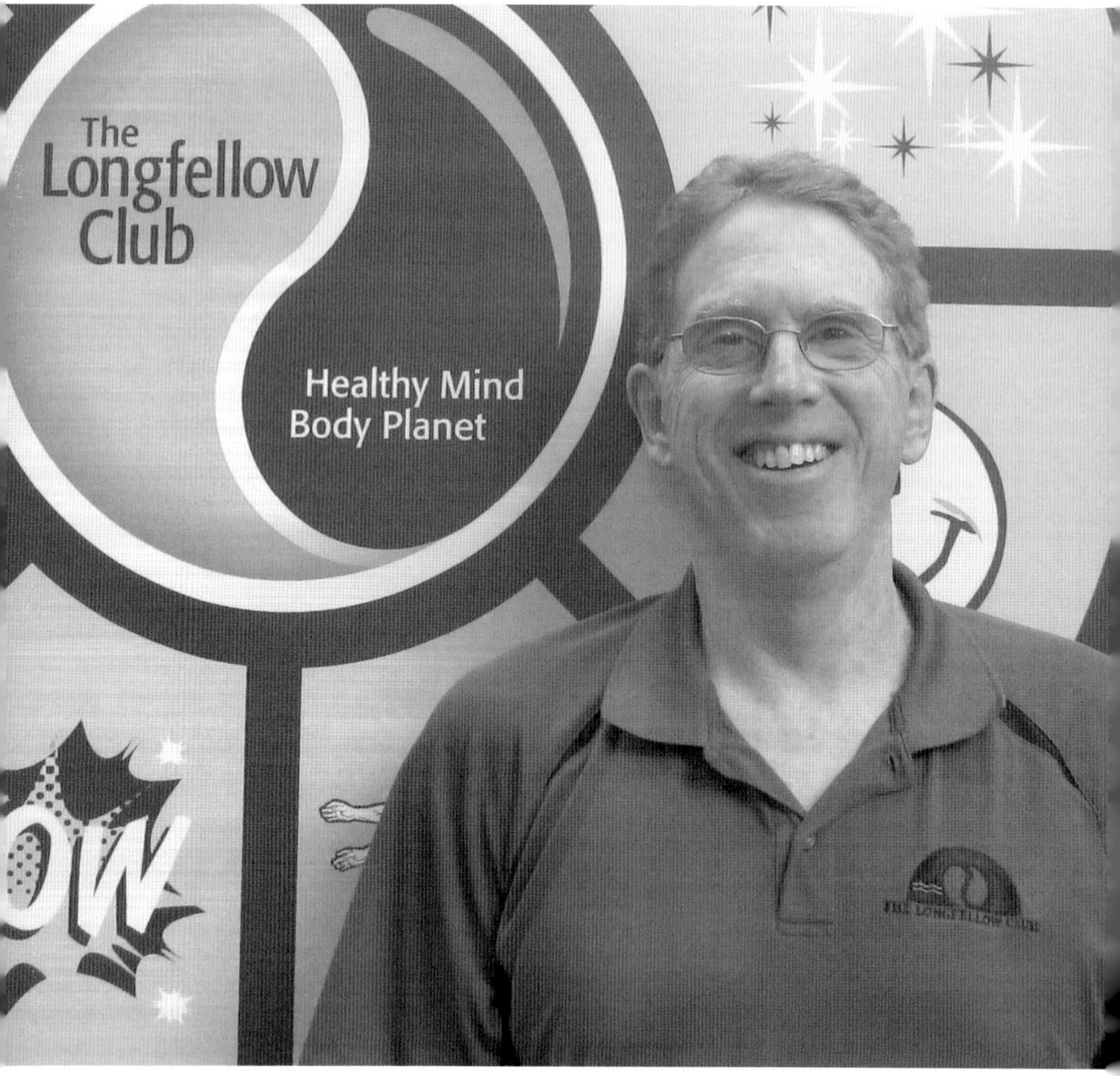

Myke Farricker

Myke Farricker purchased the Longfellow Tennis Club in 1980 with his partner, Laury Hammel. Today, the club has the largest instructional and junior tennis programs in New England. Club facilities include state-of-the-art exercise equipment, swimming pools, pickleball courts, and health and healing facilities. When the town was in need of childcare during school vacations, the partners opened a day camp in an adjacent facility to accommodate local families. Faculty members host the Special Olympics, sponsor tennis tournaments for Oxfam, cycling events for ALS patient care and research, and lead walks to raise money for the Jimmy Fund and Breast Cancer Research. (Author's collection.)

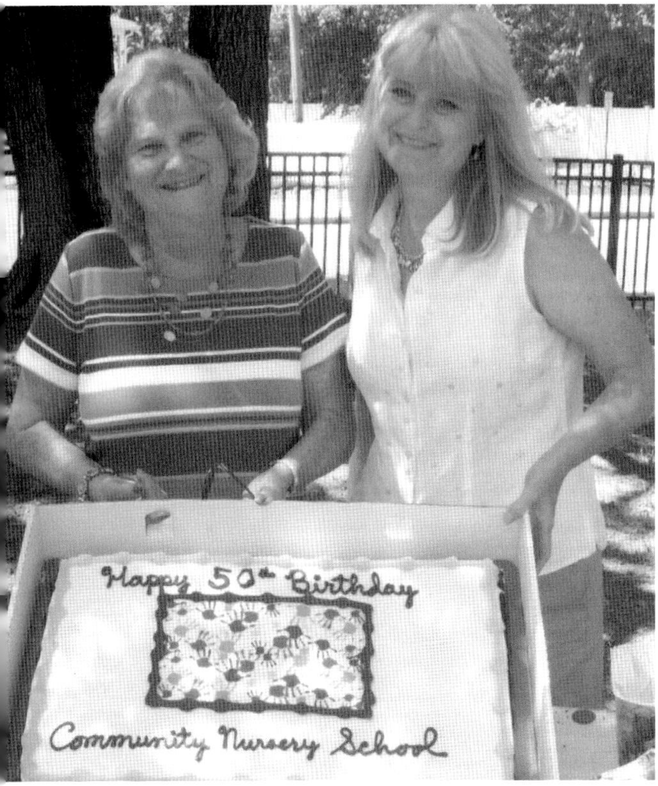

Roberta Wambolt and Beth Fuce
More than 50 years ago, a group of young mothers saw the need for local nursery schools. Roberta Wambolt responded by establishing Community Nursery in Cochituate Village. Focusing on confidence building, a positive self-image, and healthy relationships, her school's philosophy appealed to both working and non-working mothers. Today, Roberta's daughter Beth Fuce, also a teacher and mother, is co-director. Roberta's daughter-in-law Beth Wambolt is a full time teacher, and Roberta contributes several mornings a week. (Left, courtesy of Roberta Wambolt; below, author's collection.)

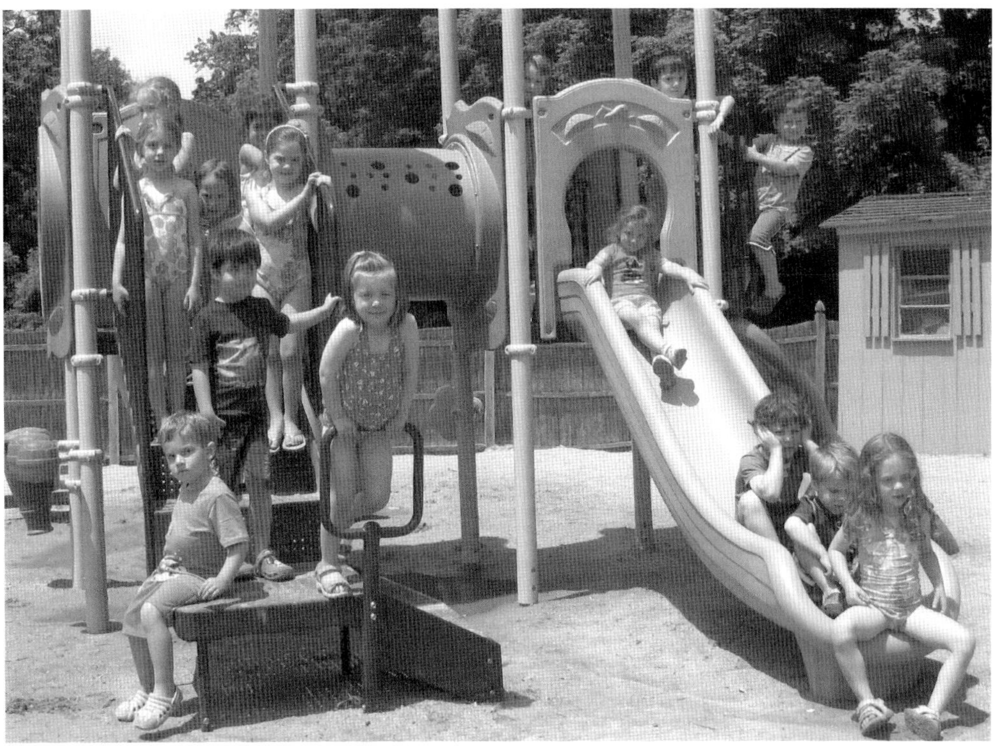

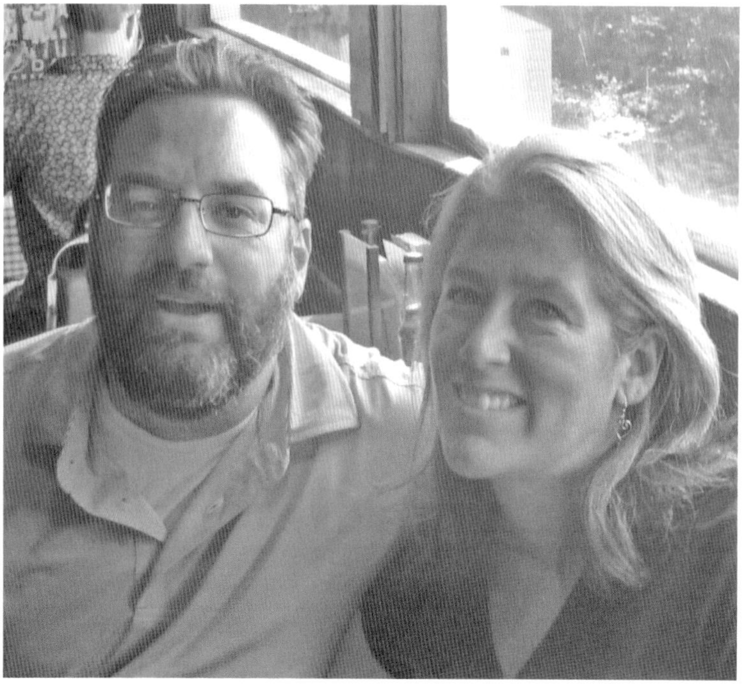

Kenneth "Ken" Phillips and Mandy Phillips

Ken and Mandy Phillips have made the Dudley Chateau, or the Chat, as it is known among regulars, a comfortable eatery for today's generation of customer. Despite the new family-friendly attitude, the Chateau boasts a colorful history. Built in the early 1920s as a private fishing lodge, it became a speakeasy during the Prohibition era. Later, it was turned into a men's club, frequented by baseball legends such as Babe Ruth and Ted Williams. Situated on the eastern edge of Dudley Pond, the Chateau serves up sparkling sunsets, a wide choice of signature burgers, and beverages for all ages and stages in life. (Both author's collection.)

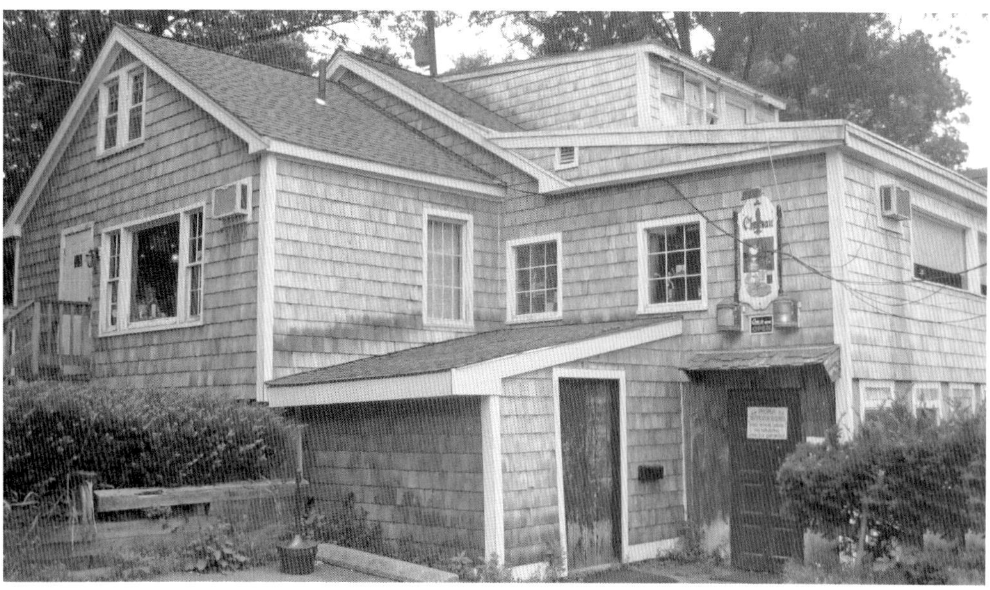

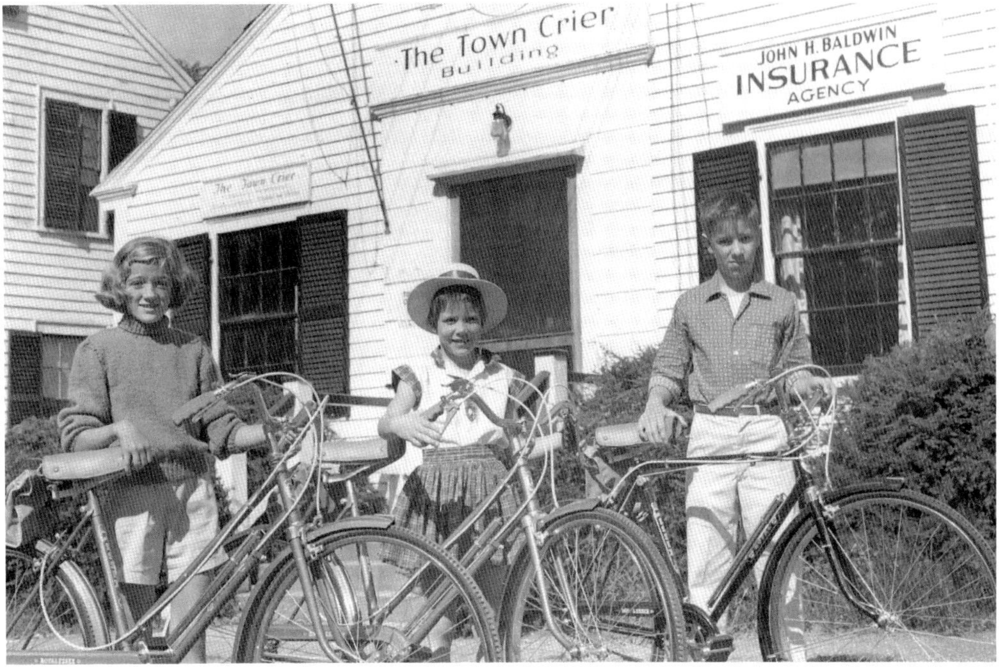

Wayland Town Crier

After the two local newspapers, *Village Bugle* and Cochituate's *Jeep*, ceased publication in February 1946, the need for a local newspaper became apparent. Three years later, early editions of the *Wayland Junior Town House Crier* were published, and eventually the current *Wayland Town Crier* became the local newspaper. Today, the paper is owned and published by Gatehouse Media Inc.

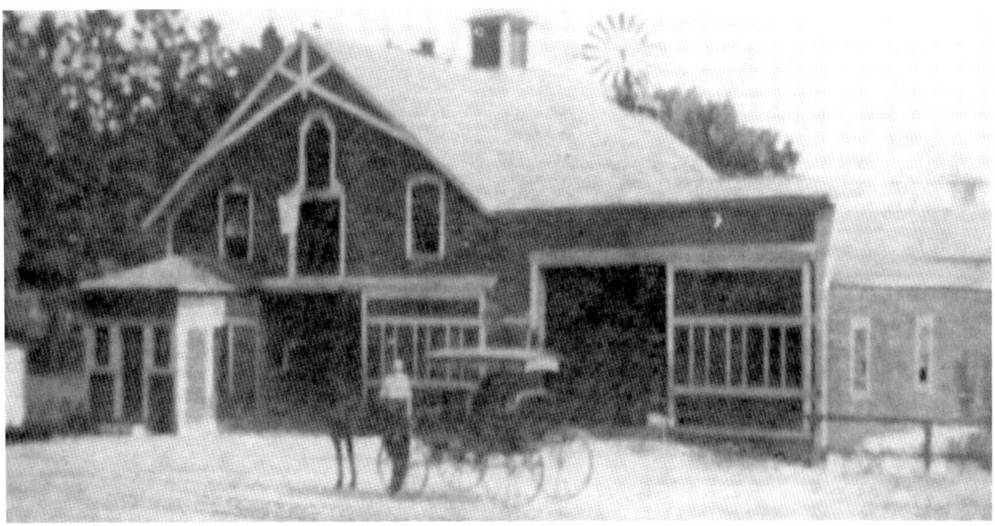

William "Bill" Begg (1914–1994)

Bill Begg worked with his father's trotters on the North Shore as a youth and became a trainer at the Flying Horse Stable in Hamilton, Massachusetts, at the age of 16. He was later hired to manage the stables at Greenway Farm in Wayland (pictured), where he worked for the rest of his life. He launched many riders on successful careers, including Karen Skives, who anchored the US equestrian team at the 1984 Olympic Games.

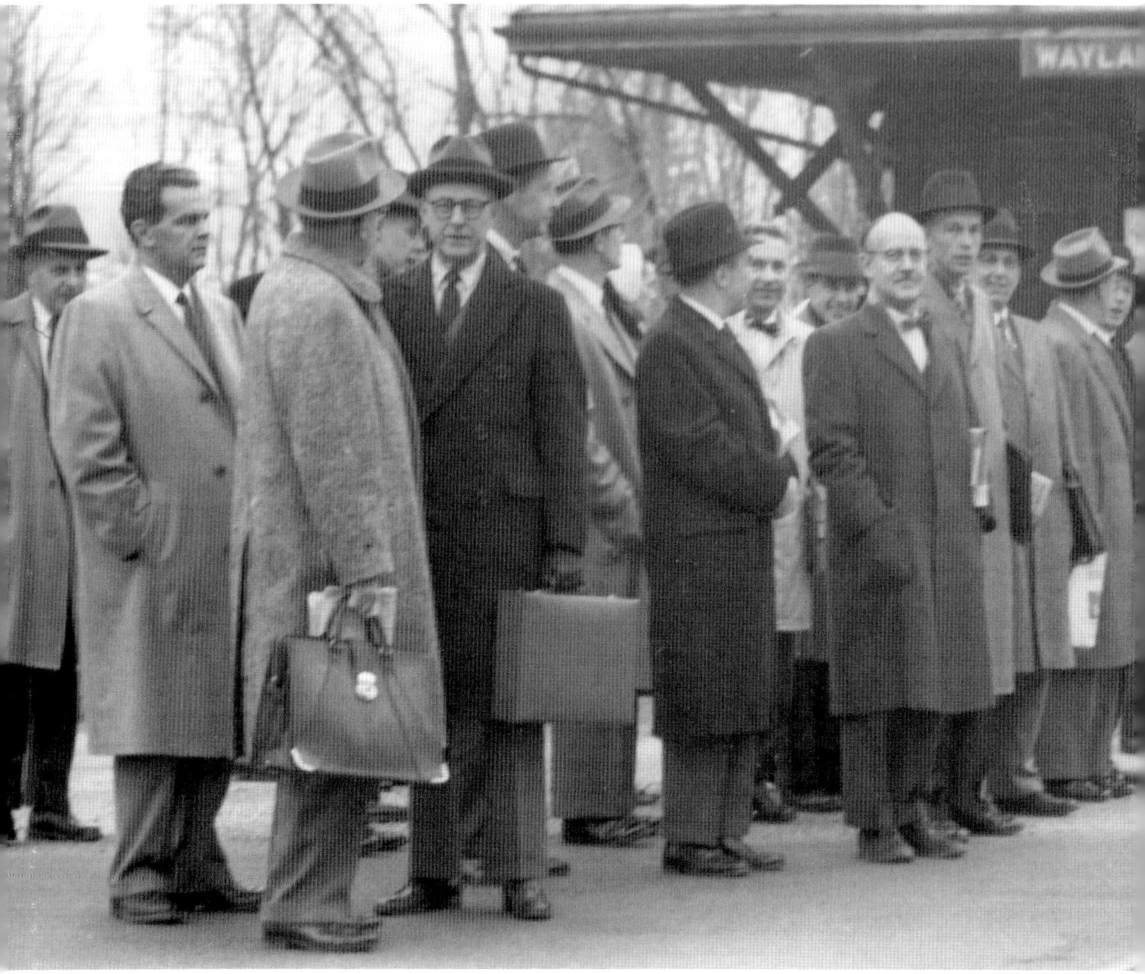

Wayland Depot

The Depot train station stopped serving in 1971, when the last train came through town. Today, the building is a National Historic Landmark and has operated as a consignment craft shop benefitting the town since 1980. The shop, a member of the National Federation of Women's Exchanges, is staffed by 70 volunteers and run by a board of directors elected by the membership. Proceeds have been donated to the Parmenter Food Pantry, Wayland Cares, and Wayland Habitat for Humanity. Pictured on the opposite page from left to right are (first row) M.C. Garfield, Barbara Hart, Ruth Wilkinson, Mary Morss, Linda Hanifin (depot president), Doss Wellins, Joan Morgello, Gene Brockington, Judy Canty Graves, Barbara Finlay, Margery Baston, and Gail Morrissey; (second row) Lois McKown, Debby Jones, Beth Barovick, and Susan Culver. (Opposite, courtesy of Julie Torres.)

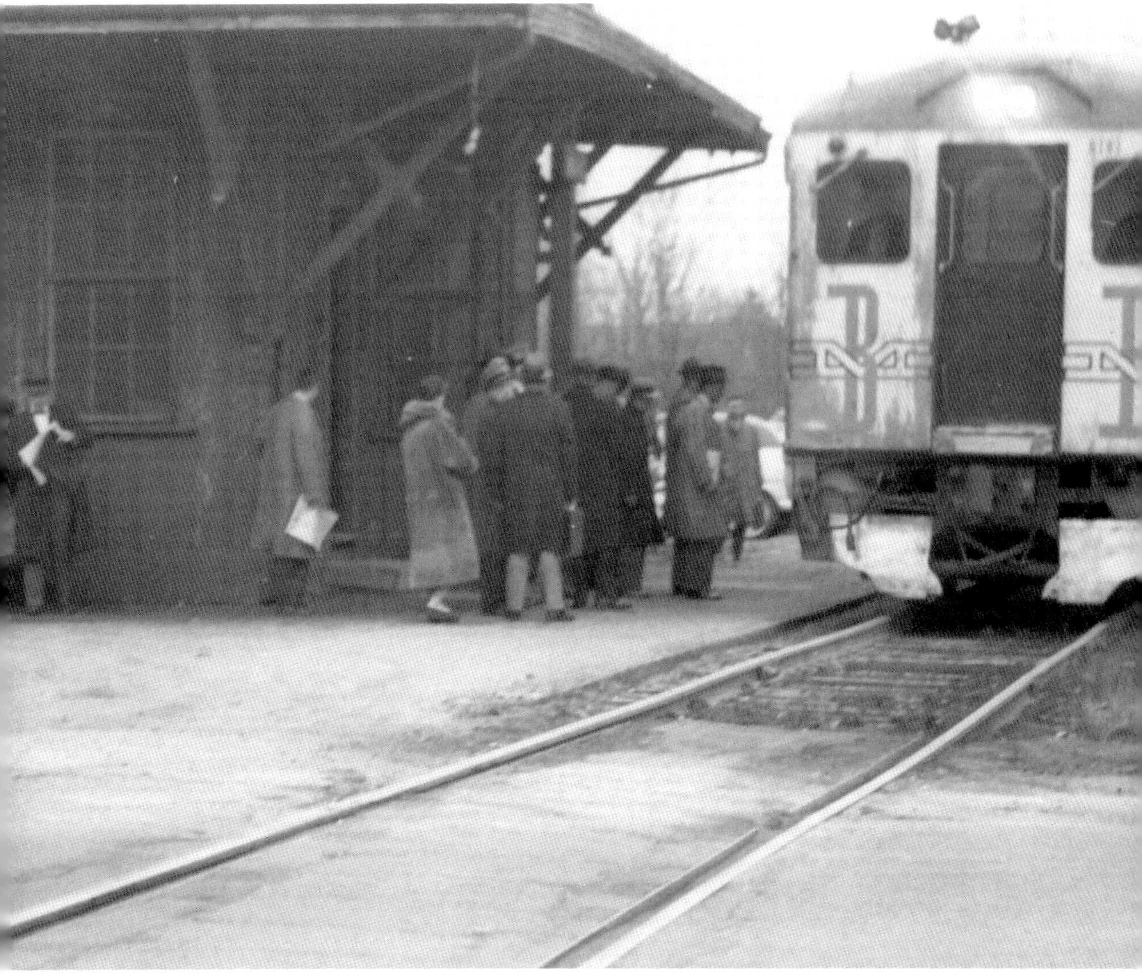

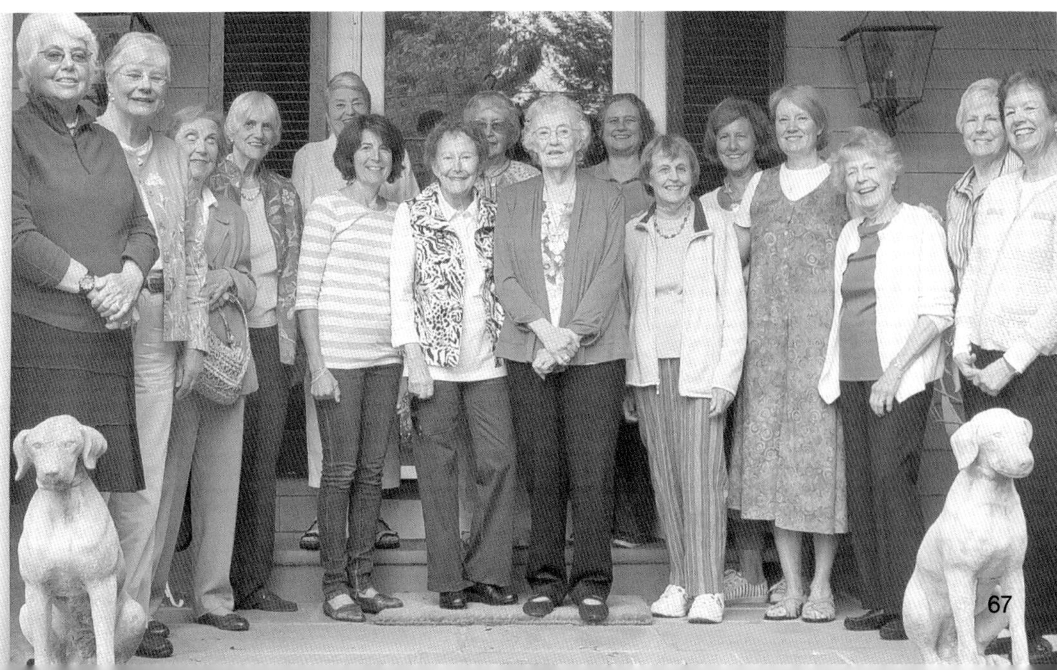

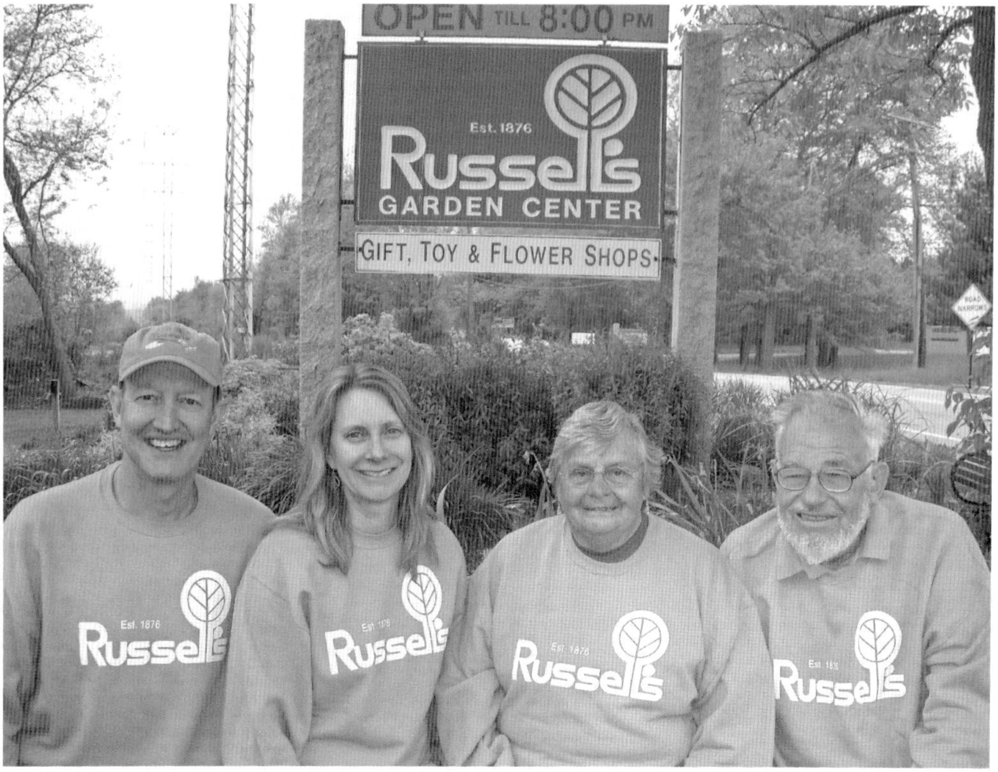

Lewis Russell Jr., Charlotte Russell, Elizabeth Russell Skehan, Timothy "Tim" Skehan, Jack Russell

Sam Russell established the first Russell's business in town in 1876, a grocery store and meat market. The third generation, Lewis Russell Jr. and his wife, Charlotte, 138 years later, have expanded the business to include a wide variety of annual and perennial plants, shrubs, and trees, in addition to flower, candle, and Christmas shops. Lewis specializes in custom-selected Christmas trees, chosen from tree farms in Maine and Canada. His daughter Elizabeth created a fully stocked gift section in 1981, which now includes everything from clothing to toys. With her husband, Tim Skehan, and cousin Jack Russell, this fourth generation caters to customers who come from all over New England for one-stop shopping. Farmers' markets, on Saturday in the winter and Wednesday in the summer, began in 2005, offering fresh produce and locally prepared foods. Russell's has always contributed to local charities and is an active presence in the Wayland Business Association and with Wayland Beautification. (Both courtesy of Suzie Shapiro.)

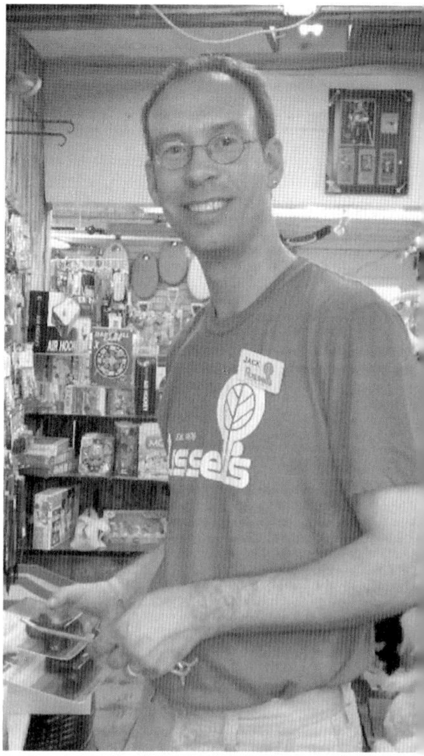

Mike Giakoumakis and Kathleen "Kathy" Giakoumakis

Mike and Kathy Giakoumakis have owned and operated Liberty Pizza since 1985, and their generosity to the schools and community are legend. The Giakoumakises do more than feed hungry mouths; they nurture good sportsmanship and academic excellence. The Liberty Pizza Scholarship Fund is awarded to three seniors annually; the Wayland football team receives 10 large pizzas, plus drinks, after winning a game; and Wayland High School cheerleaders hold their annual car wash alongside Liberty Pizza. One season, the Wayland football team won 13 games, and Mike and Kathy served athletes 130 pizzas. A large jug sits on the counter for donations to the Daniel G. Burgess Scholarship Fund, named for a local athlete who died young. The fund is sponsored by Good Shepherd Church, and at the end of each year, the jug, often containing close to $1,000, is delivered to the church. During the summer, under the lights, a Wayland/Cochituate Amateur Sports Development (WAYco) softball team, sponsored by Mike and Kathy, plays at the Cochituate/Griffin Ball Field behind their establishment. (Author's collection.)

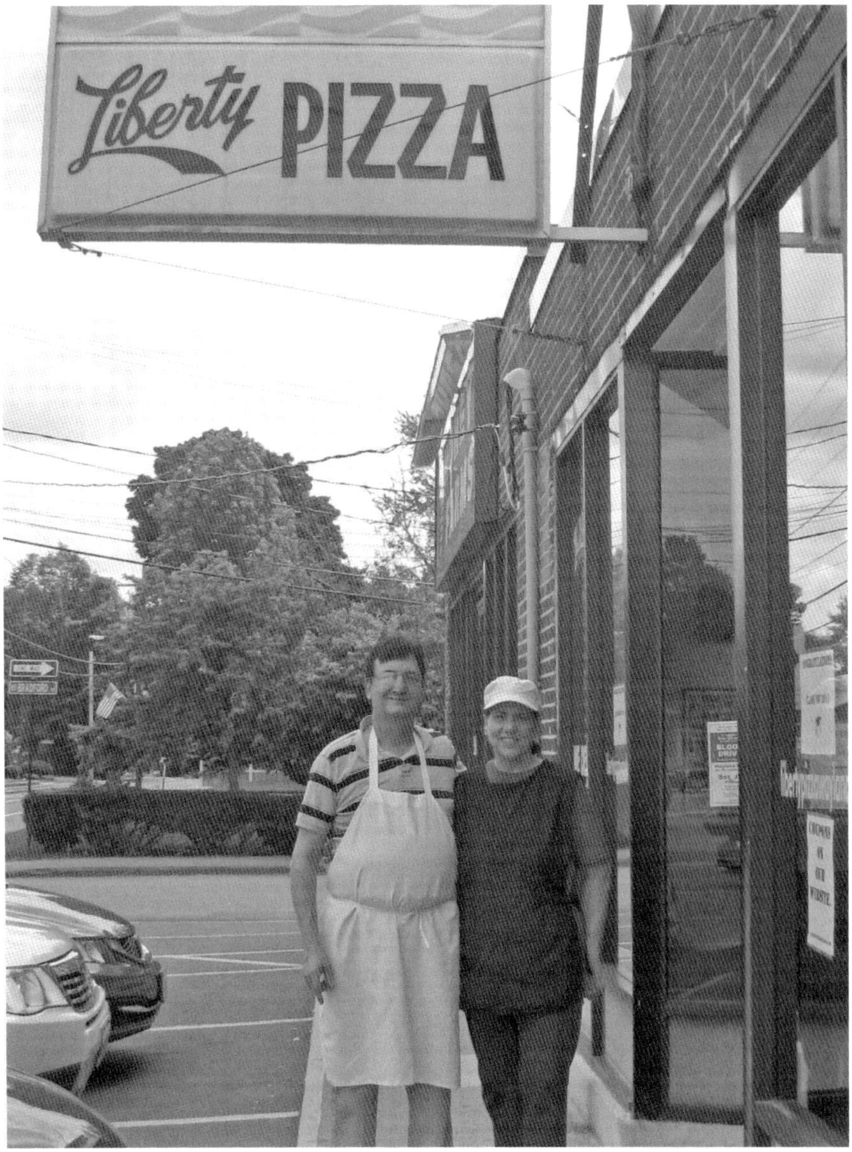

John Bryant (1924–2005)

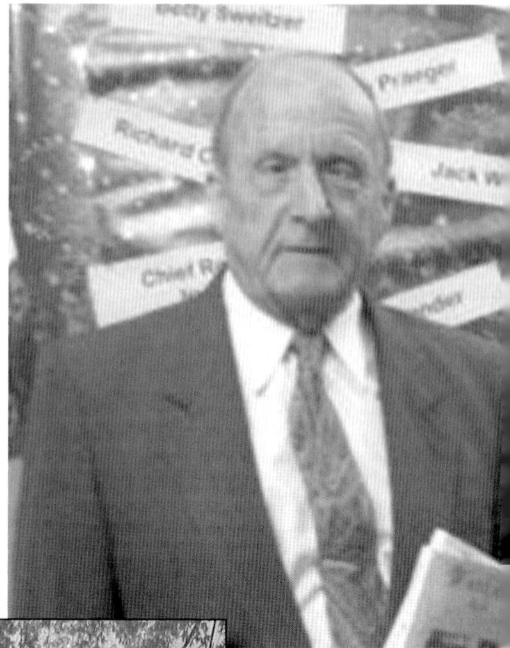

A lifelong resident of Wayland, Bryant enlisted in the Army Air Corps after graduating from Wayland High, serving two years in China, Burma, and India. Upon his return home, he started his own business, eventually employing some of the finest carpenters in the Boston metro west region. He married a local girl, Lorraine Campbell, and the couple had three children. In addition to his business, Bryant decided to pursue other interests as well. He apprenticed at the Gibbs Funeral Home in Cochituate, and by 1965, had graduated with highest honors from the New England Institute of Funeral Directing and Anatomy. Three years later, he opened his own funeral establishment. He was the go-to person for Cochituate history and became unofficial historian of the village of Cochituate, serving on many town boards and committees. John's kindness, honesty, and service to the town are legendary. (Right, courtesy of Steve Engler; below, author's collection.)

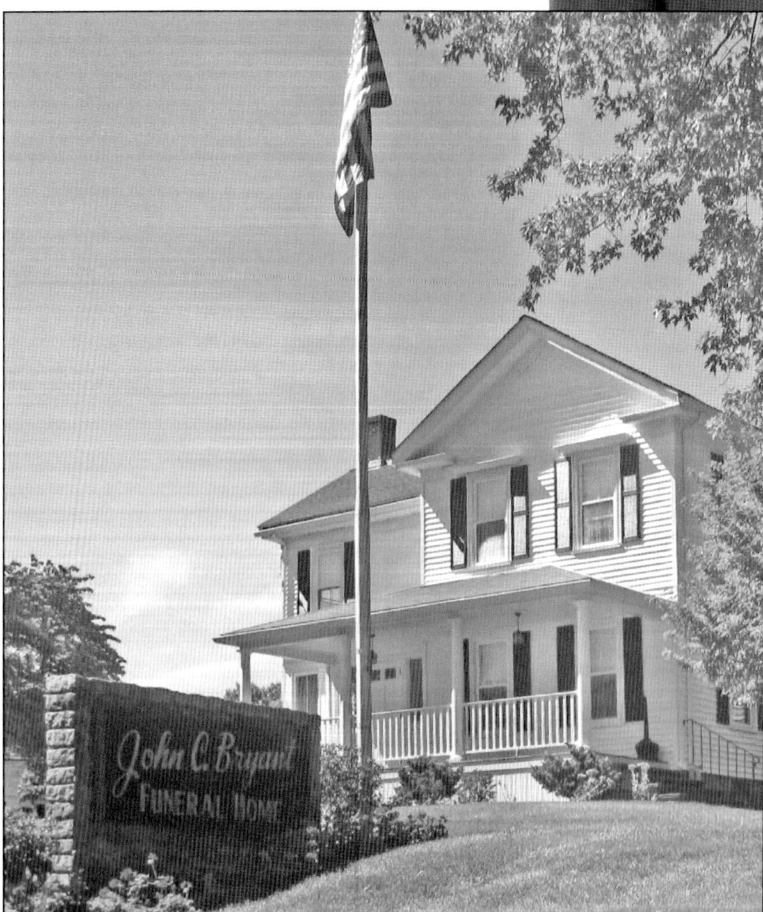

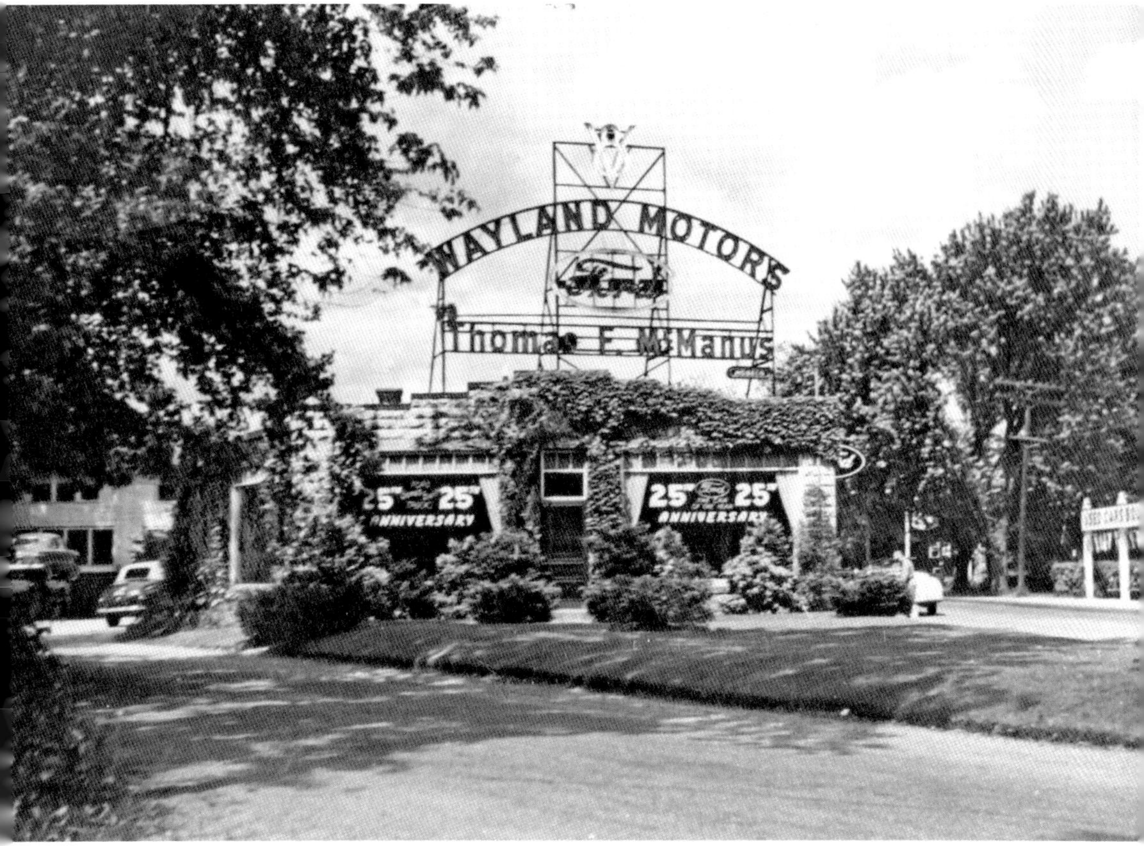

Thomas L.M. McManus (1920–2007)

In 1915, Thomas opened Wayland Motors, a dealership for Overland cars, at the corner of the Boston Post and Pelham Island Roads. His father, Lawrence, who had been working as a blacksmith since his youth, had purchased Jeremiah Mullen's blacksmith shop on the site in 1884.

A decade after Wayland Motors opened for business, Henry Ford persuaded Thomas to switch to selling Ford cars. Thereafter, a shiny new Ford car was always displayed on the lot, and the business remained in the hands of the McManus family until 1979. After the business closed, the town bought the land, demolished the building, and created Blacksmith Green in its place.

Elijah Bent (1715–1779)

Elijah Bent built the Pequod House (Inn) in 1771 when the town was still named Sudbury, to provide refreshments and a gathering place for tired travelers and townspeople. The Public Safety Building now stands in its place. The inn was one of the favorite stops along the route from Sudbury to Stony Brook in Weston, Massachusetts. There was ample room for overnight guests, shelter for wagons, and side stalls for horses. The town watering trough and pump were located in front of the inn on Cochituate Road. The inn had a series of owners until it was purchased in 1920 by private citizens. Eight years later, the inn was torn down and the land donated to the town as a site for a new town hall.

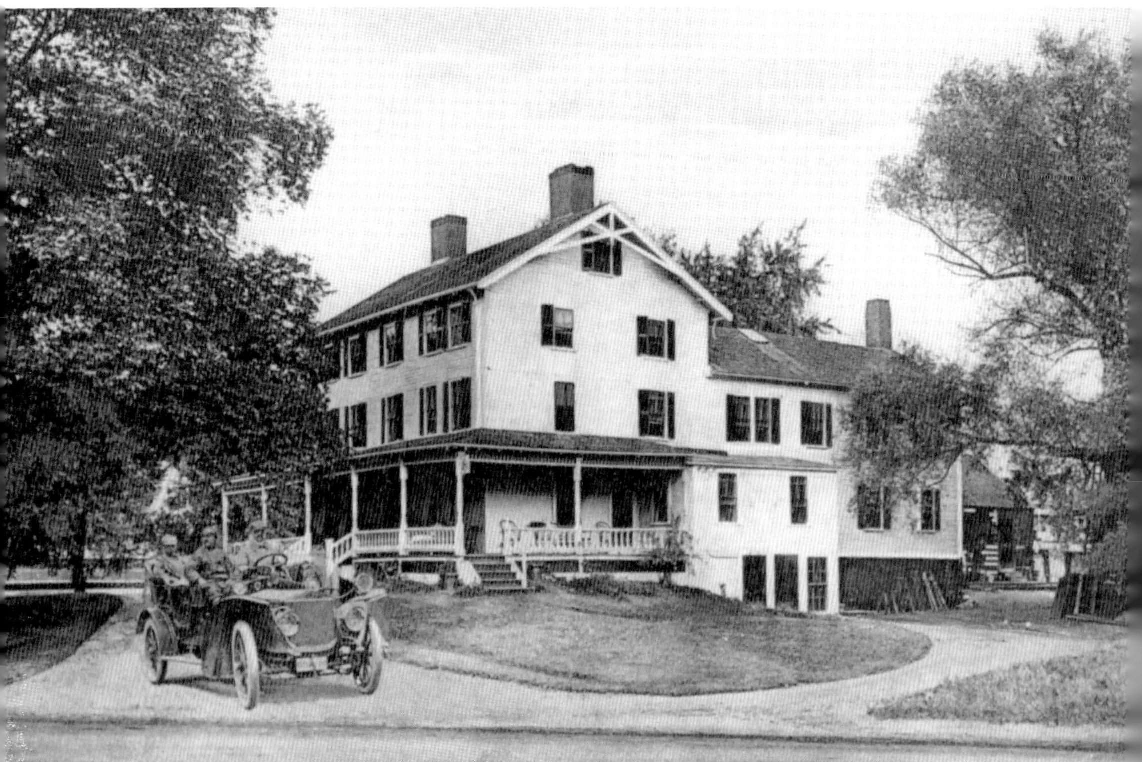

CHAPTER FOUR

Heroes and Heroines

Courage is found in unlikely places.

—J.R.R. Tolkien

For almost 400 years, brave young men and women have served the town as soldiers. In 1676, with little support from Mother England, Sudbury men and women fought with axes, shovels, and a limited number of weapons against King Philip and his Wampanoag warriors. King Philip planned to wipe out every settlement until he reached Boston, but suffered a significant setback in Sudbury. Fortunately, Ephraim Curtis, a Sudbury soldier, managed to get a message through enemy lines, and Philip's war campaign ended in Sudbury. After the war, Curtis returned to his family and became an important figure in the community. He served many years as a representative in the General Court.

A century later, in 1776, Sudbury found itself confronted by the Revolutionary War. When the call for action came, Sudbury's militia was prepared, and 348 men responded. Soldiers marched to Concord, just seven miles away, to join the revolution and raise arms against their English brethren. The soldiers were led to Concord by 80-year-old deacon Josiah Haynes. He survived until later in the war, when he and Thomas Bent were killed by musket balls in Lexington.

A little more than eight decades passed before Sudbury soldiers were asked once again to fight in the Civil War. Over 70 Wayland men enlisted, and they saw action throughout the South or spent their service in Boston Harbor. After the war, John Calvin Butterfield returned home to serve as undertaker and superintendent of Lakeview Cemetery, and Frank W. Draper served for two decades as state medical examiner.

Many men and women served at home and abroad during World War II. Shirley Barnes and Marian Draper, Army Air Corps nurses, attended wounded soldiers in France, and Leila Sears and her half-sister Mary Sears served in the Navy in Washington, DC.

During World War II, the *Village Bugle* and *Jeep* were produced in town and mailed to young men abroad, keeping them in touch with family and friends. Following World War II, John Dyer served in the Korean War as a navigator and captain in the Air Force. Richard Turner served in the Vietnam War as coxswain on a river craft in Vietnam, for which he earned a Purple Heart. The veteran of the most wars was the late George Dergalis, who served in World War II, Korea, and Vietnam before settling in Wayland to practice his art.

Important town heroes, whether or not a war is raging, are the many firefighters who protect Wayland. Since the first all-volunteer fire department battled blazes in the Cochituate shoe factories, Wayland firefighters have fought to save homes throughout town. In the 1950s, the town's all-volunteer fire department handed the job of firefighting over to professional firefighters, and citizens continue to be well protected by these heroes.

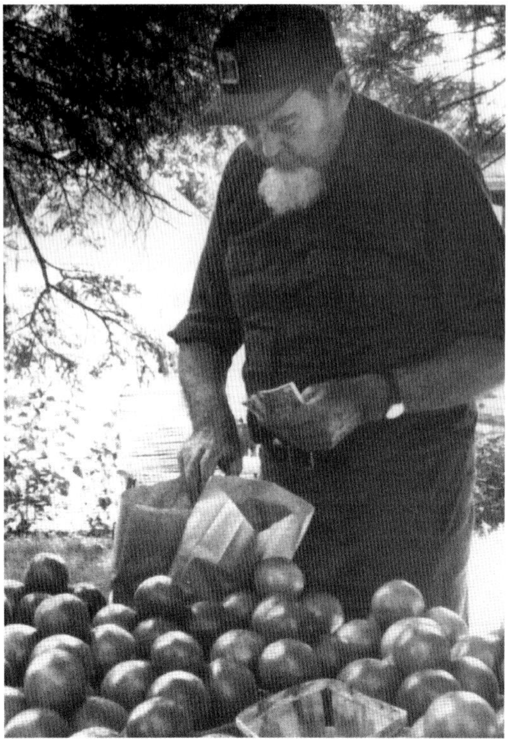

Clarence Ames (1913–1997)

Clarence "Farmer" Ames was in the Navy during World War II, working at the Natick government transit depot. But he never stopped farming. He dropped out of school during the Great Depression to work on his uncle's 350-acre farm in Wayland. Later, he raised produce for sale at a roadside stand in front of his home on Main Street. He tended a chicken coop and sold strawberries, blueberries, corn, pumpkins, and hay.

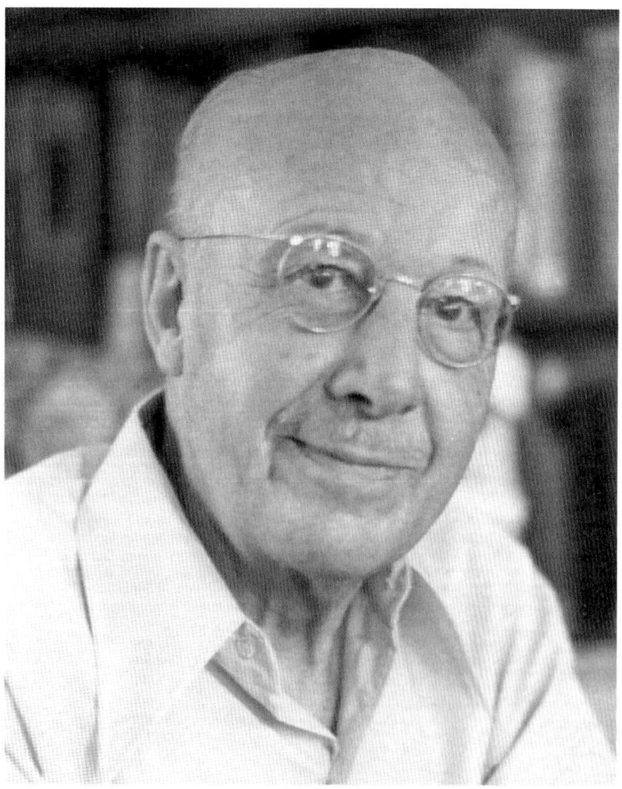

George Bogren (1900–1992)

George Bogren was a major with the Western Pacific Base Command in the Fiji Islands during World War II and received the Bronze Star for outstanding service. A professional engineer, he was active in Wayland for more than eight decades, serving on several town boards and as a charter member of Charles H. Alward Post 133 of the American Legion. He was a trustee of the Hannah Williams playground, Wayland Historical Society, and Parmenter Health Center.

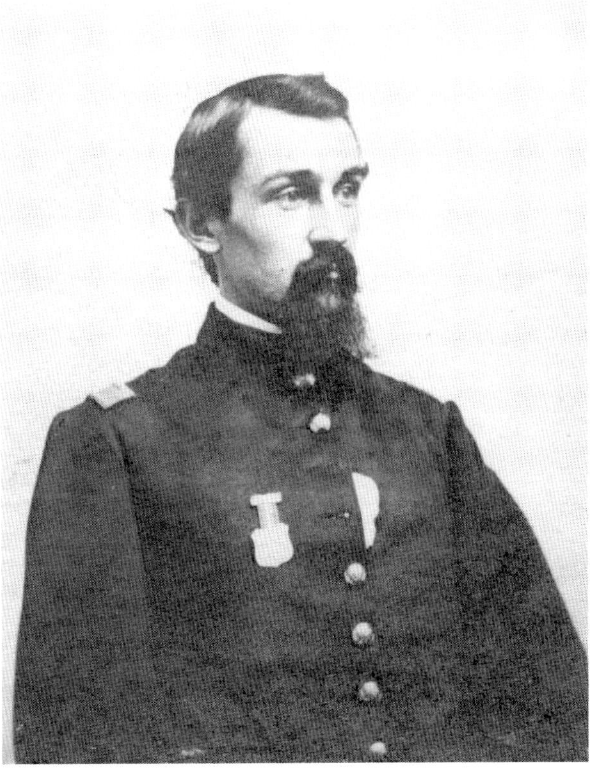

John Noyes Morse (1844–1935)

Morse enlisted for service in the Civil War at the age of 18 and was assigned to Company D, 35th Massachusetts Infantry. In 1862, he was promoted to the rank of first lieutenant. He was one of the town's oldest citizens, long prominent in town and veterans' affairs. Three volleys were fired and taps sounded at Mount Auburn Crematory before his ashes were taken to Wayland for burial.

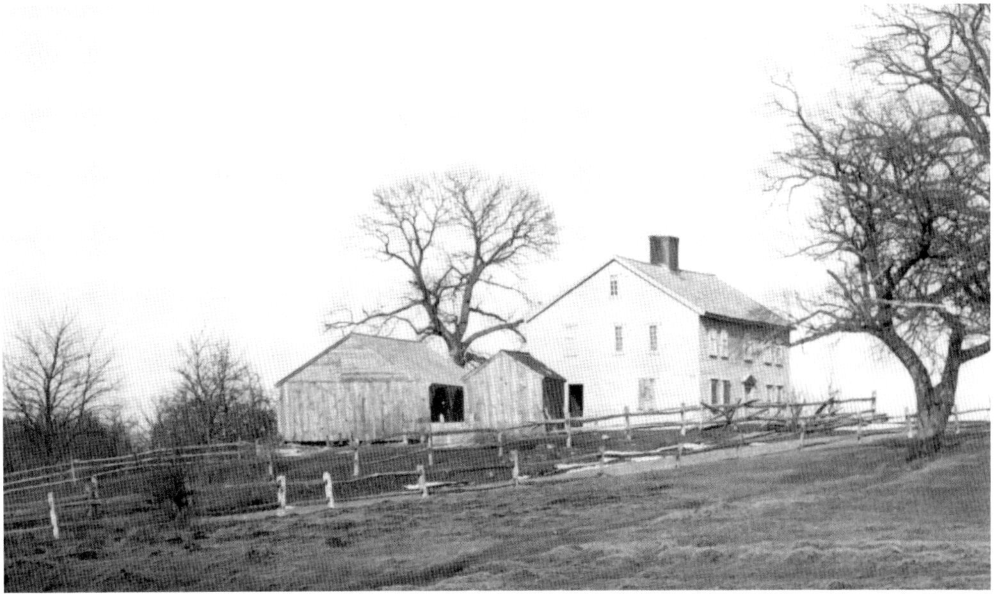

Thomas Bent (1706–1775)

Thomas Bent left this home on Pelham Island Road and marched off to Concord along with his four sons on April 19, 1775. He was 68 years old. Bent had fought in the French and Indian War as a young man. He took a musket ball in the leg at Concord against British troops and died three months later. His wife, who had cared for him, died that same morning. They were buried together in a single grave.

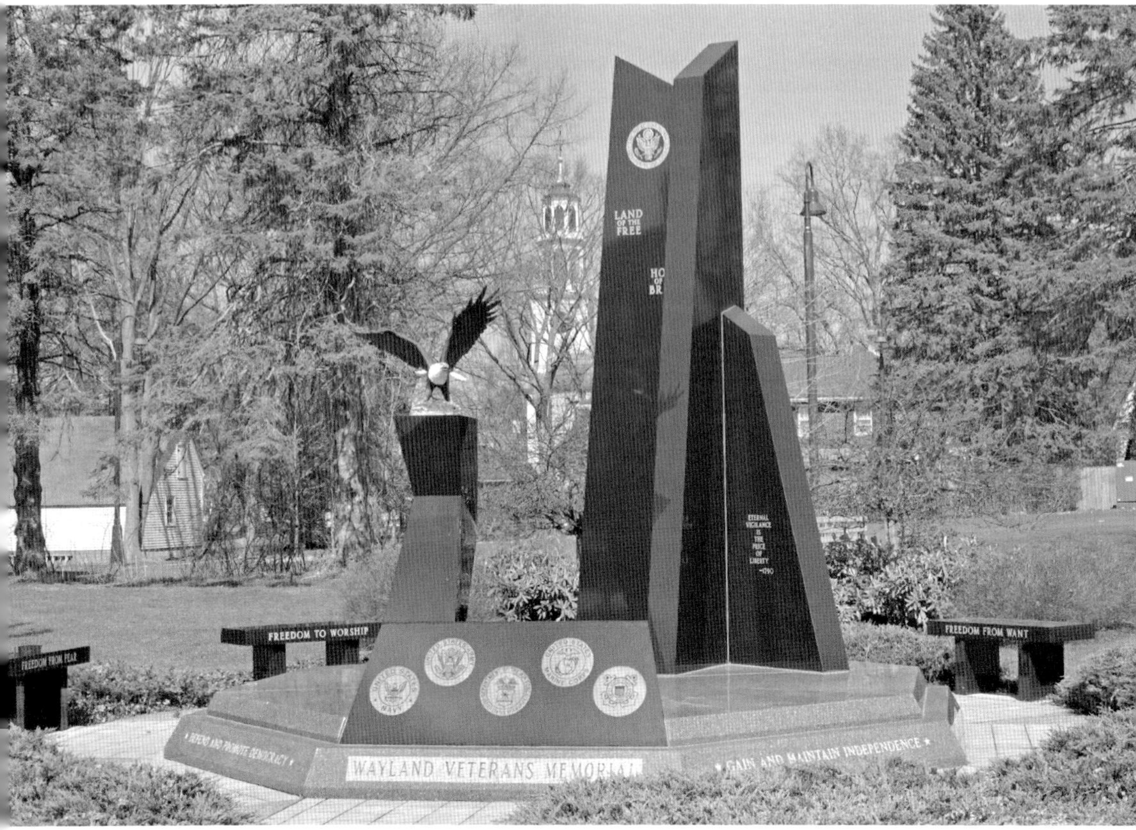

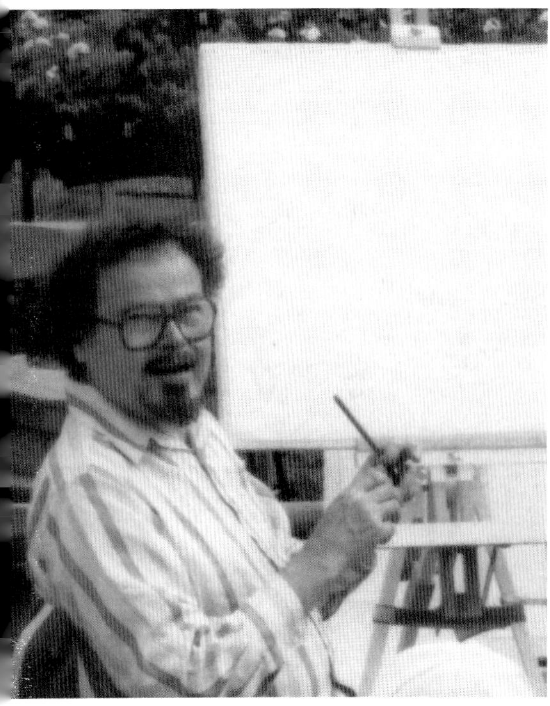

George Dergalis (1928–2012)

Dergalis, a survivor of three wars—World War II, the Korean War, and the Vietnam War—moved to Wayland in 1969. Born in Athens, Greece, he was drafted into the Greek army at the age of 15. Three years later, he was captured by the Germans and sent to a concentration camp. He later escaped to Italy, where he earned a master's degree from the Academy of Fine Arts in Rome, with the highest honor. Upon his arrival in the United States, he held menial jobs until he was drafted into the Air Force. During the Vietnam War, he served as a combat artist, painting Vietnamese battlefields throughout a country he deemed beautiful. After being discharged, Dergalis continued his art education at the Museum of Fine Arts in Boston, where he became a lecturer. He also taught at the DeCordova Museum in Lincoln and at home. Grateful to have been able to immigrate to the United States and become a citizen, Dergalis volunteered to design the town's Veterans Memorial (above), which was completed and dedicated in 2005. (Above, courtesy of Dorothea Callen.)

George B. Howe (1844–1940)
Howe was Wayland's last surviving Civil War veteran and remained active in town affairs until two days before his death. He came to Cochituate in 1875, was first employed in the shoe industry, and later owned a grain and coal business. He drove a stagecoach between Marlboro and Stony Brook Station on the Weston town line as there was no connection between these points prior to 1881. Full military honors were accorded at his funeral.

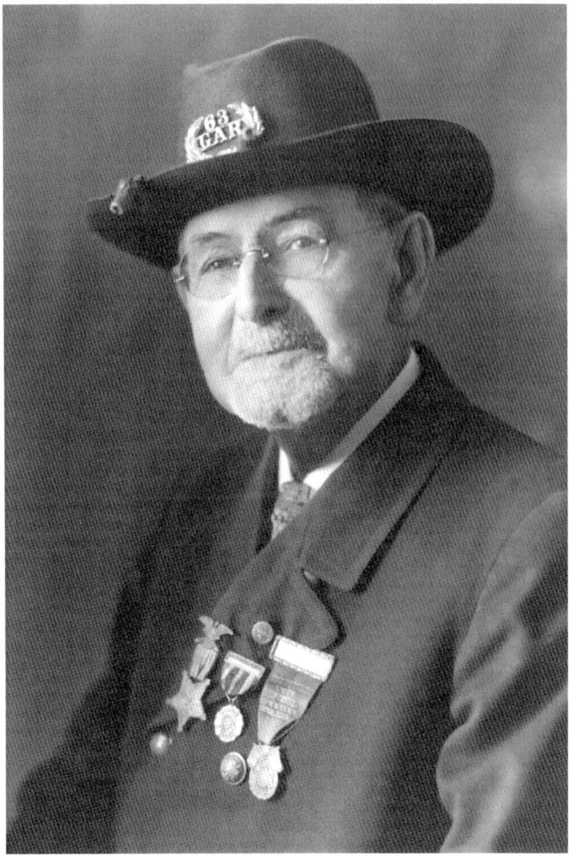

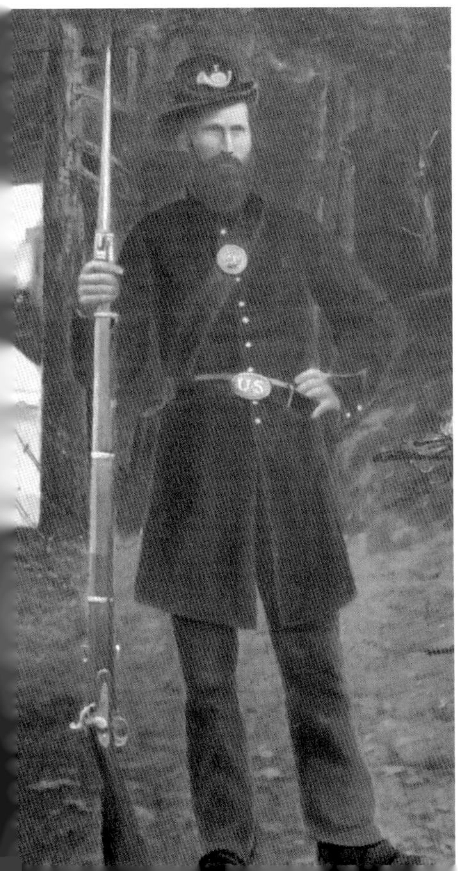

George T. Dickey (1826–1862)
Dickey was a 35-year-old father of three when he enlisted in the Union Army in 1861. A year later, while on duty in Maryland, he contracted pneumonia and died. Dickey was one of eight Wayland soldiers to die in the Civil War.

John Calvin Butterfield (1816–1909)
Butterfield volunteered to join the Union Army along with two of his sons, the only family in town to do so. After the war, he became a shoemaker in Cochituate Village and served as undertaker and superintendent of the Lakeview Cemetery. As overseer of the poor, he saw that drunks and transients locked up overnight were fed a meal. In 1865, he became superintendent of the new Episcopal Methodist Society in Cochituate.

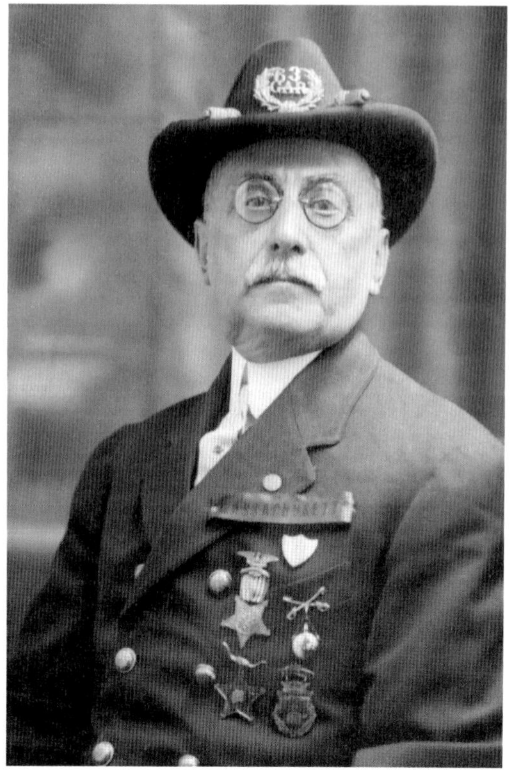

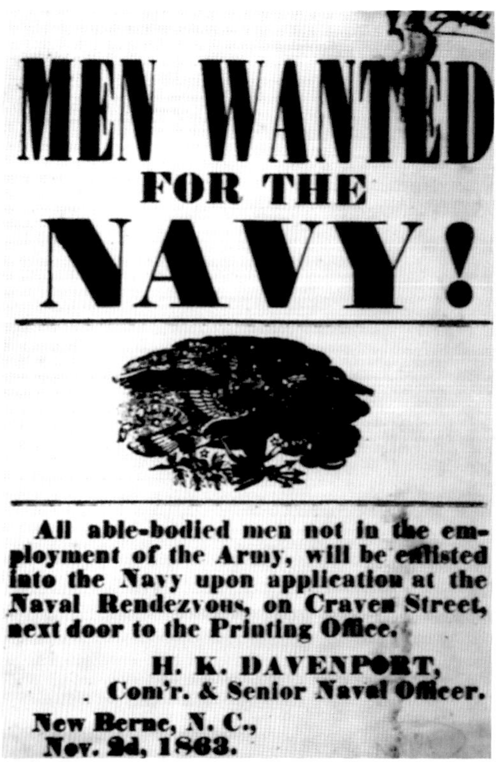

Charles B. Butterfield (1844–1919)
Charles was the son of John C. Butterfield, a prominent citizen of Cochituate. He enlisted in the Civil War with his father in 1862 at the age of 18. His brother William Henry Butterfield had signed up the previous year. Of Wayland's 78 men who participated in the Civil War, six were captured, including Charles. After the war, Charles raced horses in winter on an ice track on Dudley Pond. The Boston Water Board tried unsuccessfully to stop him.

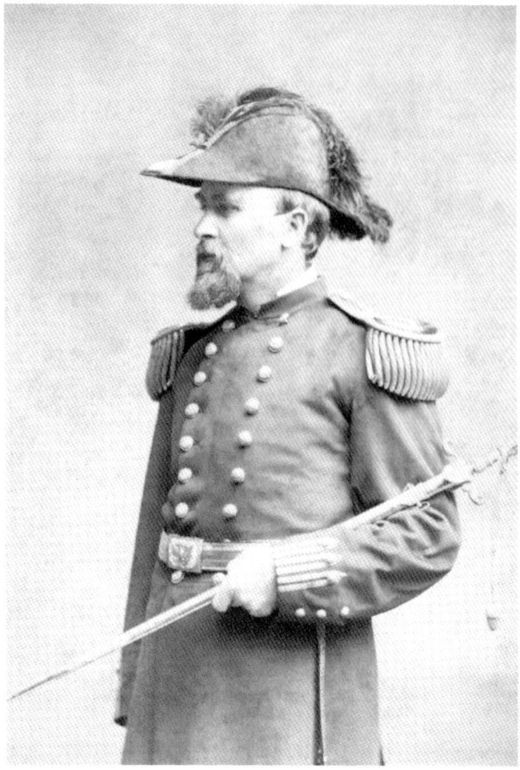

Frank W. Draper (1843–1909)
Frank Draper left Brown University in 1862 to serve in the Civil War. His service included marching in review for Pres. Abraham Lincoln and commanding a unit of African American troops. After the war, he entered Harvard Medical School, where he taught for 35 years. He was appointed state medical examiner in 1877 and served for two decades. Active in 38 murder cases, he was present at the trial of Lizzie Borden.

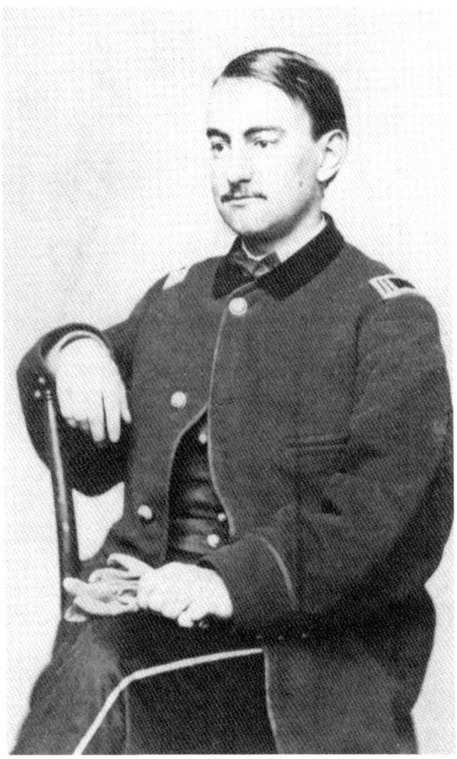

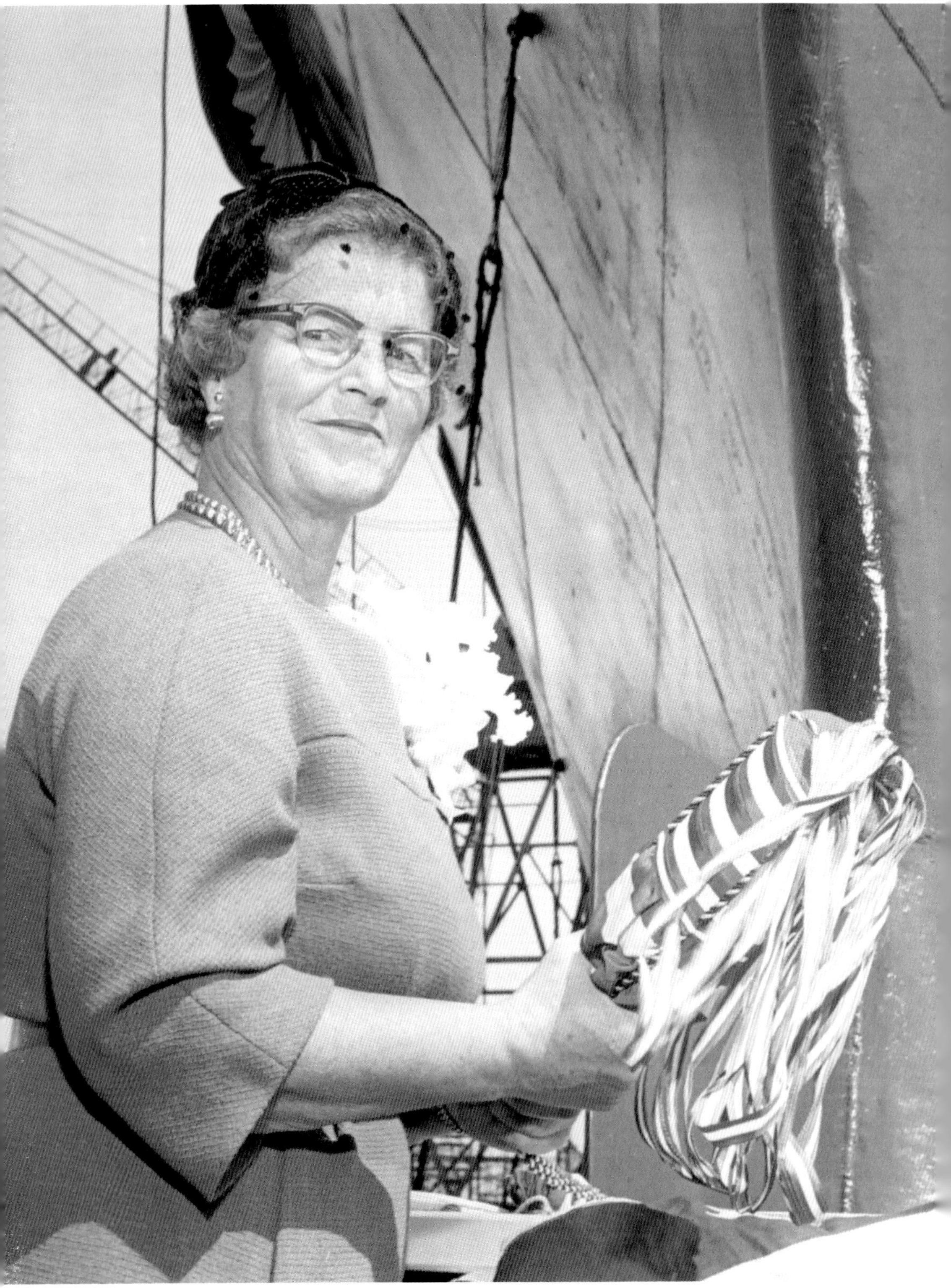

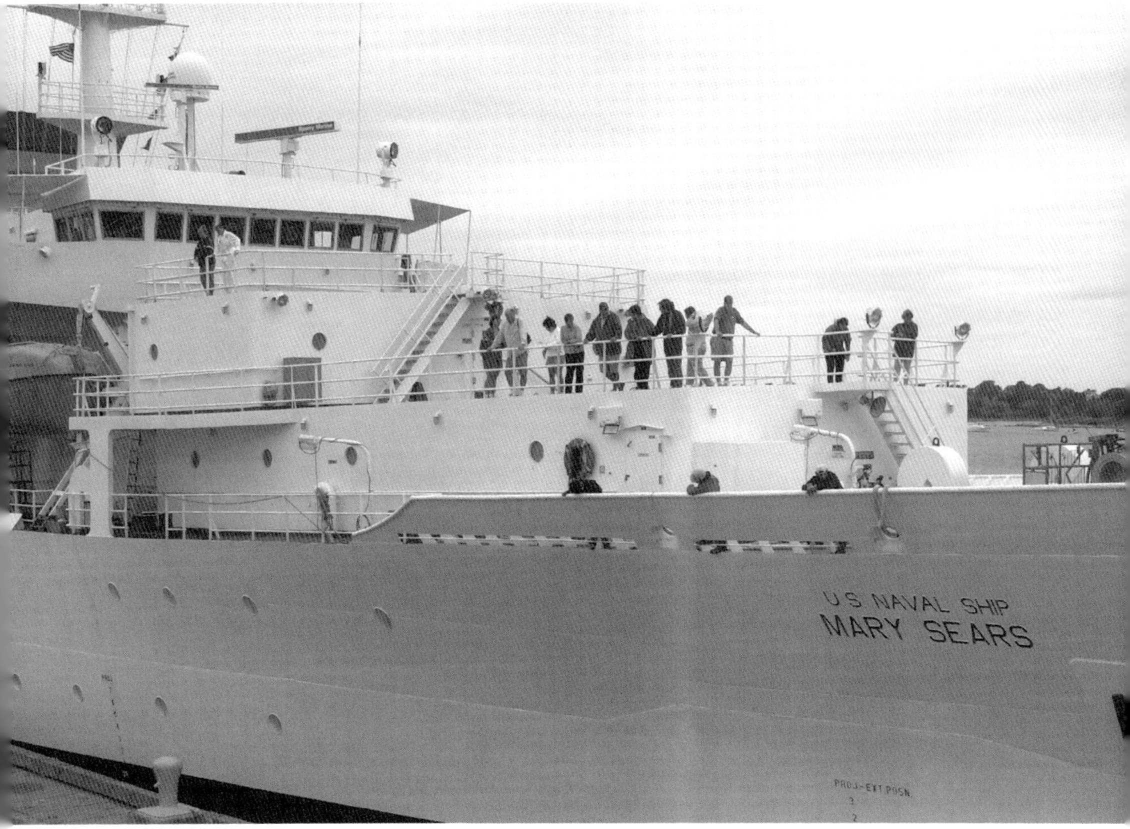

Mary Sears (1905–1997) (OPPOSITE)
Mary Sears was born and raised on Pelham Island Road, daughter of Edmund and Leslie Buckingham Sears. She was commissioned a lieutenant junior grade in the Navy WAVES in 1943 and called to Washington, DC, where she organized and headed the new Oceanographic Unit of the Navy Hydrographic Office. She taught the Navy how to hide its submarines from the Japanese Imperial Navy between different temperature layers in the Pacific Ocean and helped plan guidelines for amphibious operations. In 1947, she transferred to the Navy Reserves and retired as a commander in US Naval Research. In 2000, the Navy launched its newest oceanographic survey ship, USNS *Mary Sears*, at the Halter Marine shipyard in Moss Point, Mississippi. Sears was one of the first staff members of the Woods Hole Oceanographic Institution and a guiding force in its development. (Above, courtesy of Tom Kleindinst at Woods Hole Oceanographic Institution; opposite, courtesy of WHOI Archives.)

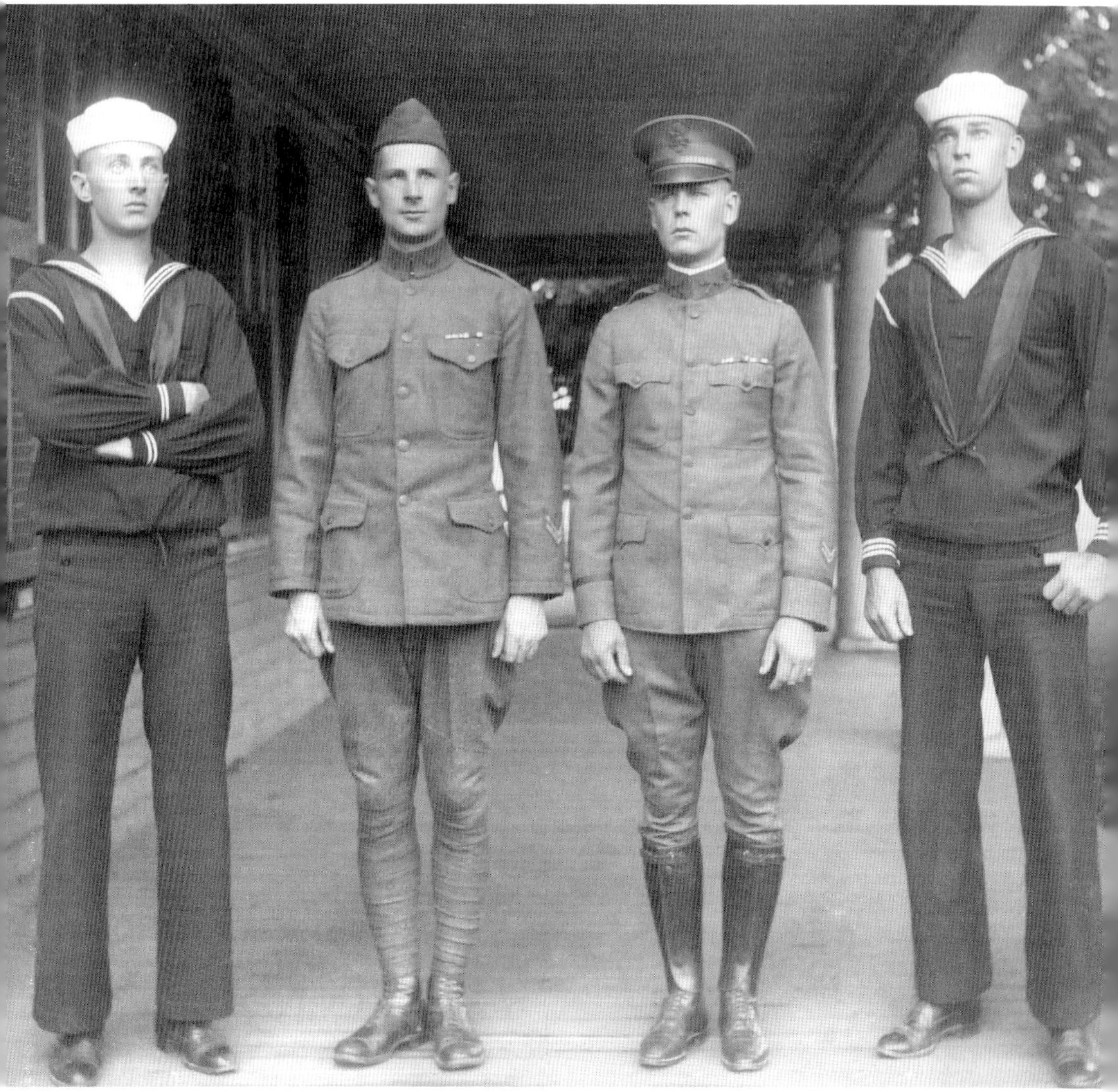

Morrell Brothers

The Morrell brothers are pictured here on the porch of their home in Wayland on July 4, 1919, the welcoming home celebration day for World War I veterans. From left to right are Kenneth (Navy), Willard (Army), Malcolm (Army, battlefield commission), and Allen (Navy). Kenneth Morrell went to Tufts University, married Margaret Bent, a town historian, and became a businessman. He was the only brother to remain in Wayland. Willard, who had been in the 55th Artillery in France, reenlisted in the Army Air Force in World War II. Malcolm and Allen both graduated from Bowdoin College. The former became an athletic director, and the latter a prominent businessman.

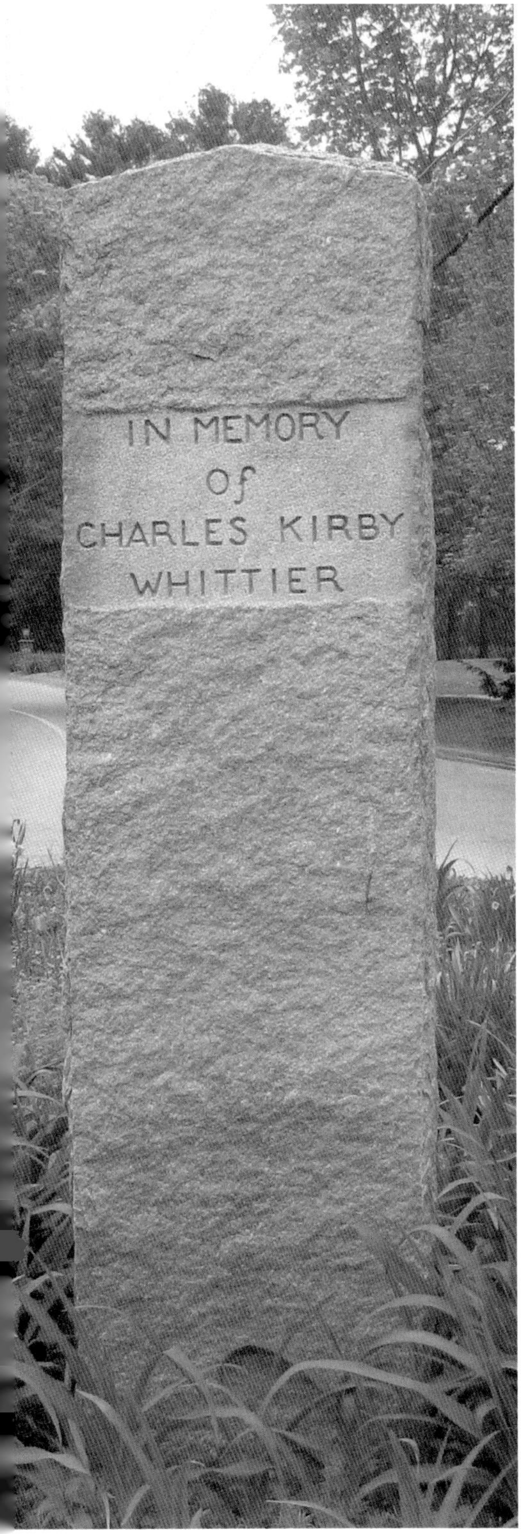

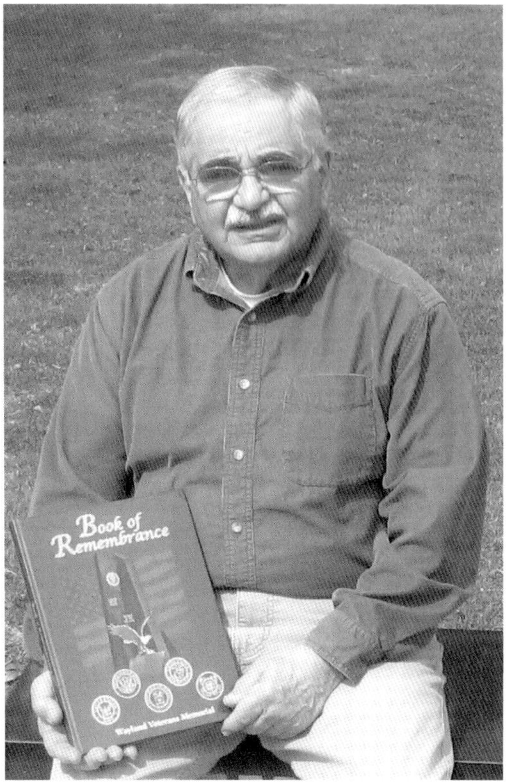

John Dyer
Dyer, a Korean War veteran, was a navigator and captain in the Air Force. A dedicated volunteer, he oversaw the Planned Unit Development bylaw for the Mainstone property while chairman of the Planning Board. He was a member of the Metropolitan Area Planning Council for eight years, and on the Septage and Public Ceremonies Committees for a decade each. He chaired the town's new Veterans Memorial Committee. (Author's collection.)

Charles Kirby Whittier (1883–1942) (LEFT)
Charles Whittier was born in Cambridge but moved to Wayland when he was a young child. He attended local schools and lived on Concord Road until he enlisted in the Merchant Marines. He attained the rank of chief engineer before leaving the service. Whittier worked as a civilian until World War II broke out, when he joined the Merchant Marines once again. In 1942, he went down with the SS *William J. Salman* when it sank in the Atlantic.

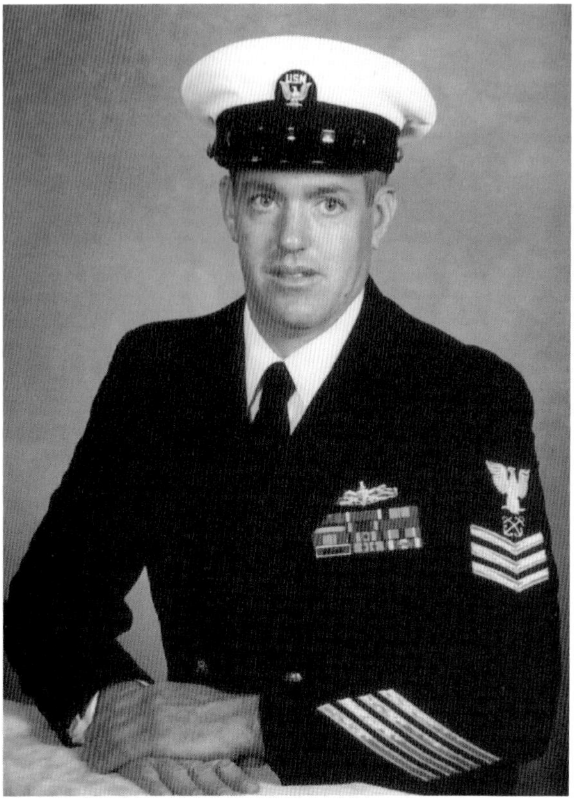

Richard Turner

Richard Turner joined the Navy in 1964, two years after graduating from Wayland High School. He was sent to Vietnam and assigned to River Assault Squadron 15 as the coxswain on a river assault craft. During one mission, the craft was hit by the Vietcong hidden along the shoreline, and Turner was wounded in the leg by a rocket-propelled grenade. After a short recovery period, he was sent back to active combat due to a shortage of trained boat coxswains to maintain and carry out the daily operations of the squadron. He was awarded a Purple Heart and a variety of combat medals. Since 2002, he has served the town on the Public Ceremonies Committee, as liaison to the Veterans Memorial Committee, the Cable TV Advisory Board, and volunteer for Friends in Service Helping. (Both, courtesy of Richard Turner.)

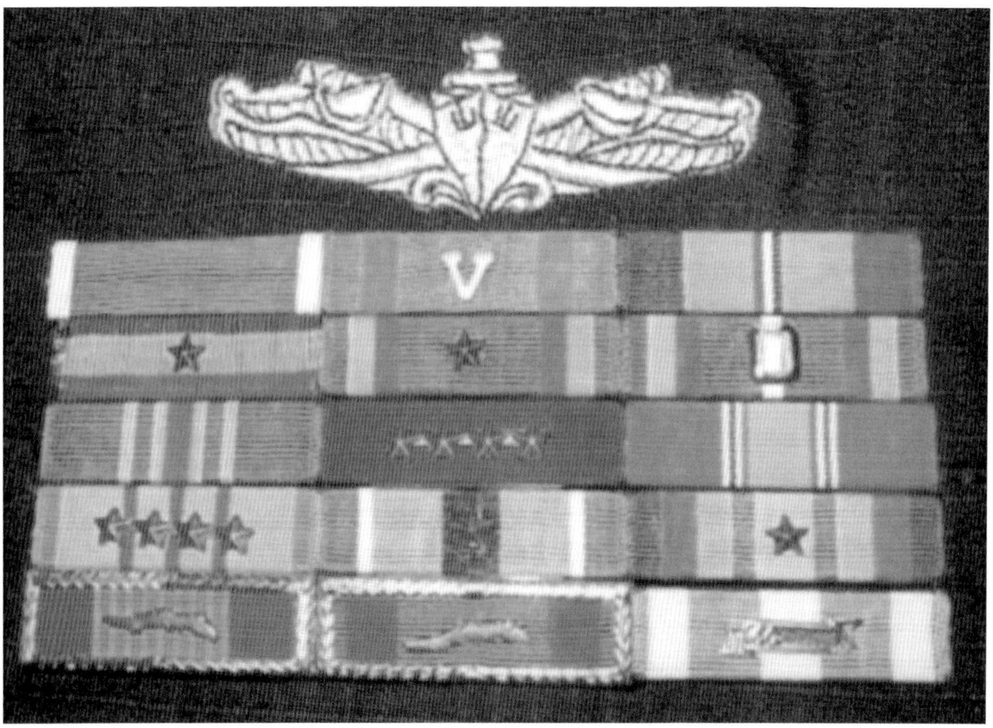

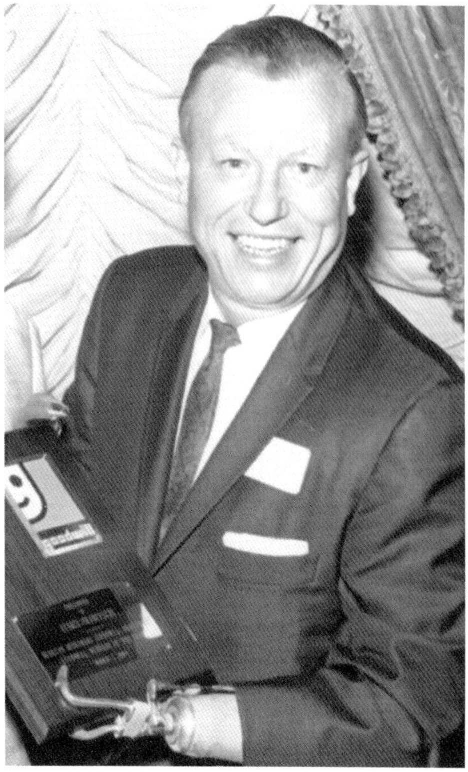

Harold Russell (1914–2002)
Russell lost both hands at Camp MacKall, North Carolina, in 1944. After learning to use hooks for hands, he made a training movie for the Army and was cast in the film *The Best Years of Our Lives.* He received two Oscars, one for supporting actor and one for being an inspiration to returning veterans. He later graduated from Boston University and starred in four more films. He is buried in Wayland's Lakeview Cemetery.

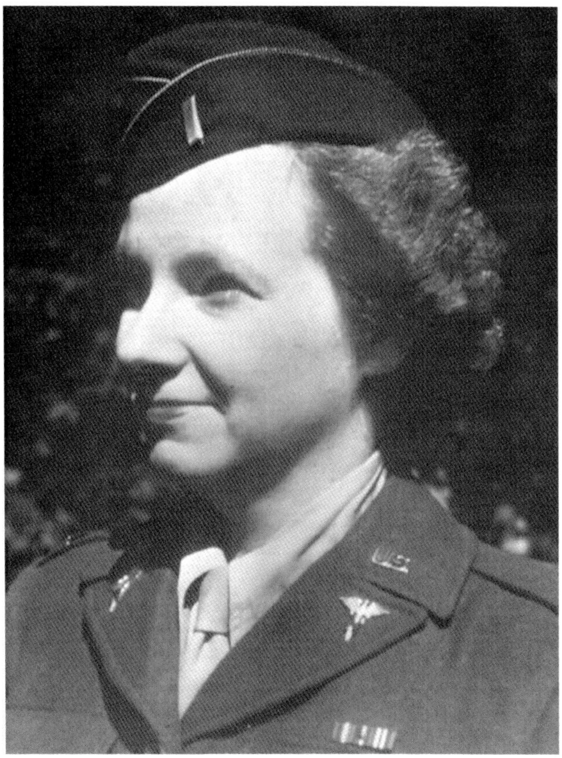

Marian Draper (1914–2009)
Marian Draper trained at Yale School of Nursing while serving in the US Army Nurse Corps in 1943. During World War II, she worked in the 62nd General Hospital outside of Paris. After the war ended in 1945, she stayed on until patients had been sent home. She was discharged a first lieutenant in December 1945. Marian was a descendant of the very public-spirited Draper family, and like many relatives, she continued in their good stead.

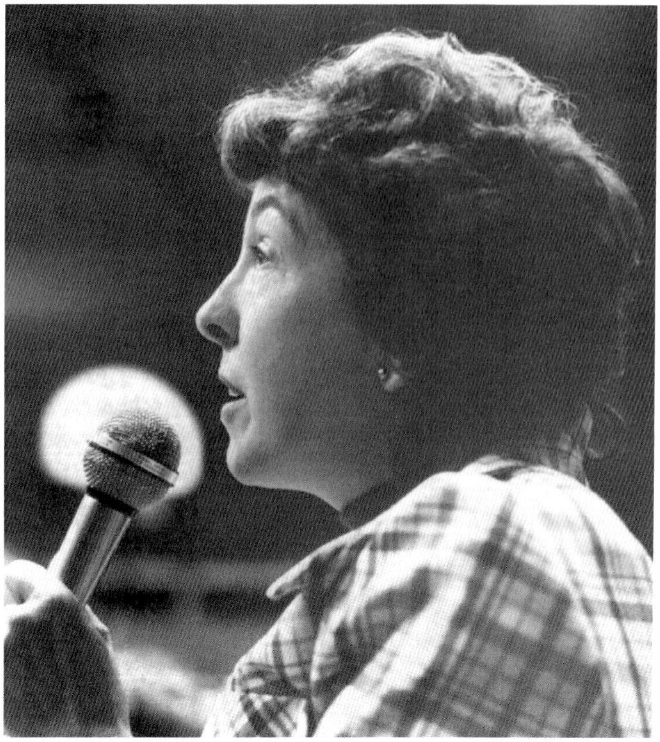

Shirley Barnes

After basic training in Greensboro, North Carolina, in 1944, Shirley Barnes served in the Army Air Nurse Corps and was discharged in 1948 with the rank of captain. In 1961, she and her husband, Robert, settled in Wayland. Since then, she has been on the Conservation Commission, was instrumental in saving the town's historic north training field, and campaigned to preserve portions of the Watertown Dairy for passive recreation.

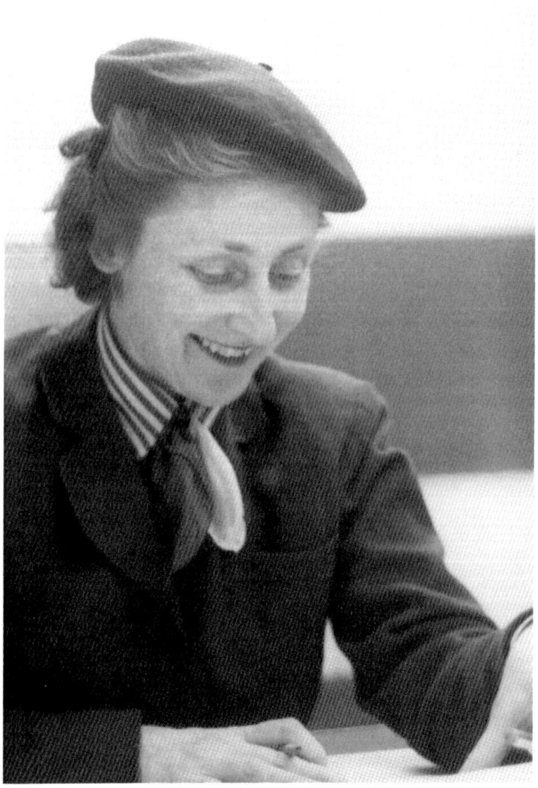

Leila Sears (1919–2008)

Leila Sears was a popular figure in town, serving two decades as town clerk. She raised golden retrievers and west highland white terriers on Pelham Island Road and was a member of the Wayland Historical Society and the Elbanobscot Foundation. But few were aware of her service during World War II. She had been stationed in Washington, DC, working in the Navy's decryption unit, delivering dispatches to Fleet Adm. Chester A. Nimitz. In 1972, she moved to New York City and joined the executive staff of the American Kennel Club.

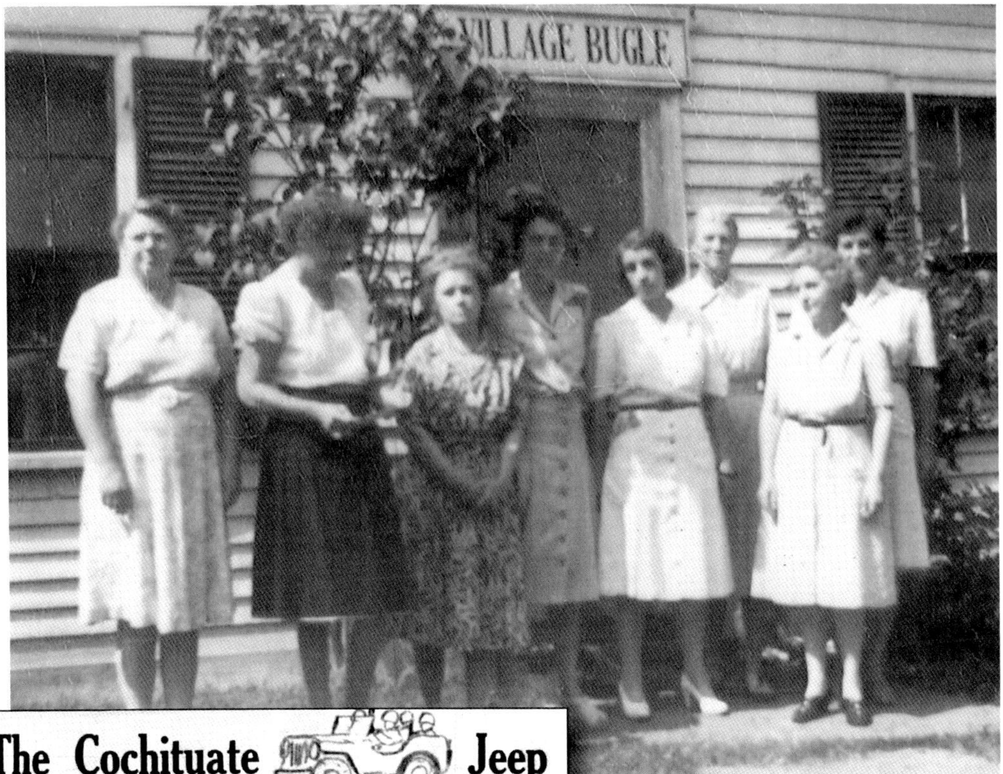

The Cochituate Jeep

Conveyor Of News From The Folks At Home To Their Service Men And Women Everywhere

No. 2 | February 24, 1945 | MAIL ADDRESS P. O. Box 70, Cochituate, Mass.

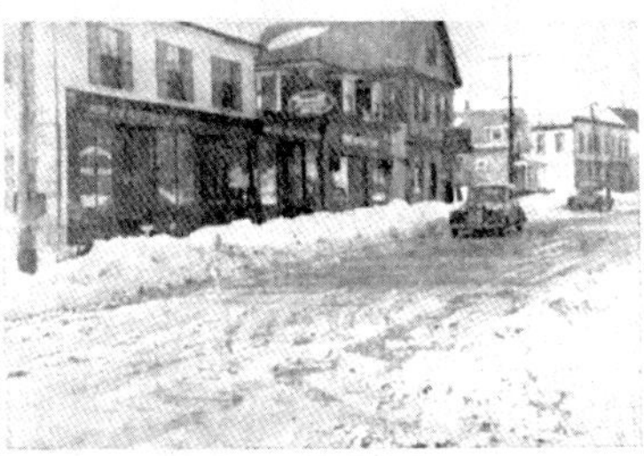

Correction

Sorry to have made errors and omissions in the honor roll of our first edition, it was unintentional and hope you will bear with us.

On the Honor Roll, the surnames of Francis J. Hartin and his brother Bill were listed as "Martin."

The name of Harold C. Hurlbut, husband of the former Alice Forbes, should have been included, as well as Wm. Burgin, C. Russell Thomas, Wm. V. Young, Robert Merritt, John Hampstead.

Discharged From The Service

Several men who have been discharged from the service were not listed on the Jeep Honor Roll. They are as follows:

Kenneth A. Baker
Roy F. Hallenbrook
Gurney O. Nichol
Chester R. Rafus
Arthur A. Therrien
George Toohill
Charles Maher

Cochituate boys who registered elsewhere and are in the service, but not on the Honor Roll are:

Charles Waters
Rowland W. Ashley
Ralph M. Bent
Richard W. Bishop
Chester H. Dusseault
Francis L. Fisher
Alie Petrocelli
Raymond Snell
Percy H. Steele
John O'Connor
Raymond MacMillen
Paul Thomas
Henry Stanley
Wm. A. Hammond
Wm. A. Hammond, Jr.

To You And You

Climb aboard the Jeep
The townsfolk want a peep
A bit that's new
From all of you
Just be a pal—'twill boost morale.

GERTRUDE PERODEAU

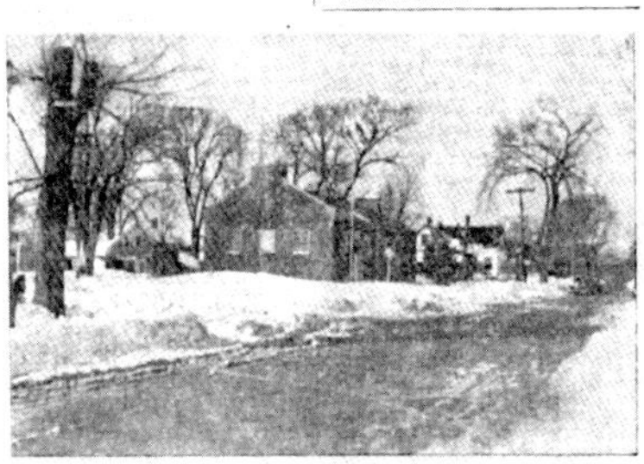

Village Bugle **and** *Cochituate Jeep*
World War II also had heroes and heroines working at home. In 1942, a group of Wayland women, spearheaded by Eleanor Upton, compiled, edited, and typed the *Village Bugle*, a mimeographed sheet filled with hometown news for soldiers abroad. Later, residents in Cochituate began publication of their own servicemen's newspaper called the *Jeep*. The *Jeep* had more pages and included photographs. Both papers, mailed free of charge, included editorials and a heavy dose of hometown news. Soldiers replied with enthusiastic letters of thanks.

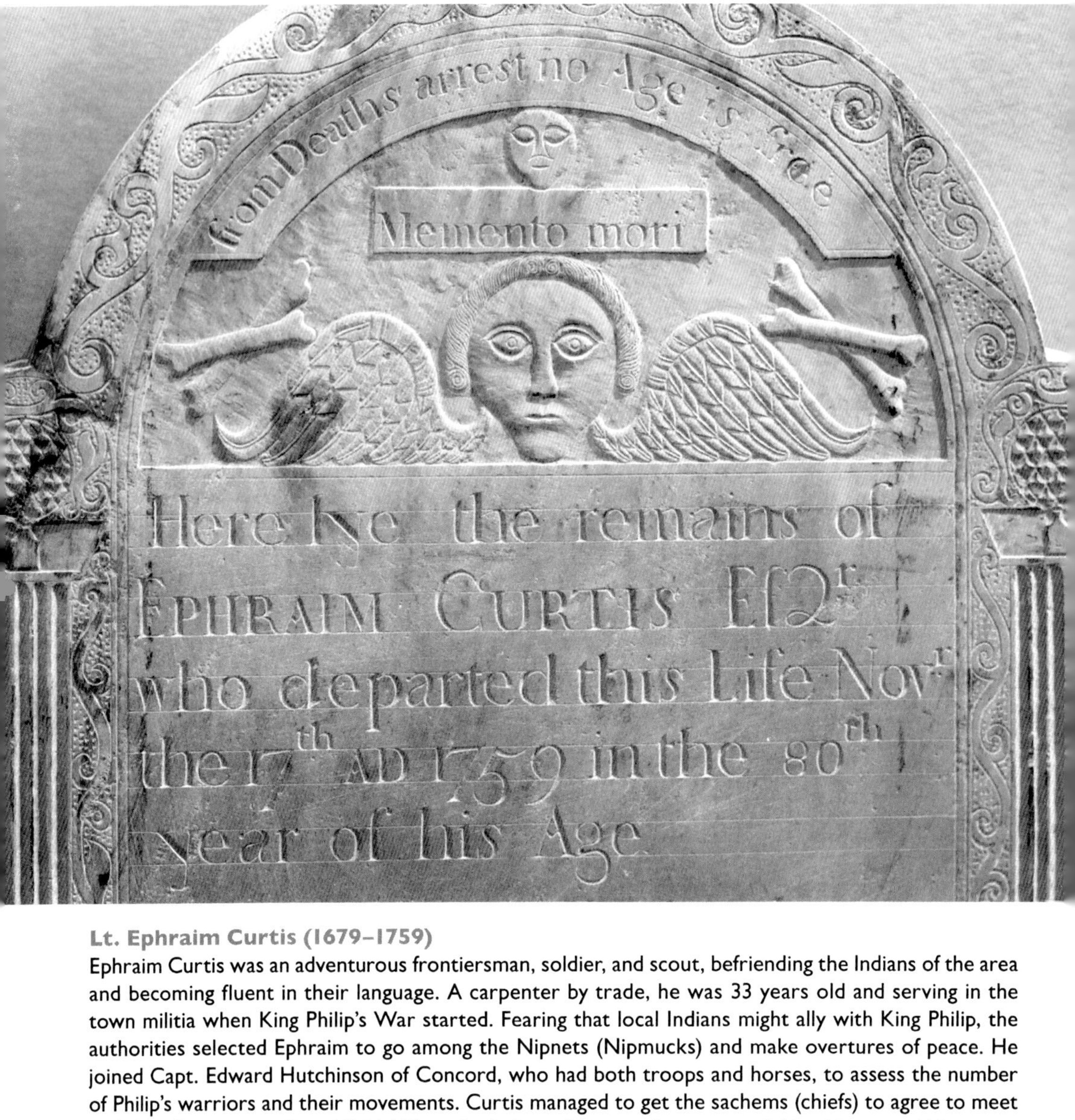

Lt. Ephraim Curtis (1679–1759)

Ephraim Curtis was an adventurous frontiersman, soldier, and scout, befriending the Indians of the area and becoming fluent in their language. A carpenter by trade, he was 33 years old and serving in the town militia when King Philip's War started. Fearing that local Indians might ally with King Philip, the authorities selected Ephraim to go among the Nipnets (Nipmucks) and make overtures of peace. He joined Capt. Edward Hutchinson of Concord, who had both troops and horses, to assess the number of Philip's warriors and their movements. Curtis managed to get the sachems (chiefs) to agree to meet with Hutchinson near Brookfield. When the Indians did not arrive as agreed, Hutchinson and his troops set out to find them, against the advice of his guides. Much to their surprise, 200–300 Indians lay in wait to ambush them, killing one and wounding two. Hutchinson and his men quickly retreated to the nearest garrison house. Curtis and Henry Young, from Concord, were sent on to Boston to seek help. But the town was under siege, and the two men were forced to return to the garrison. Henry Young was soon shot and mortally wounded through a window in the garrison, and, after three desperate attempts to get through enemy lines, Curtis finally made it to Marlboro. There he met with Maj. Simon Willard and Capt. James Parker of Groton and told them of the siege at Brookfield. The major and captain, along with 46 men, left immediately to rescue the Brookfield survivors. King Philip and his allies were eventually turned back at Sudbury, although skirmishes between Indians and settlers continued for a time. After the war, Ephraim served as justice of the peace, major of a regiment, and for many years, representative in the General Court.

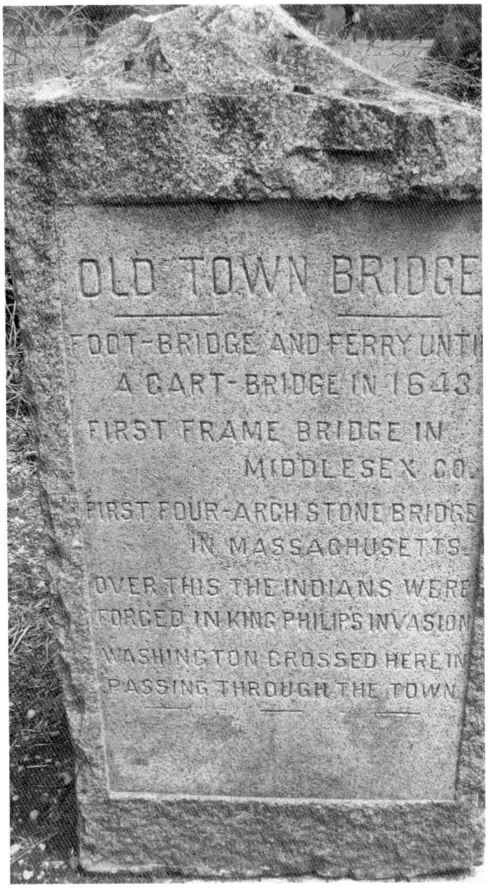

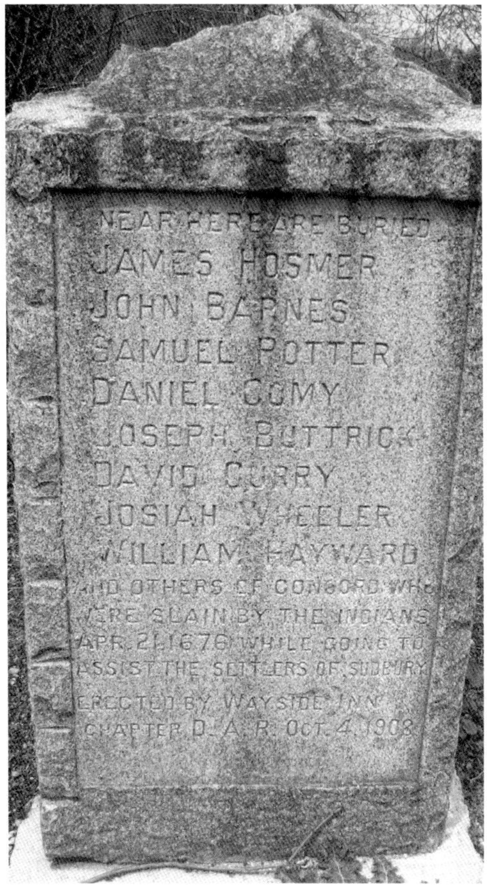

King Philip's Soldiers

When King Philip's warriors attacked the Haynes and Goodenow Garrisons, eight brave men from Concord came to assist the soldiers of Sudbury Plantation on the morning of April 21, 1676. The men were ambushed in the meadow on the east side of the Sudbury River, and only one made it alive to Haynes Garrison. Three of the men who were killed had been born and raised in nearby Concord. The fathers of Samuel Potter, Joseph Buttrick, and James Hosmer had come to Concord with the first settlers. Luke Potter, Samuel's father, was deacon of the church at the time of the war. (Both, author's collection.)

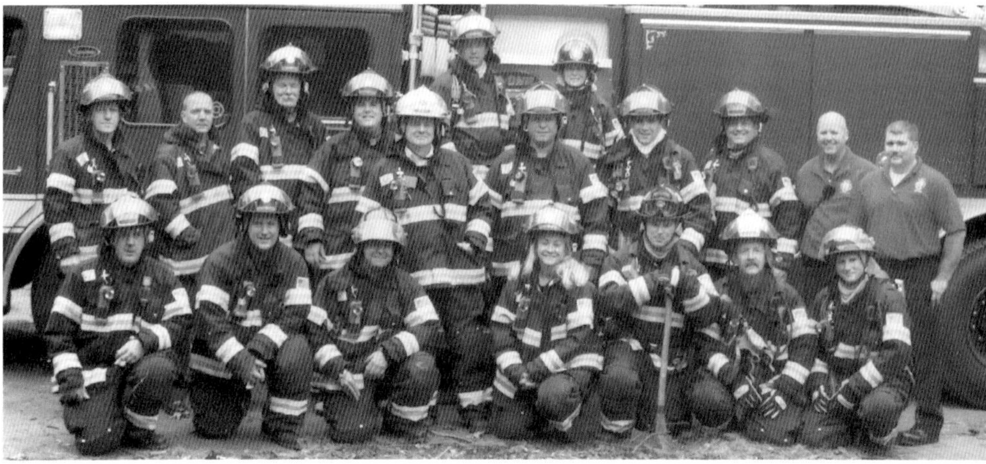

Wayland Firefighters

Wayland has had publicly financed fire protection since the first station opened in 1878 on Harrison Street in Cochituate Village. Today, in town center, on the northeast corner of Boston Post and Cochituate Roads, the police and fire departments, along with a joint communications center, are housed in the new, state-of-the art Public Safety Building. The town has had a long and successful tradition of recruiting young men who have grown up in the town to join the town's fire department. A training exercise in 2009 provided a unique opportunity for the entire team to come together for training and to capture a group photograph. Some members in this photograph have retired, and some have been promoted since 2009; firefighters raised in Wayland are marked WN (Wayland native). Pictured here from left to right are (first row) Lt. David Houghton (WN), Timothy Dempsey, Peter Regan, Alexiss Wheeler, Daniel Spurling, Lt. Robert Knox, and Todd Winner (WN); (second row) William Ash, Brian Burgett (WN), Ronald Rokes (WN), Robert Dorey (WN), Deputy Chief Kenneth Hart (WN), Gregory Tauer (WN), Jeffrey McLeod, Lt. James Gemelli (WN), Lt. Gregory Halfpenny (WN), and Capt. Daniel Buentello; (third row) William Leone (WN), and Debra Duran. The building in the photograph below would have required enormous courage to enter had the fire not been set for training purposes. This 1998 training session prepared many firefighters for future fires similar to one that had burned a local home to the ground in 1972. (Above, courtesy of Heather Dorey; below, courtesy of Robert Dorey.)

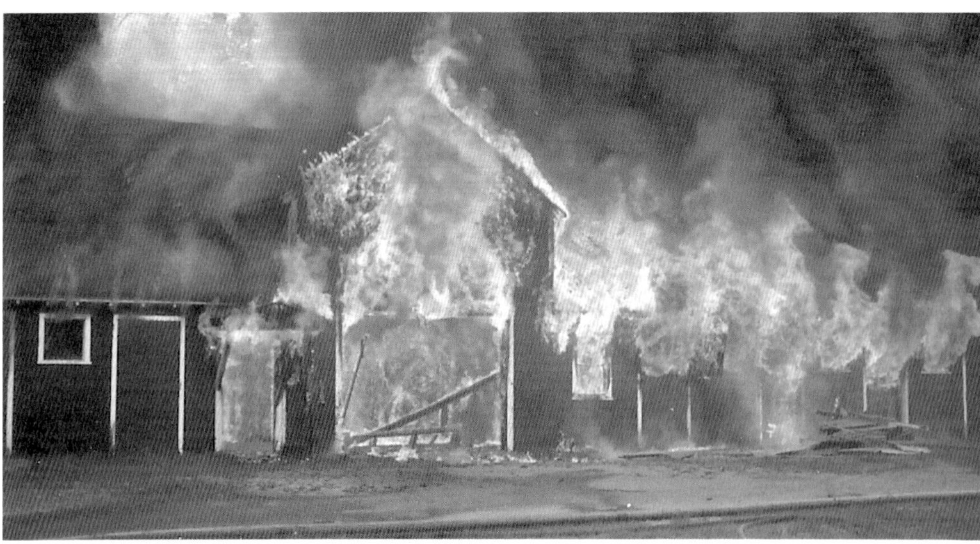

CHAPTER FIVE

Achieving Athletes

Durability is part of what makes a good athlete.

—Bill Russell

The most famous athlete in town was Alberto Salazar. As a track star at Wayland High School, local women financed him to compete while still a student. His Boston Marathon victory in 1982 put Wayland on the map.

Wayland has had a long sports history, starting in the early 20th century when shoe factory workers in Cochituate Village began to organize baseball games. The teams sported names like Cochituate Shop Ends, Natick Eagles, and Natick Mystics, and played against the Wayland Meadow Hens from the north side of town. Teams enjoyed a rivalry for many years. The Cochituate/Griffin Ball Field remains in use today by men's and women's softball leagues.

A parent-run organization, the Wayland Baseball & Softball Association organizes baseball and softball programs for boys and girls in kindergarten through 12th grade. The organization is staffed by volunteers and supported by the Wayland Park and Recreation Department.

Wayland's first high school, located on Cochituate Road across from First Parish Church, sported both softball and baseball teams long before the town had formal fields.

Between the 1950s and 1970s, Wayland's famous dogsled musher, Dr. Roland Lombard, was preparing his beloved huskies to race in a track behind his home. Lombard won eight Anchorage Fur Rendezvous World Championship sprint races, and was an eight-time Rondy champion.

Over the years, citizens of the town have demonstrated their commitment to athletics by funding dozens of well designed and maintained playing fields. The town currently has five baseball fields, five softball fields, six soccer fields, two outdoor basketball courts, ten tennis courts, one artificial turf field, two T-ball fields, and nine multi-use flat fields.

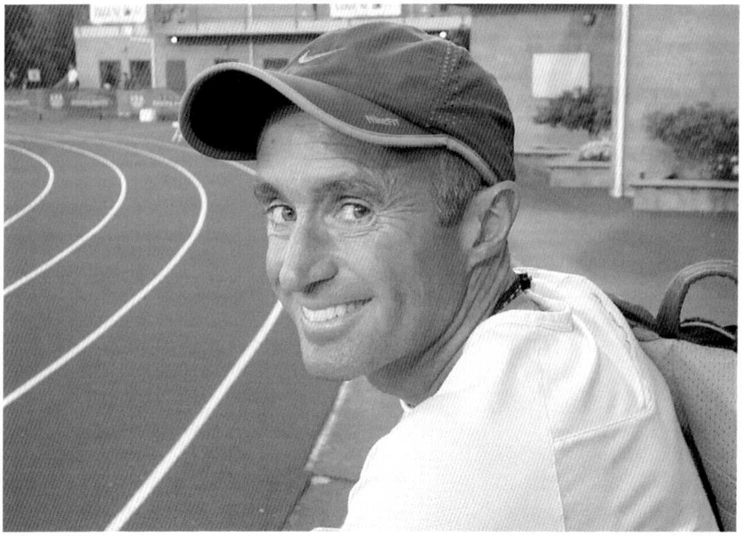

Alberto Salazar

Salazar, born in Cuba, dominated eastern Massachusetts high school track and cross-country while at Wayland High School. Local women raised money to send him to the National Junior Olympics in North Carolina when he was 16. As a college senior, he won the New York City Marathon, second only to Bill Rogers. In the 1980s, he ran in several New York City Marathons and won the Boston Marathon in 1982. He established track records in Stockholm, Sweden, and Oslo, Norway, that same year. Salazar often teetered on the edge of death, suffering from dehydration and heart problems after running. In 2006, he ran in the New York Marathon at age 48 as a pacesetter for cyclist Lance Armstrong. Salazar has since coached for the Nike Oregon Project, and in 2012, he took two Olympic-caliber athletes to the London Summer Olympics. Salazar resides in Portland, Oregon. (Above, author's collection.)

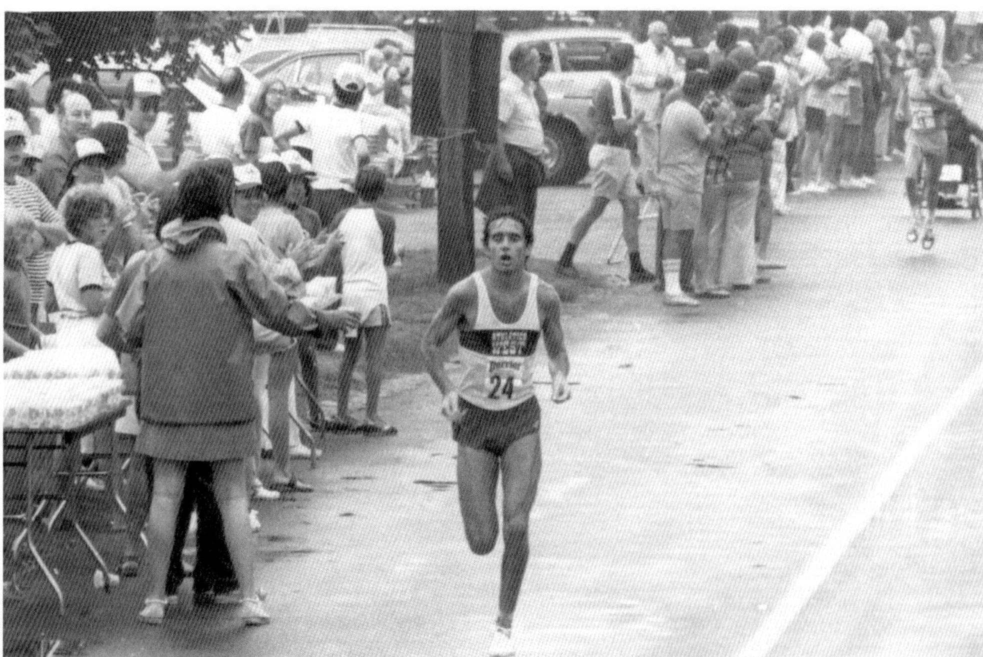

Charlotte Russell

As partner with her husband, Lewis, in the family's garden center and mother of three active daughters, Charlotte Russell has made time for her many sporting activities for more than five decades. But it was not until recently that she decided to test her athletic prowess by preparing for her very first triathlon. In 2012, she entered the Danskin Woman's Only Triathlon in Webster, Massachusetts. At the age of 79, Charlotte came in first in her age group. The race consisted of a half-mile swim, 12-mile bike ride, and three-mile run. (Author's collection.)

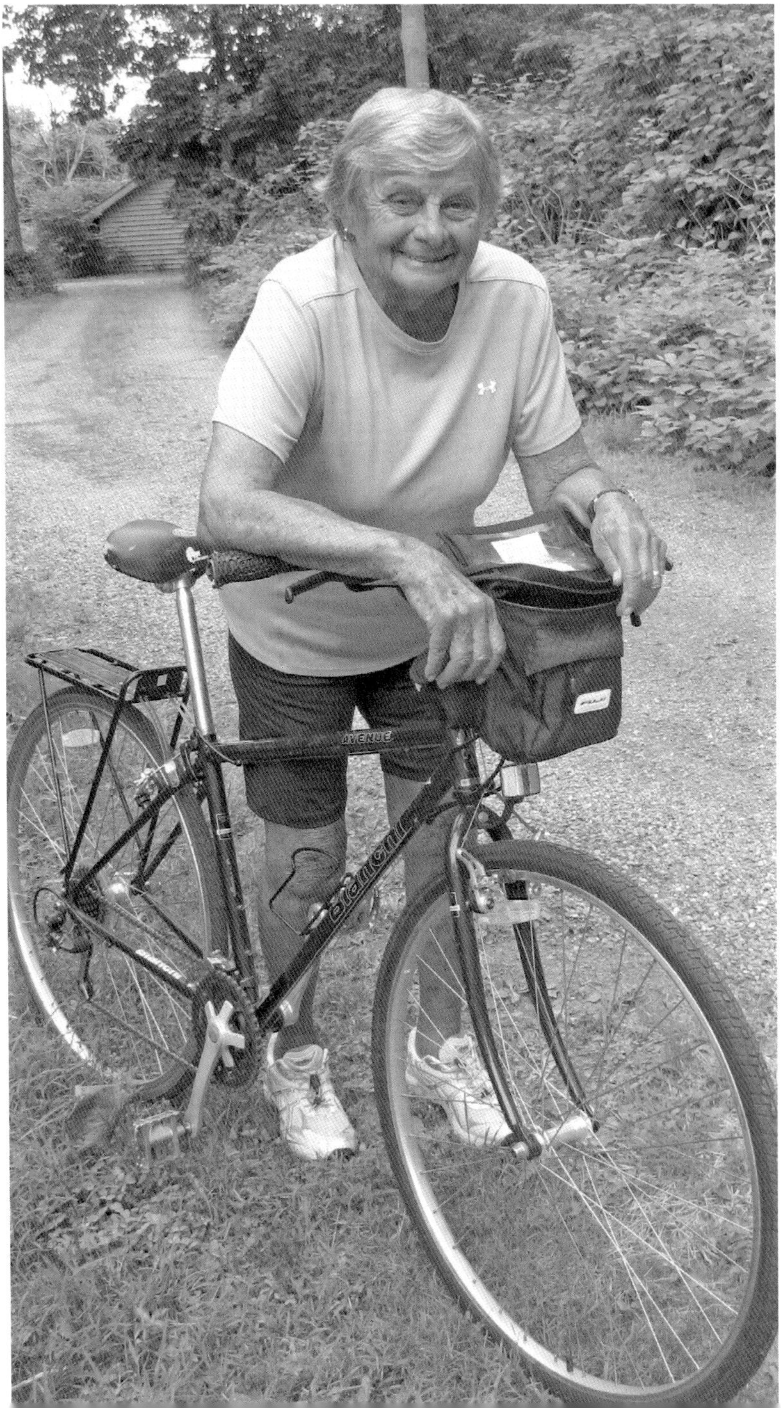

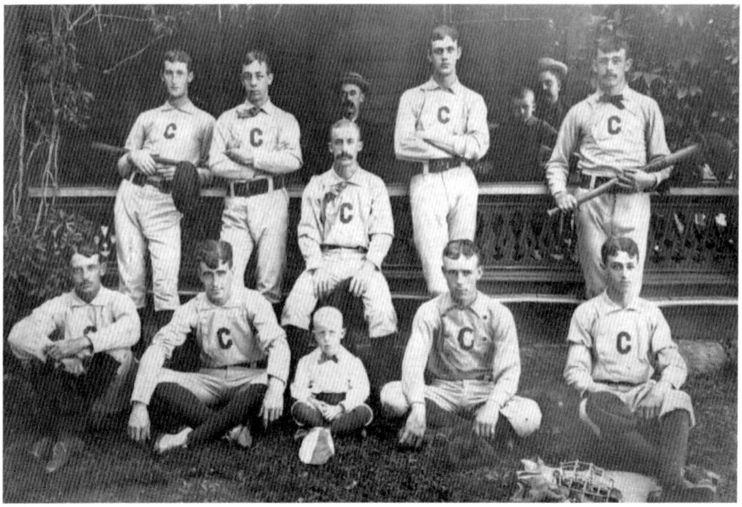

Elmer Bent (1863–1954)

Elmer Bent (among those pictured here in an unknown position) was a pitching star and did some coaching of the Harvard College team. A member of the Bent family, he played for the Cochituate baseball team. In the late 1800s, the Bent Shoe Factory employed hundreds of workers in its factory on the corner of what is now Commonwealth Road and Main Street. Smaller factories, employing fewer workers, were clustered throughout Cochituate Village. On Saturdays, the factories closed early, and informal groups of employees played baseball on the Cochituate/Griffin Ball Field still in use today. The Cochituate Shop Ends, Natick Eagles, and Natick Mystics developed a devoted following.

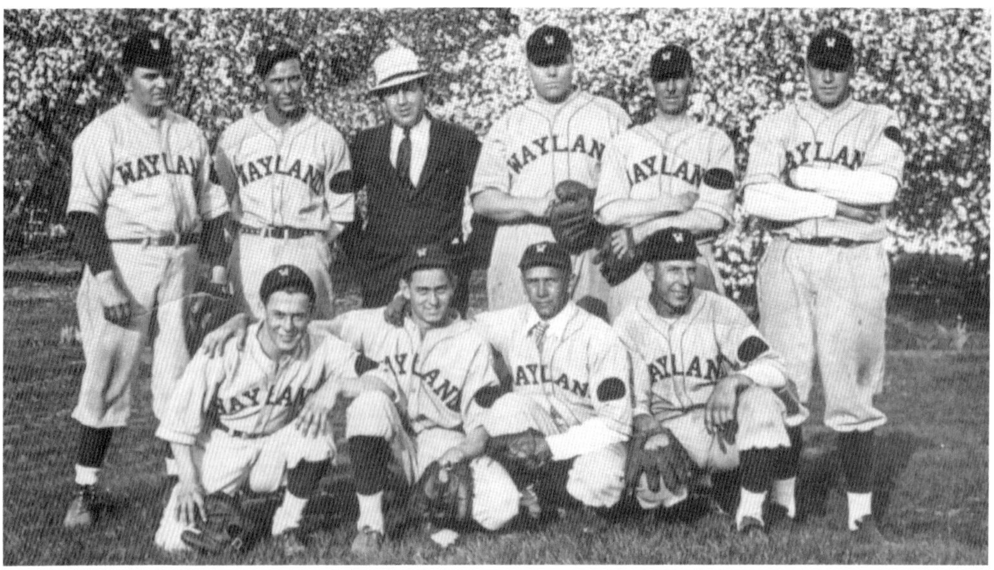

John Bryant (1924–2005)

John Bryant was a member of the Wayland Lodge of the Odd Fellows, and a member of the group that formed the Wayland Meadow Hens, a team from the north side of town. The Odd Fellows Hall stood on Cochituate Road in Wayland Center, and games were played on the field behind the school, which today is a fenced baseball field. Teams enjoyed great rivalry with their Cochituate Village neighbors, as well as teams from Weston, Lincoln, and neighboring towns.

Dr. Roland Lombard (1914–1990)

Dr. Lombard ran many miles each year practice-racing his huskies on a track behind his home in Wayland. His interest in dog mushing began when he started his veterinary career in 1938. He loved and understood his dogs, and they loved and understood him. In Alaska, he became known for innovative ideas about dog care, including methods for making a stronger race dog. At the top of his game in the late 1950s, 1960s, and into the 1970s, he won eight Anchorage Fur Rendezvous World Championship sprint races. He was an eight-time Rondy champion who finished fifth in a field that included sprint racing pioneer Earl Norris and 1975 Iditarod champion Emmitt Peters.

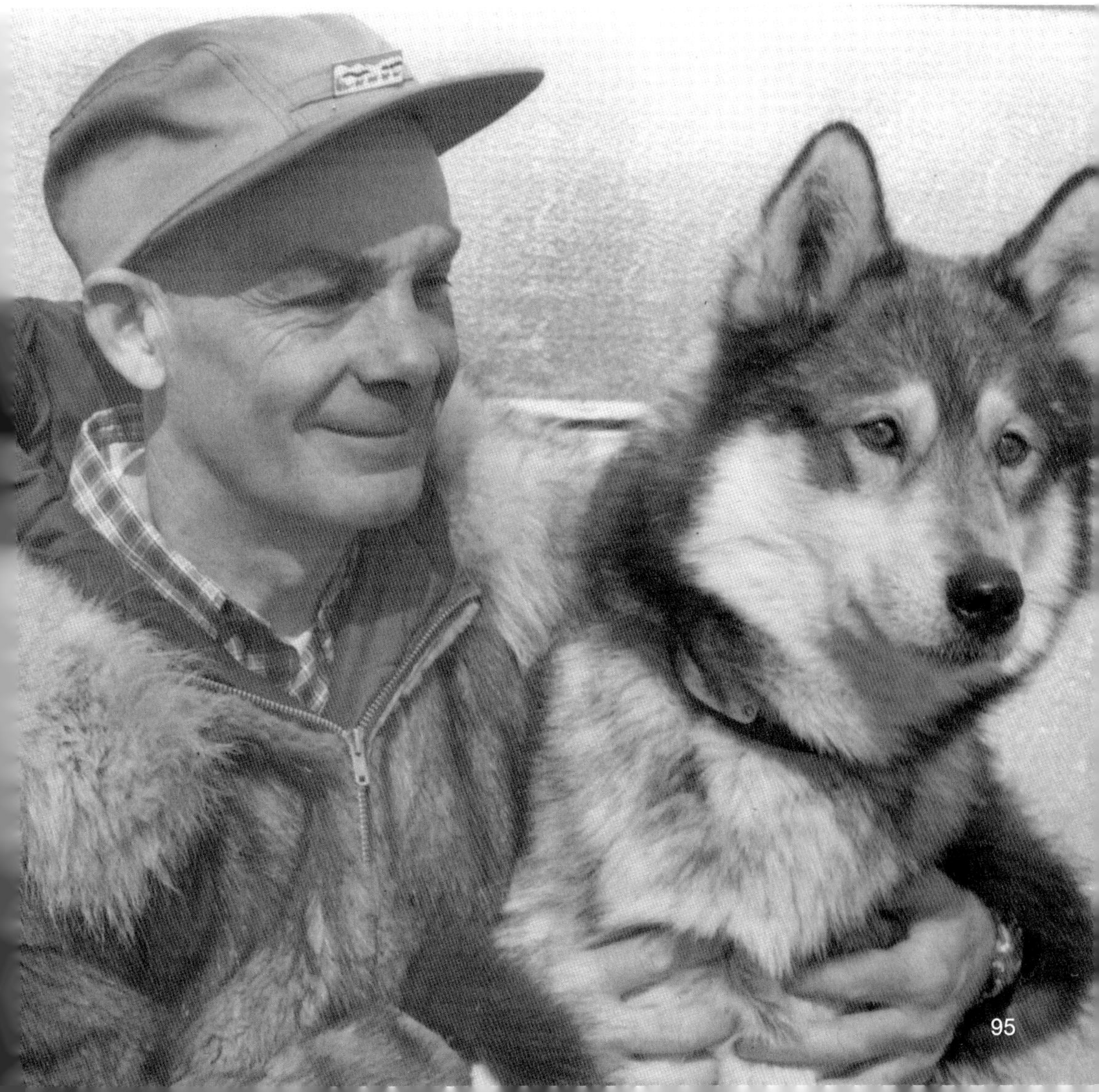

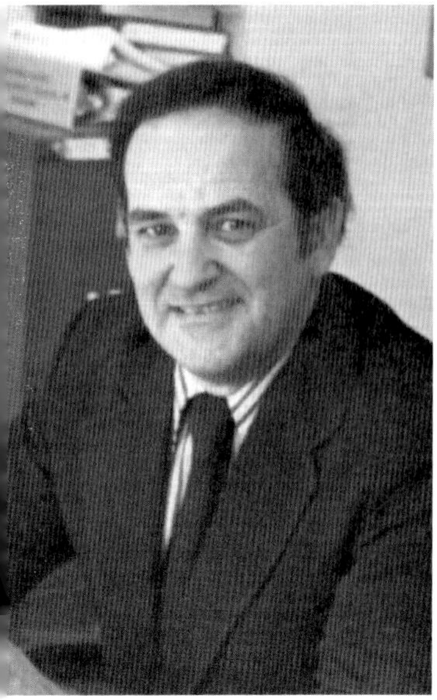

Robert "Bob" Anastas

Bob Anastas, a retired hockey coach and teacher at Wayland High School, created a prolific organization when he founded Students Against Drunk Driving (SADD) in 1981. The school had recently suffered the deaths of two students in unrelated drunk driving accidents, and Anastas decided to do something about it. Three decades later, SADD now stands for Students Against Destructive Decisions and has expanded beyond alcohol abuse. Anastas was honored as Massachusetts Teacher of the Year in 1981. (Left, courtesy of Jostens Publishing; right, author's collection.)

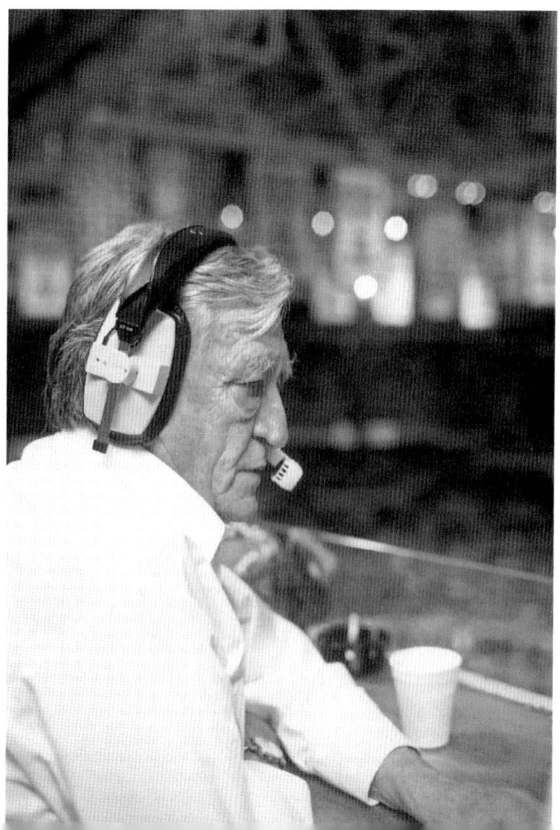

Johnny Most (1923–1993)

Johnny Most could often be heard in Mel's and the Villa restaurants, his raspy voice made famous on Boston Celtics radio for almost 40 years. He is most remembered for his excited call during the final moments of game seven of the 1965 NBA Eastern Division finals, when he roared, "Havlicek stole the ball!" He was a legend to Boston Celtics fans during the franchise's golden era and to his Wayland friends and neighbors who seldom missed a broadcast. (Author's collection.)

CHAPTER SIX

Movers and Shakers

A small body of determined spirits fired by an unquenchable faith in their mission can alter the course of history.

—Mohandas Gandhi

When people settle on a place to live and devote their time and energy into making it a better place, everyone benefits. Wayland has had more than its share of these civic-minded people. Sally Newbury, Ted Newbury, Ken Moon, and Tom Sciacca have worked for decades protecting local wetlands essential to feeding the town's aquifers and keeping the town wells filled with pure, clear water. Although two Metropolitan District Water (MDC) aqueducts crisscross the town, supplying water to many towns along the way into Boston, Wayland has never had to join the system. The town's pure drinking water is taken from wells throughout the town and is a major attraction to potential residents.

Likewise, the town's rich archaeological heritage has been protected by the efforts of Paul Gardescu, Tonya Largy, and Bobby Robinson, who have mobilized dozens of volunteers to excavate known archeological sites threatened by development. As a result of a 1970s survey, Wayland recorded 20 protected sites. The Wayland Archeology Group has been recognized as the only volunteer archeology group of its type in the commonwealth, and volunteers have unearthed artifacts 8,000 years old.

Volunteers working behind the scenes are seldom publicly recognized but are essential to the well-being of the community. Preservationist Gretchen Schuler has been instrumental in guiding development toward preserving open space, and conservation member Roger Backman helps to safeguard the quality of those spaces. Cythnia Mayher, Charles Raskin, and Mary Antes help provide housing and health services to those in need, and Ann Becker and Lynn Trimby offer both human and animal helping hands. Mike Patterson's work behind the scenes provides important short-term emergency finance assistance to residents suffering long-term unemployment or serious health problems. He, along with a small staff, quietly solicits funds to help a wide variety of residents.

Then there are folks who work many hours to preserve Wayland's long history, joining the Historical Society, Historic District, and Historic District Commission. Unofficial historians and the general public still turn to Jo Goeselt for the facts regarding the town's history. Dick Hoyt, a popular speaker, tells citizens how and when their roads were named and relays facts and anecdotes about First Parish Church from its historic beginnings in 1815 to the purchase of a new organ in 2014. Kevin Delaney, head of the social studies department at the high school, sends his students into the community each year to research a historical subject firsthand, creating tomorrow's historians.

Essential to the efforts of civic-minded volunteers are the political advocates who support them. Wayland's guardians of truth and transparency include Linda Segal and George Harris, as well as past state representatives Lucile Hicks and Susan Pope.

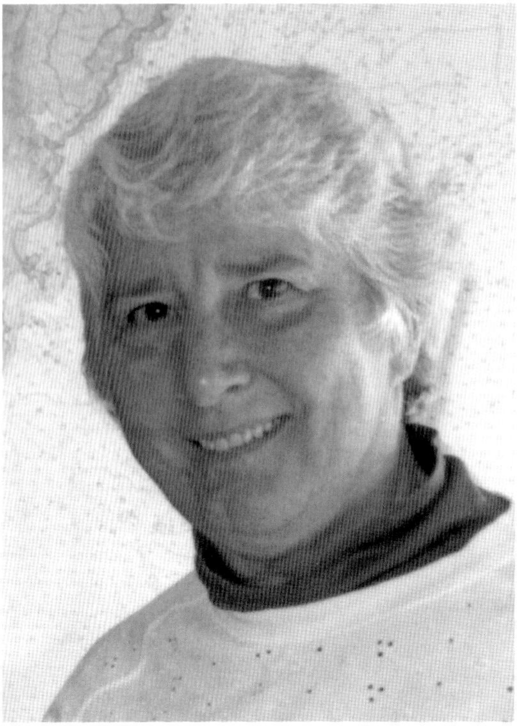

Elizabeth "Jo" Goeselt

Jo Goeselt was serving on the Wayland Historical Commission when, in 1983, she learned the Wayland Historical Society was in danger of closing. Concerned that residents would be unable to access the museum's rich holdings, she agreed to become curator. For more than two decades she organized the society's records, welcomed visitors, and arranged historical programs for schoolchildren at the museum. Goeselt has long been the town's official historian and remains the primary source for information on its 375-year history.

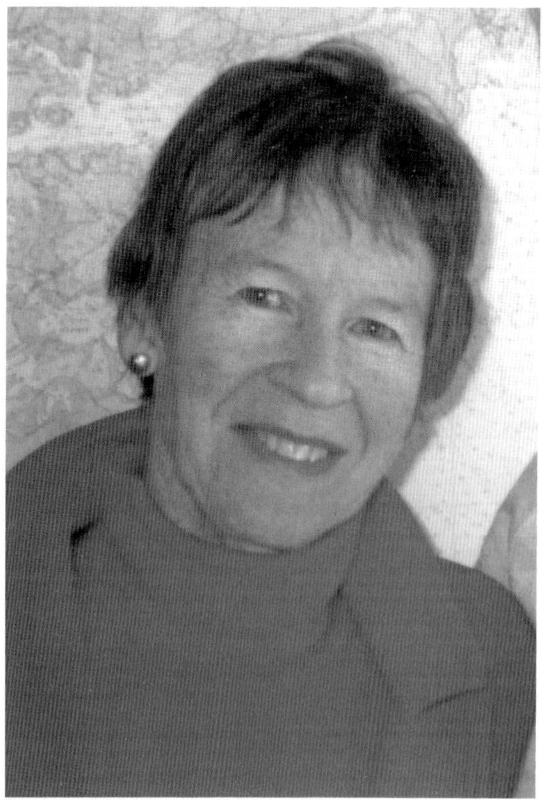

Barbara "Bobby" Robinson

Bobby Robinson lent her many talents to school and community projects including archaeology, environmental education, and local history studies. She organized hands-on historical projects on the town green for the 1976 Bicentennial, and wrote the booklet *Wayland Historical Tours*. She worked on one of the town's first master plans and initiated a state survey of archeology sites in town. Robinson's many publications remain valuable resources. She retired as director of the Massachusetts Studies Project at the University of Massachusetts.

Tonya Largy

Tonya Largy trained as a professional social worker and became interested in archaeology as a young mother. She volunteered at the town's first excavation site in the late 1970s and co-founded the Wayland Archaeology Group. She also served on the town's Historical Commission and as a trustee and president of the Massachusetts Archaeological Society. She now holds a master's degree in anthropology from the University of Massachusetts, Amherst. She is on the staff of the Zooarcheology Laboratory, Peabody Museum, Harvard University, and is a consultant to other archaeologists in her specialty. (Both, courtesy of Tom Largy.)

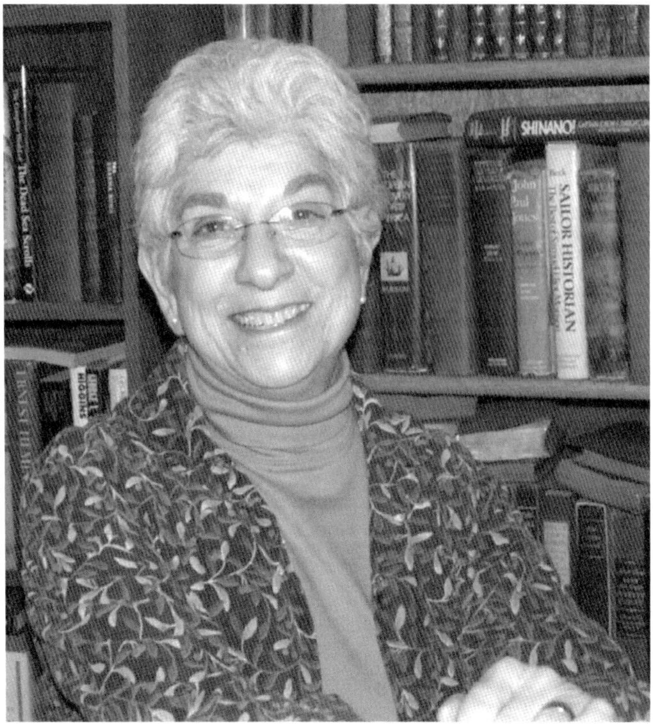

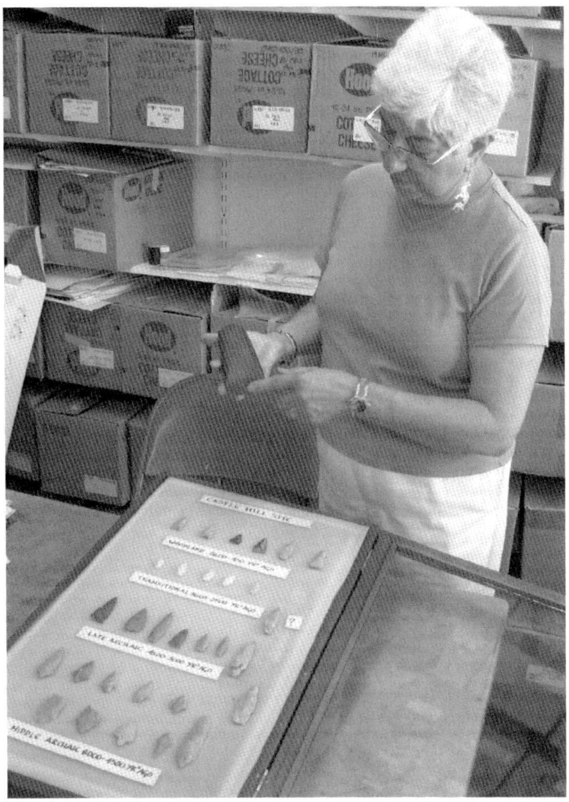

Lois Hanssen Davis

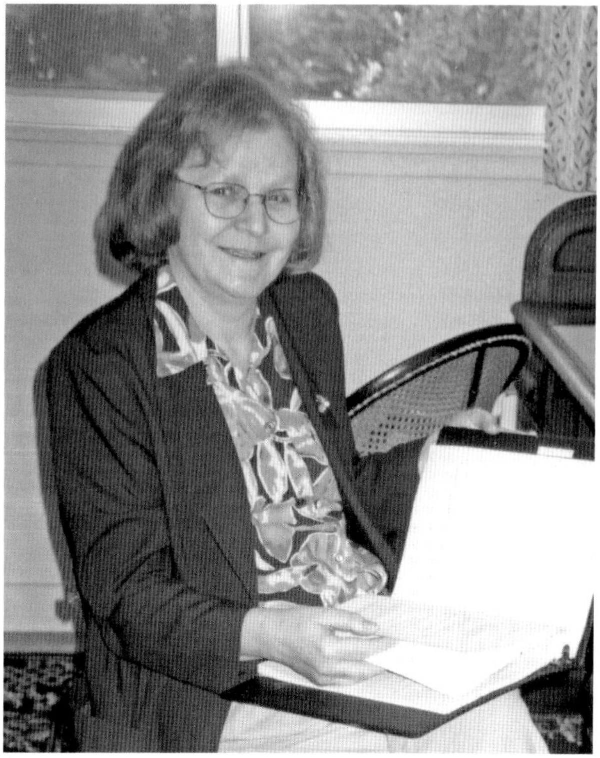

Lois Davis is a longtime resident of Wayland and a mother of two. She has been curator of the Wayland Historical Society since 2006. She oversees the collections, conducts research, and assists visitors at the Grout-Heard House and through the society's web page, which she and her husband maintain. Recently, she served on the committee that organized the town's 375th birthday celebration. She enjoys meeting and helping descendants of long ago residents.

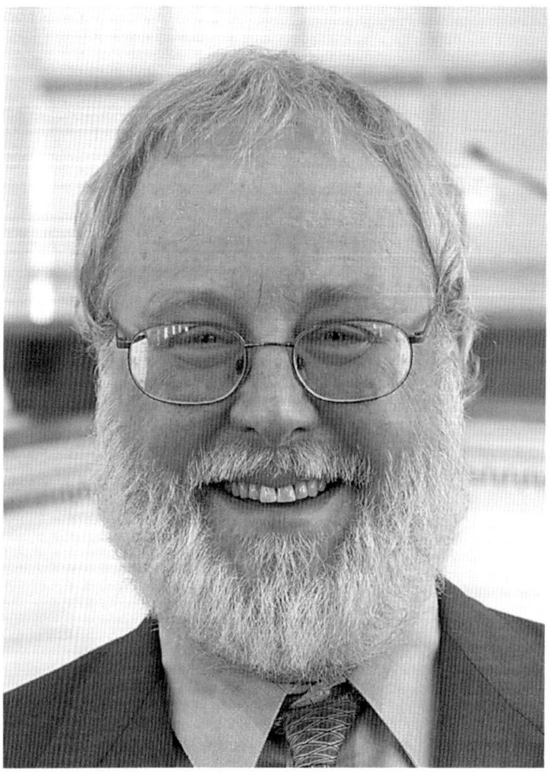

Kenneth Sawyer

Ken Sawyer retired as minister of the First Parish in Wayland in 2012 after nearly 40 years. At the time, he was the longest serving Unitarian Universalist (UU) minister to remain in one town in the United States. He was president of the continental UU Ministers Association and co-authored the book *Thematic Preaching: An Introduction*. As a newly settled minister and resident, Sawyer was editor of a 144-page guide to the trails in Wayland's conservation areas. (Courtesy of Brad Keyes.)

Nathan "Ted" Newbury III and Sarah "Sally" Newbury (1927–2014)

Ted and Sally Newbury worked tirelessly to preserve the town's natural resources. The Sudbury Valley Trustees, organized to acquire open space before it could be developed, held meetings in the Newburys' home throughout the 1970s. During the 1970s and 1980s, working in tandem with the SVT and with state and federal grant programs, the Wayland Conservation Commission negotiated the purchase of a large amount of land, especially adjacent to the river. Ted was president of SVT for a decade, during which time Sally was a member of the Wayland Conservation Commission when commissions assumed initial jurisdiction of the state's wetlands protection law; Sally volunteered before the commission had paid employees. Sally and Ted received SVT's Allen H. Morgan Award in 1991. In 1979, when the state's Metropolitan District Commission (MDC) proposed diverting Sudbury River water to augment Boston's water supply, as was being planned for the Connecticut River, Sally represented SVT on an ad hoc citizens advisory committee, later becoming a member of the official Water Supply Citizens Advisory Committee to the Massachusetts Water Resources Authority (MWRA), MDC's successor. The Water Supply Citizens Advisory Committee (WSCAC) successfully persuaded the state to employ conservation before river diversions. Sally represented Wayland on the study committee to gain federal Wild & Scenic River designation for the Sudbury, Assabet, and Concord (SUASCO) Rivers, receiving the SUASCO Stewardship Award in 2002.

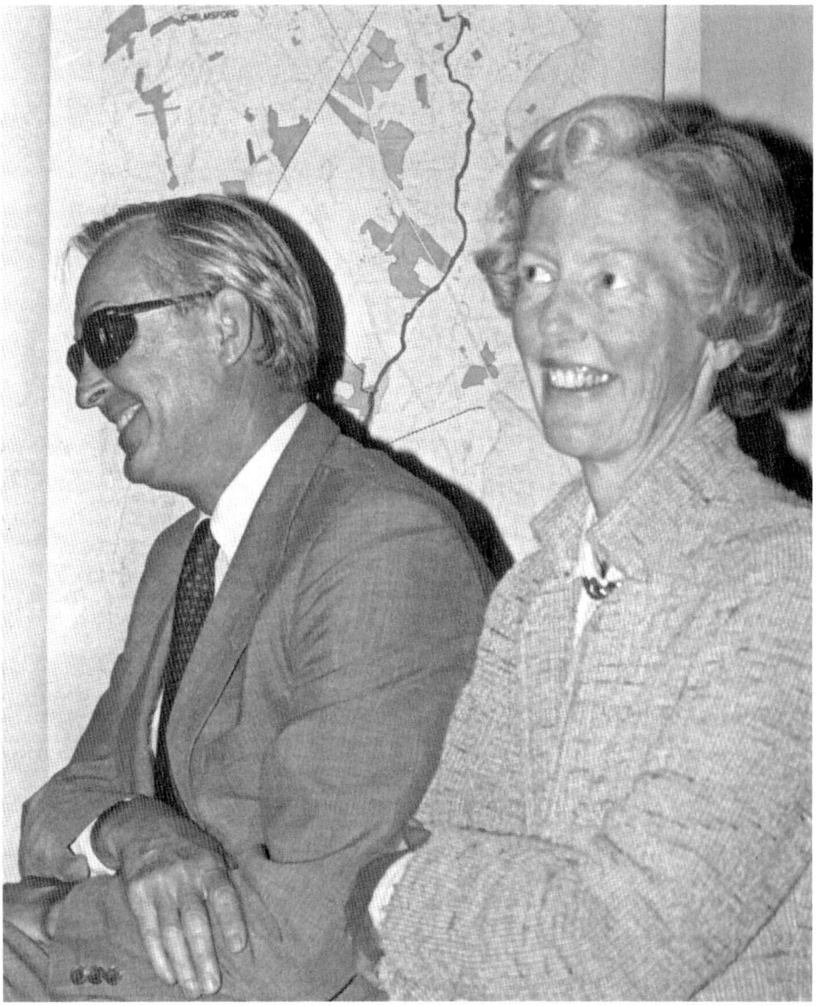

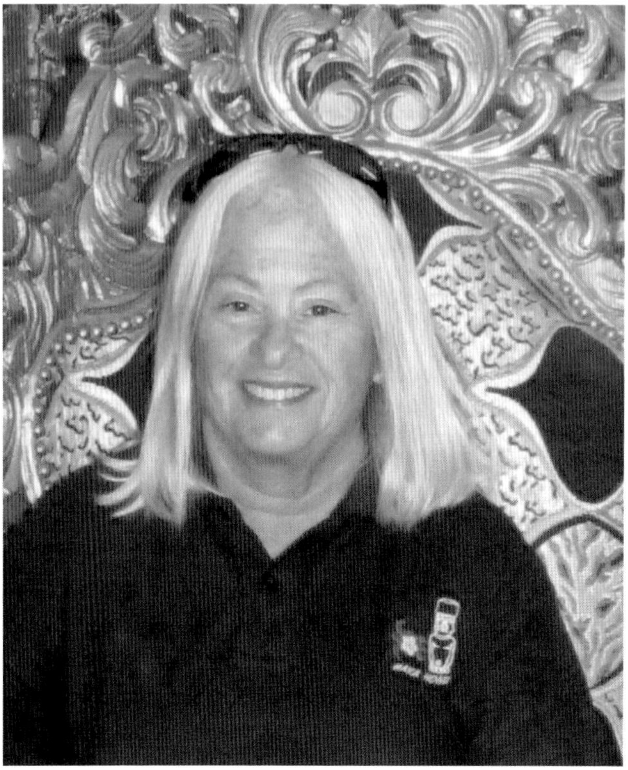

Linda Segal
Linda Segal taught Spanish for 30 years, during which she traveled extensively on her own and with students. Her 25 years of service in Wayland include the board of selectmen, zoning board of appeals, Wellhead Protection Committee, and advocate for acquisition of the former Dow site, now Loker Conservation and Recreation Area. She is a strong environmental activist, serves on the board of the Toxics Action Center, and was awarded the Toxics Action Center Citizens Award in 2009. (Courtesy of Linda Segal.)

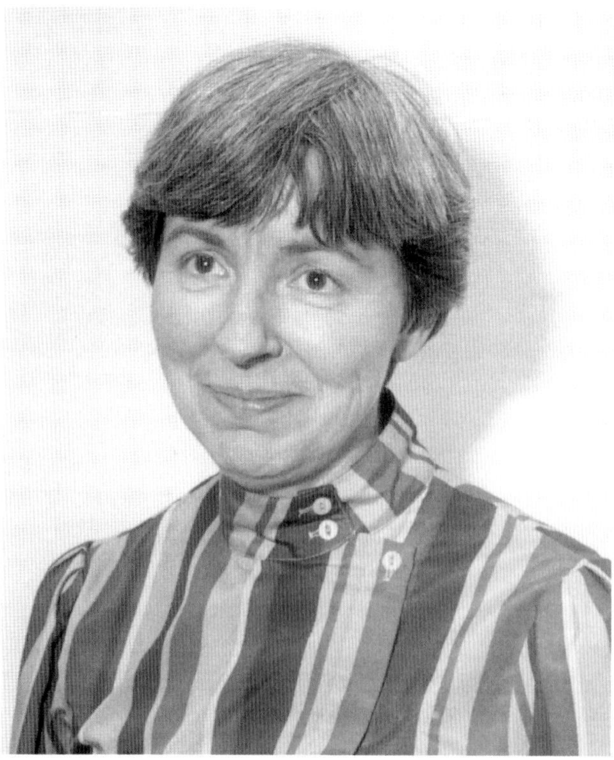

Mary Antes
Mary Antes retired in 2012 from Education Development Center, a nonprofit that carries out projects in education and health in the United States and around the world. During her 45 years in town, she has served on the Housing Authority, Housing Partnership, River Stewardship Council, 375th Anniversary Commemoration Committee, Habitat for Humanity, the board of selectmen, the League of Women Voters, and Metropolitan Council for Educational Opportunity Community Committee.

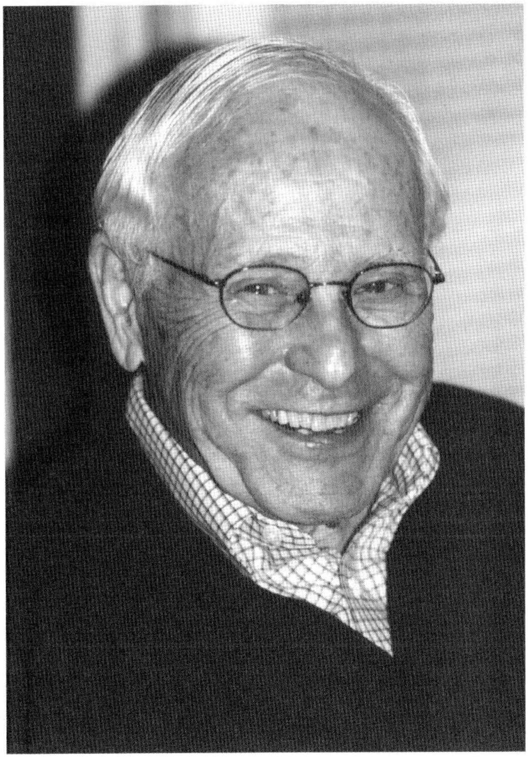

Charles Raskin

Charlie Raskin helped found Wayland Housing Associates, a nonprofit development corporation. Since 1993, he has been a member of the Wayland Housing Authority Board of Commissioners, overseeing millions of dollars of preservation and modernization work in public housing, including the demolition and reconstruction of 25 scattered site houses, and the renovation of a development for seniors and persons with disabilities. He recently received the Local Housing Heroes Award from Massachusetts Housing Partnership. (Courtesy of Charles Raskin.)

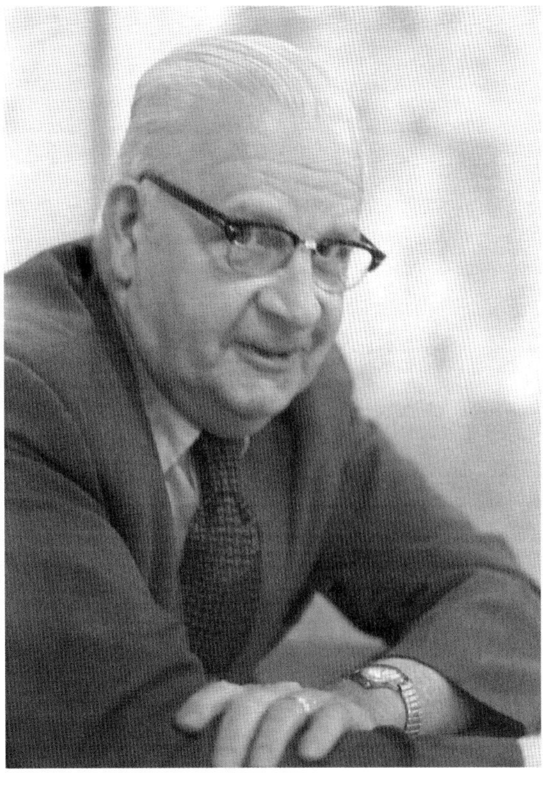

John McEnroy (1913–2002)

John McEnroy was a familiar face in town, strolling the streets and gathering information for his turn at the microphone during town meetings. Often referred to as the "Mayor of Cochituate," he served as a selectman, town clerk, and finance committee member. It was said that people who wanted to accomplish something felt they needed to consult him. He had a real constituency. McEnroy had a love affair with Wayland and believed he always did best for the town.

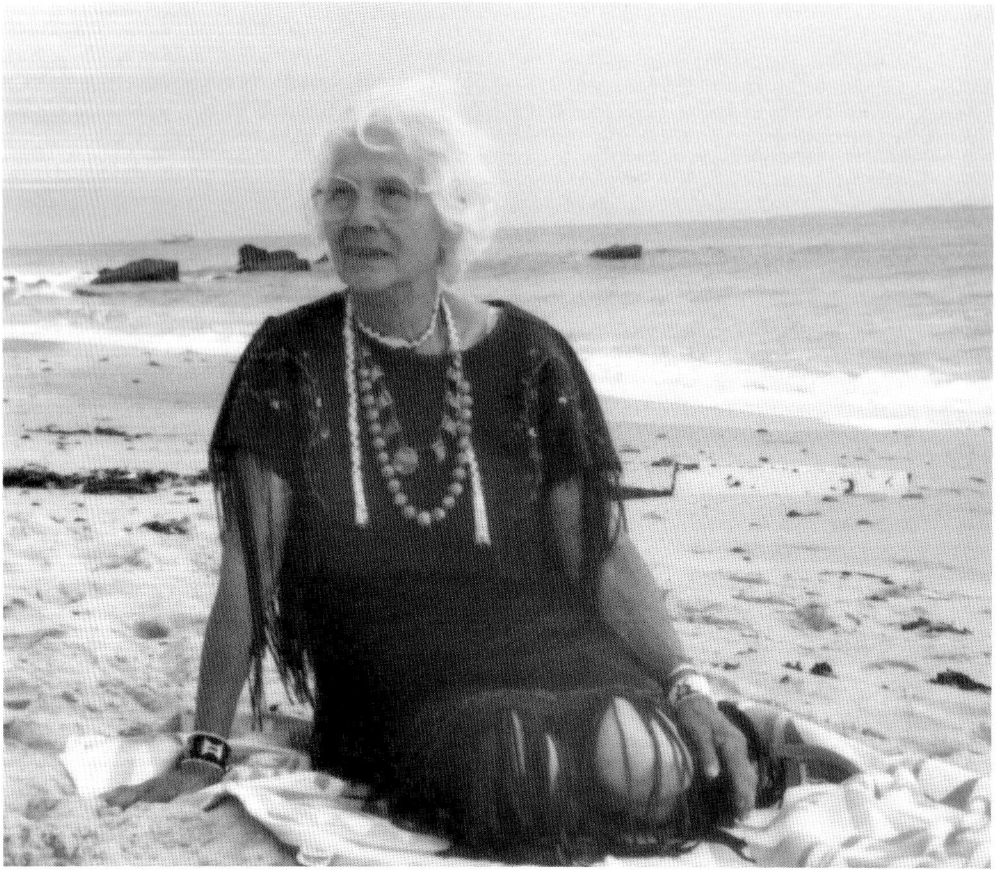

Gladys Widdiss (1915–2012)

Gladys Widdiss was a noted potter and highly respected tribal leader who led the Wampanoag Tribe of Gay Head for many years. She was president of the tribe from 1978 to 1987, a formative time for the Wampanoags. During her tenure, the tribe acquired the Gay Head Cliffs, the cranberry bogs, and Herring Creek from the town, and the Wampanoag Tribe of Gay Head won federal recognition from the Bureau of Indian Affairs. For some years afterward, Widdiss continued to serve as vice chairman of the tribal council. Born at Gay Head, she and her brother Donald, who later became chief of the Wampanoag tribe, grew up in their parents' homestead on Lobsterville Road. It had been built for her great-grandfather, the whaling man Thomas Manning, and his bride in the mid-19th century. The cottage that Gladys long called home is on the homestead property. In later years, she frequently reminisced about her happy Gay Head childhood when the village was a far simpler place than today. In those days, she recalled, fishing and farming were the principal occupations in the community, and there were wide expanses of corn and potato fields. Widdiss moved to Wayland when World War II broke out and her husband joined the Marines. While raising three children, she volunteered in Wayland schools, churches, and with the Boy Scouts, bringing her Indian heritage to life through storytelling and crafts. In addition to her artwork and Island tribal activities, she traveled the country attending Native American gatherings as a representative of the Wampanoags. In the 1960s, she was active in the Coalition of Eastern Native Americans. She was on the board of the Boston Children's Museum for many years and regularly attended the Martha's Vineyard Center for Living and the Baptist Church of Gay Head. Her husband, Leonard, died in 1987, and not long after, she returned to Gay Head where she built a cottage of her own on family homestead land. In 1993, the Gay Head Council on Aging nominated her as senior citizen of the year, declaring that she exemplified "the spirit of positive aging." (Courtesy of Dawn Widdiss.)

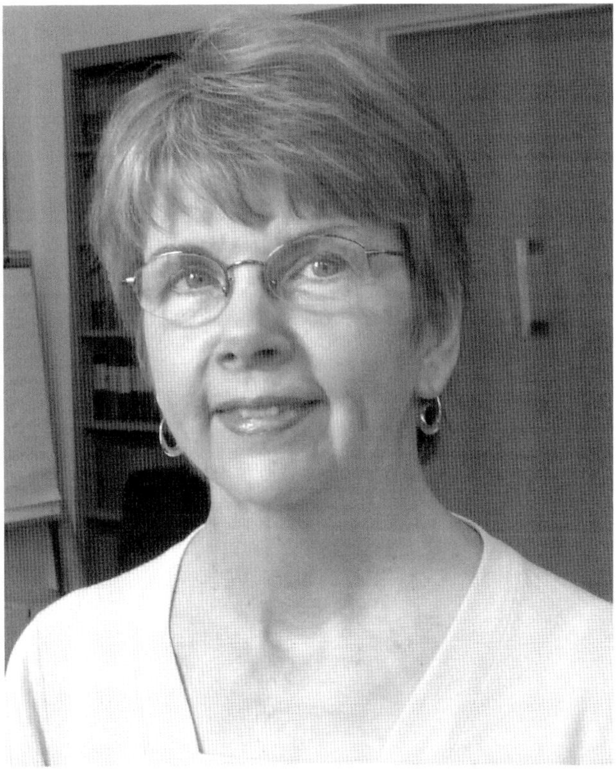

Lynn Trimby

Lynn Trimby has been on the board of Monkey Helpers since 2005, serving three years as chair of the finance committee before assuming responsibility as treasurer in 2010. Since 1979, Helping Hands: Monkey Helpers for the Disabled Inc. has been raising and training capuchin monkeys to provide daily, in-home assistance to people living with spinal cord injuries and other mobility impairments. The animals, placed free of charge, provide independence, a set of nimble hands, and welcome companionship. The staff provides lifetime active placement support for each animal. Based in Boston, this is the only nonprofit organization in the world that places these special-service animals. (Clockwise from top left, author's collection; courtesy of Ryan Watkins; courtesy of Ryan Watkins)

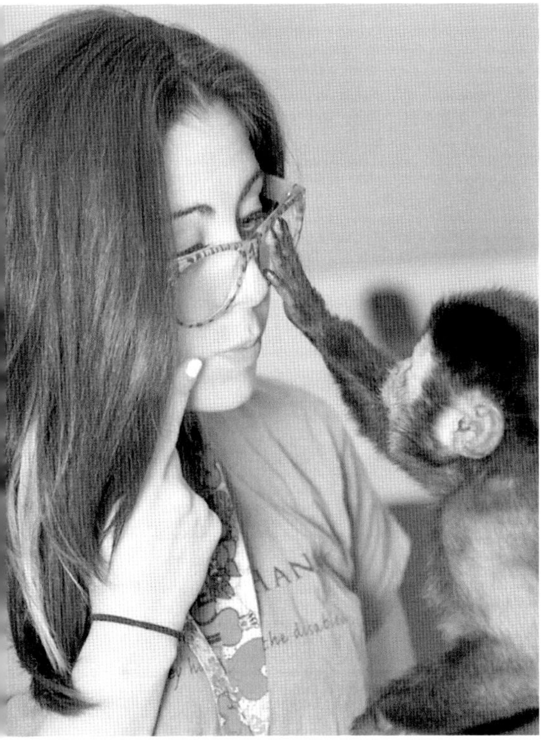

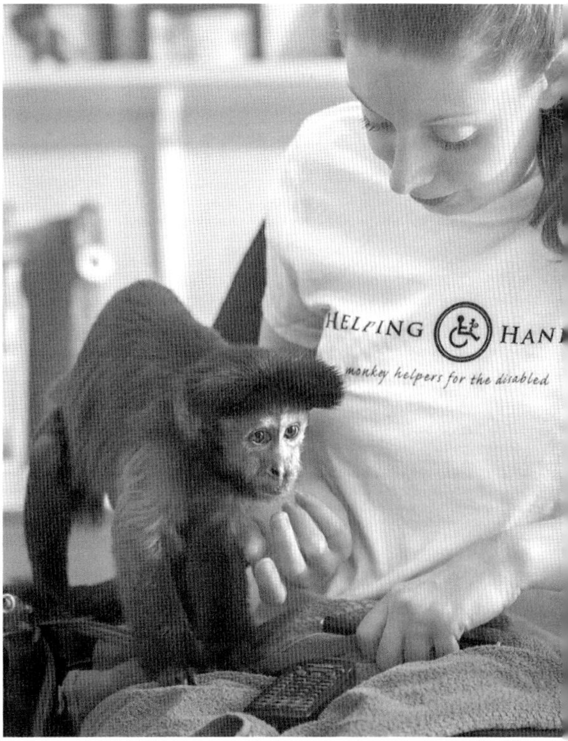

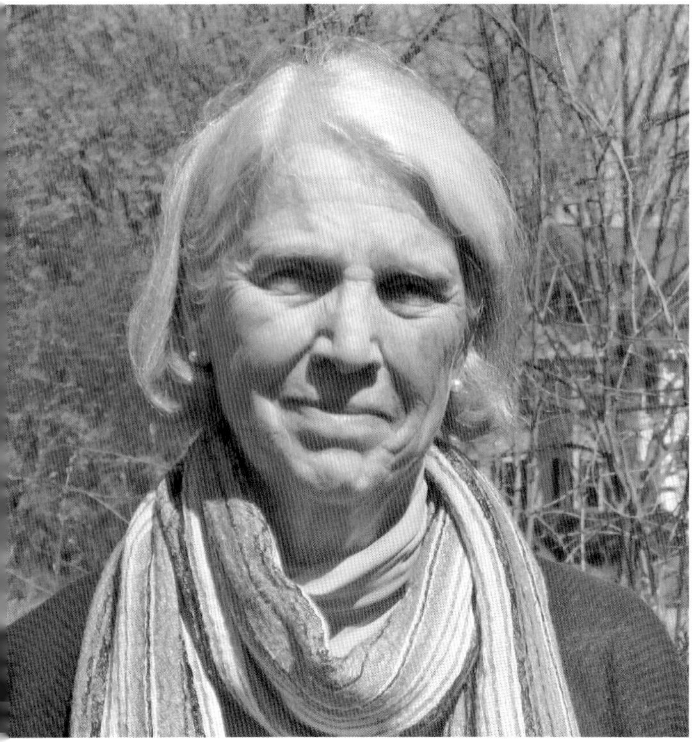

Gretchen Schuler

Gretchen Schuler was instrumental in seeing the Nike site reused for housing and open space and chaired the committee to preserve 133 acres of the Paine Estate when it was being developed. A professional preservationist, Gretchen developed a historical resource survey for the Historical Society in 2012, has served on the Planning Board, Historical Commission, and Historic District Commission. She is currently on the Community Preservation Committee as a selectmen appointee. (Author's collection.)

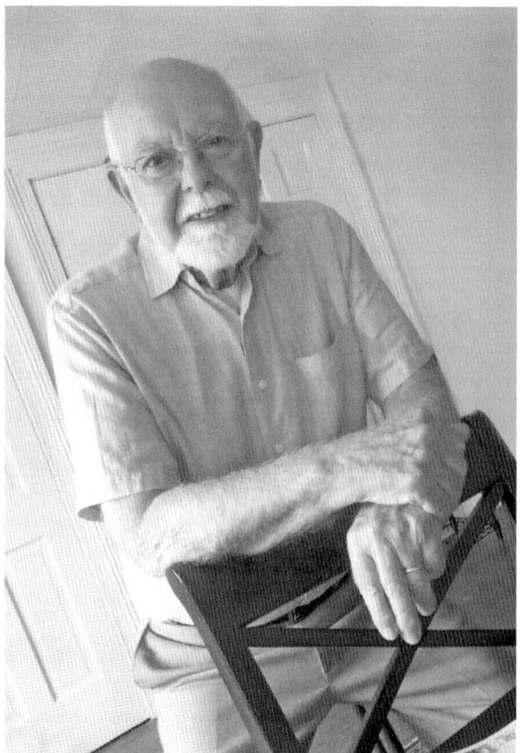

Richard "Dick" Hoyt

Dick Hoyt became an active volunteer in town after retiring from 42 years of teaching. He was president of the Brookline Educators Association and recipient of the Ernest R. Caverly Award for excellence in teaching. He was president of the Wayland Historical Society for seven years, choir singer/bass soloist at First Parish Church, served on the Wayland Veterans Memorial Committee, and co-edited *Wayland A to Z*, a book about the town's past and present. (Courtesy of David Lang.)

Tom Sciacca and Jane Sciacca

Tom and Jane Sciacca have lived in town for 44 years, and Tom has devoted many hours to the preservation of the town's wetlands. A retired engineer, he has served on the town's Conservation Commission, Energy Initiatives Advisory Committee, School Technology Task Force, and the regional River Stewardship Council. He is currently a writer and reporter for Wayland Voters Network. Jane served on the Historical Commission, was president of the Wayland Historical Society for eight years, and worked with the town's 375th celebration committee. She is also a National Park Service ranger. Over the years, she has become a specialist in early New England slavery. (Courtesy of the Sciaccas.)

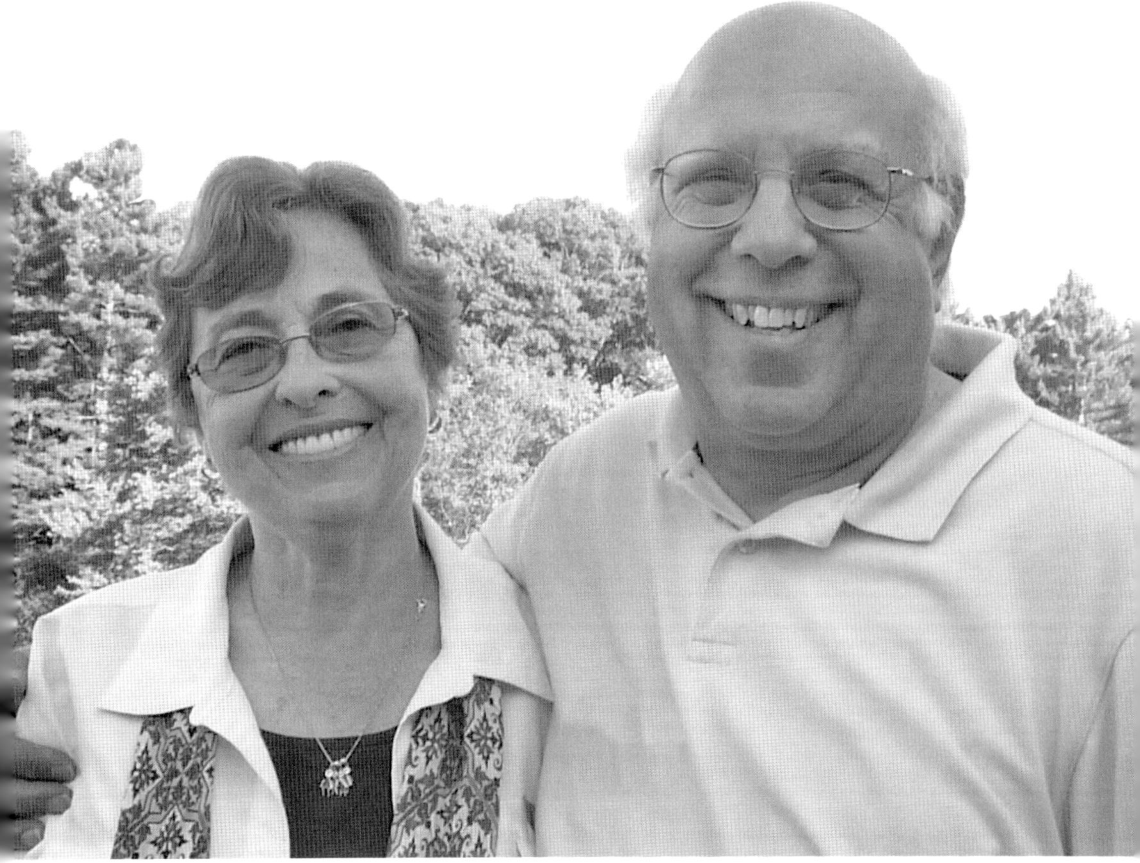

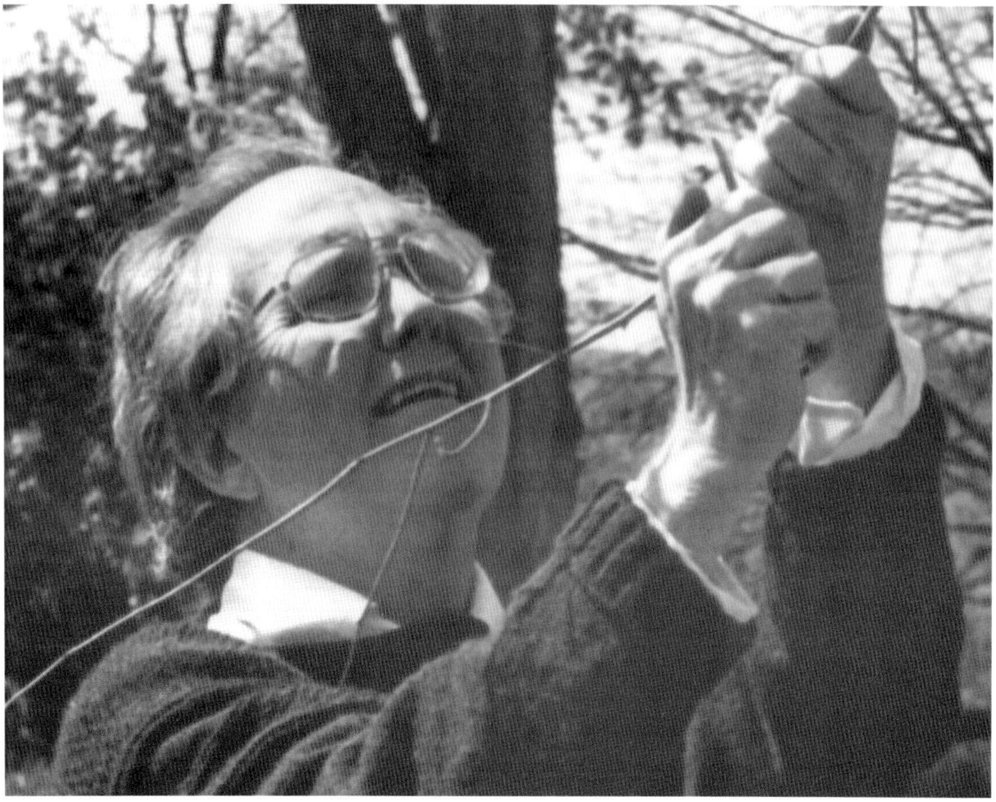

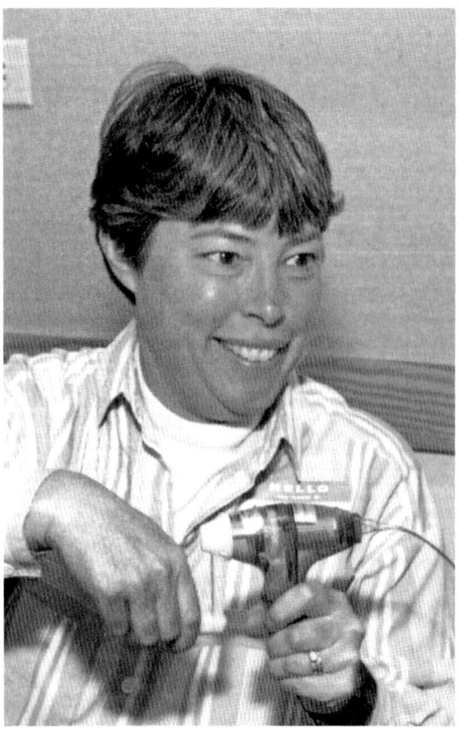

Paul Gardescu
Paul Gardescu, a former landscape architect, devoted his retirement in 1984 to the conservation of archeological sites in Wayland. An enthusiastic and committed amateur archeologist, he has recruited and trained numerous volunteers for the Wayland Archeology Group, the only group of its type in the commonwealth. A recent site yielded 8,000-year-old artifacts, which have been washed, sorted, and cataloged, along with hundreds of others, in a laboratory in the town building.

Nancy Ashkar (1948–2004)
Nancy Ashkar was a popular biology teacher who settled in Wayland in 1977. An active volunteer in the schools, she served in the Parent Teacher Organization, coached girls' soccer, and cofounded Wayland Sports Network, a community television show for which she received several awards. She was co-founder and director of the Wayland Local Studies Center and was awarded the Massachusetts State Historian's Award. She also created Animals as Intermediaries, an organization dedicated to helping people with injured animals.

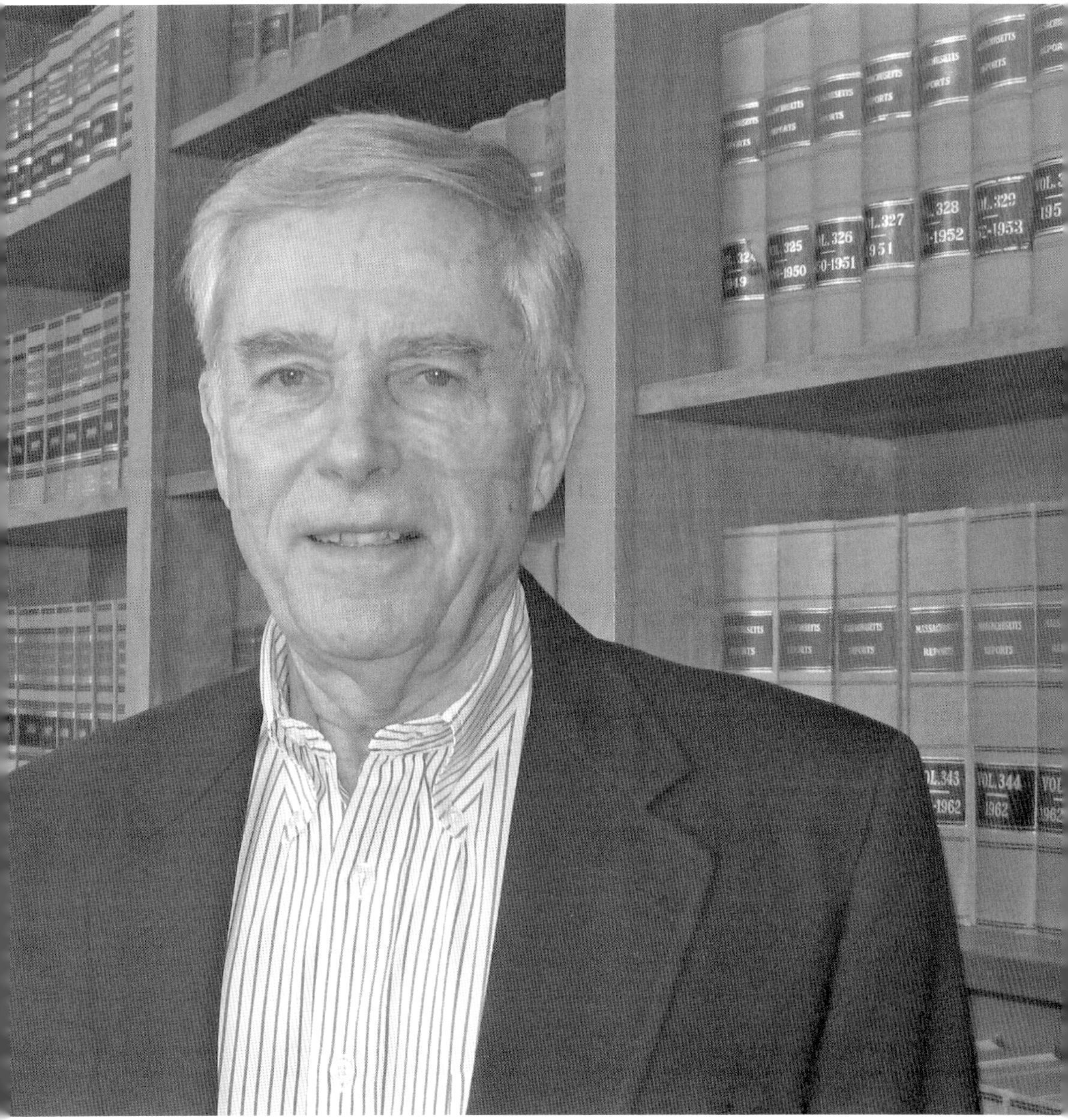

Michael Patterson

Michael Patterson, along with a staff of five volunteers, chairs the Wayland Community Fund, which provides short-term emergency financial assistance to residents in need. Established in 1997 by Patterson and the Commissioners of Trust Funds, the organization was originally funded by a bequest from the late Suzanne Leavitt. Still funded in part by this bequest, Wayland residents and local organizations also contribute. The fund has no overhead, and 100 percent of contributions go directly to residents. The fund has helped a wide variety of residents, including elderly grandparents raising grandchildren, the long-term unemployed, adults and children with serious health problems, and teenagers with no family or financial support. They have sometimes assisted women in Wayland who were reduced to living in their cars. (Author's collection.)

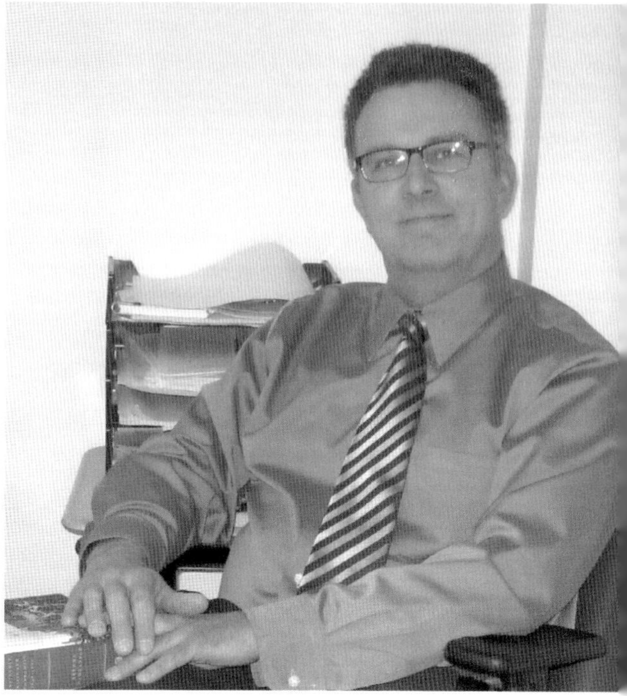

Kevin Delaney
Kevin Delaney has been teaching history at Wayland High School for 23 years, including 14 as the social studies department head. In 2001, he founded the Wayland High School History Project, a six-volume electronic archive of Wayland's history. Each edition took students two years to research, construct, and trace how national trends and developments play out in the Wayland microcosm during distinct 20th century eras. Delaney is the 2014 Massachusetts History Teacher of the Year. (Author's collection.)

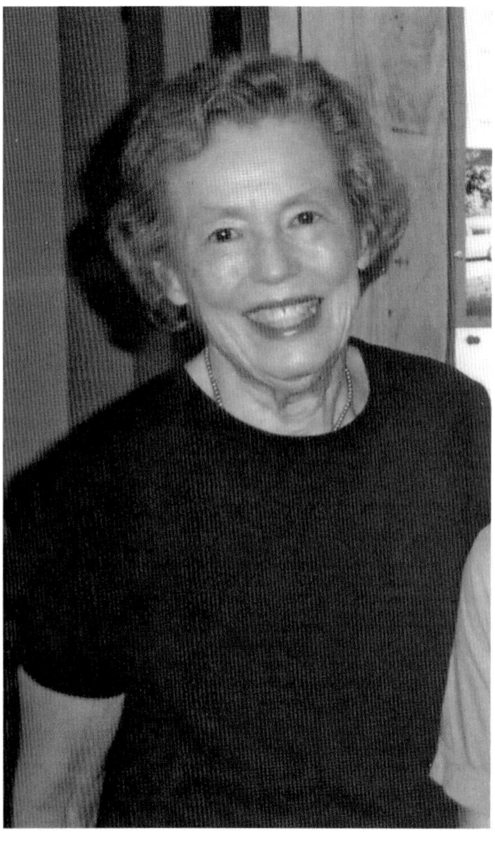

Joanne Davis
Joanne Davis has spent the past six decades in Wayland, where she raised three children. She has served as general chairman of the historical Strawberry Festival, which started in 1959, as a Conservation Commission associate, and as a longtime member of the Wayland Historical Society. She taught in the Wayland Public Schools for 24 years, most of the time teaching first graders at Claypit School. Since retirement, she has been the Wayland Historical Society's museum director.

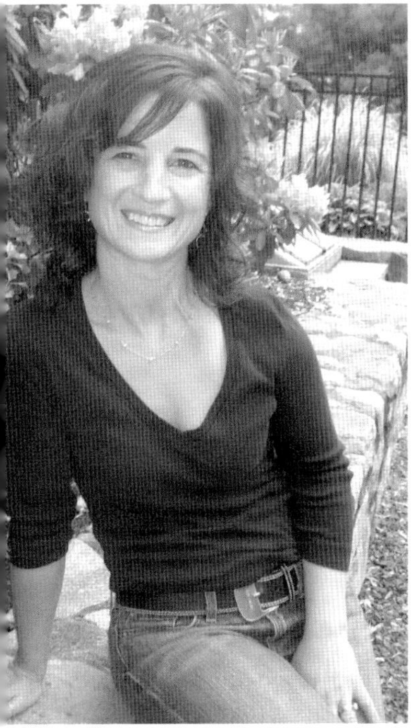

Pam Washek (1965–2012) and Anne Becker

When Pam Washek (left) and a friend, Jean Seiden, were battling cancer, their friends came together to give their children rides, organize meals, walk dogs, and clean homes. They were called the Wayland Angels. After Seiden died in 2010, Washek, knowing they could not have made it without the help of their friends, turned the Angels network of volunteers into the Neighborhood Brigade. Even though Washek had caring family and friends nearby, the experience taught her that not everyone was so lucky. She served as executive director of Neighborhood Brigade until her death in 2012. Today, Anne Becker (below) is co-leader of the founding chapter. She has lived in Wayland for 30 years and was inspired to join the organization after meeting Pam and Jean. Wayland's Neighborhood Brigade has over 500 volunteers willing to respond when a friend or neighbor in the community needs some assistance. The brigade has delivered 1,000 meals, provided countless rides, and helped with dog walking, local errands, and grocery shopping for many residents. They also support local churches with holiday meals for needy families. Neighborhood Brigade has become a household name in Wayland, offering community support to all in need. (Left, courtesy of Jessica Washek; below, courtesy of Anne Becker.)

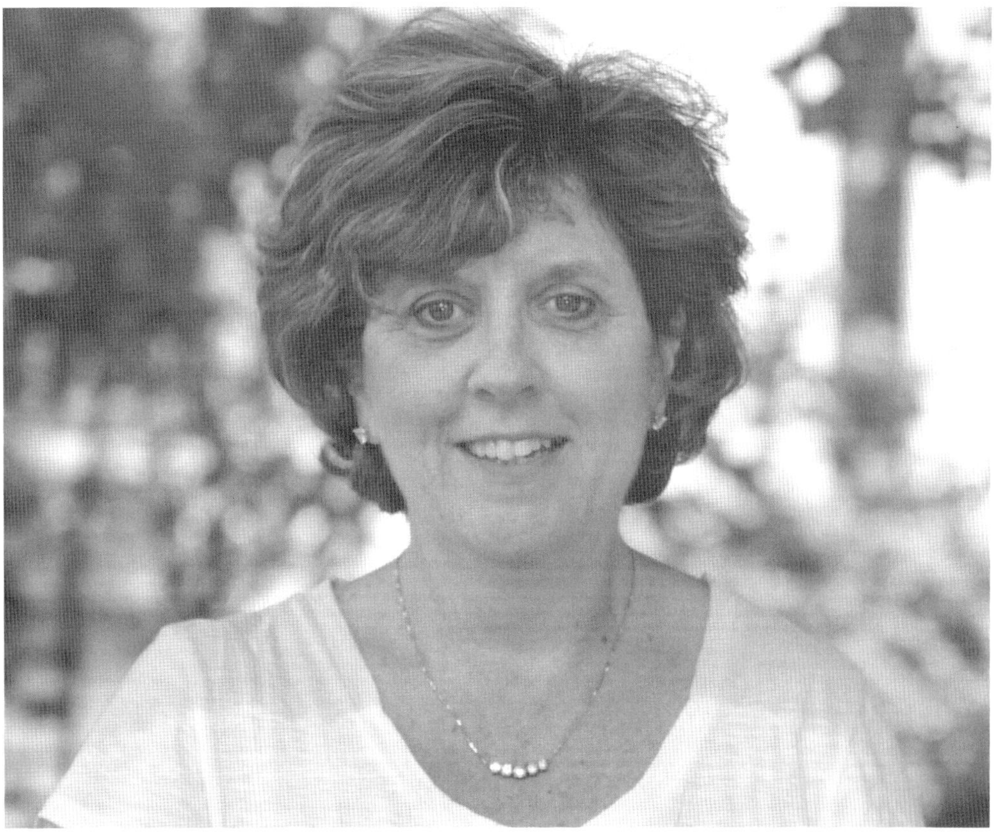

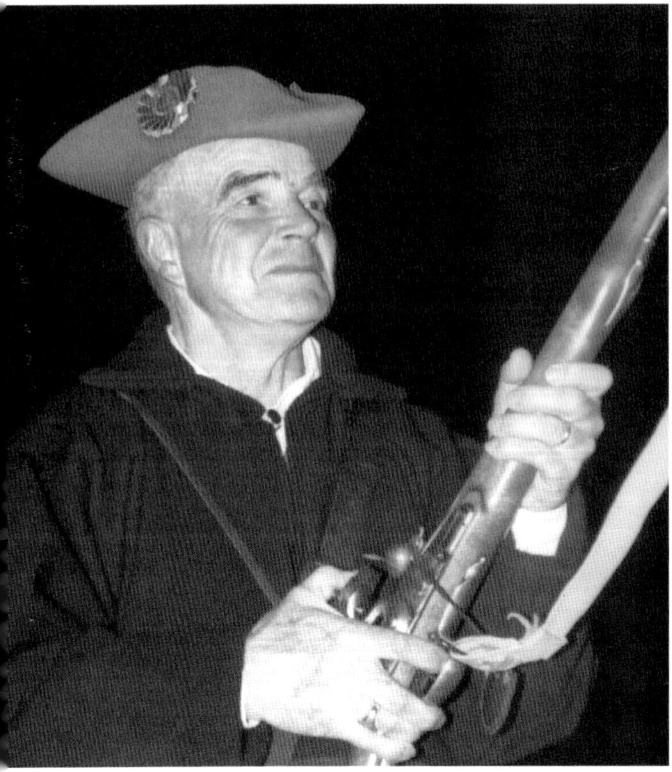

Roger Backman

Roger Backman settled in town more than six decades ago and has been a committed and valued volunteer ever since. He has served 43 years as a member of the Wayland East Company of the Sudbury Minute & Militia, been a member of the board of the Wayland Historical Society for 29 years, served on the Conservation Commission for 17 years, and for 23 years has been volunteering at Drumlin Farm in Lincoln.

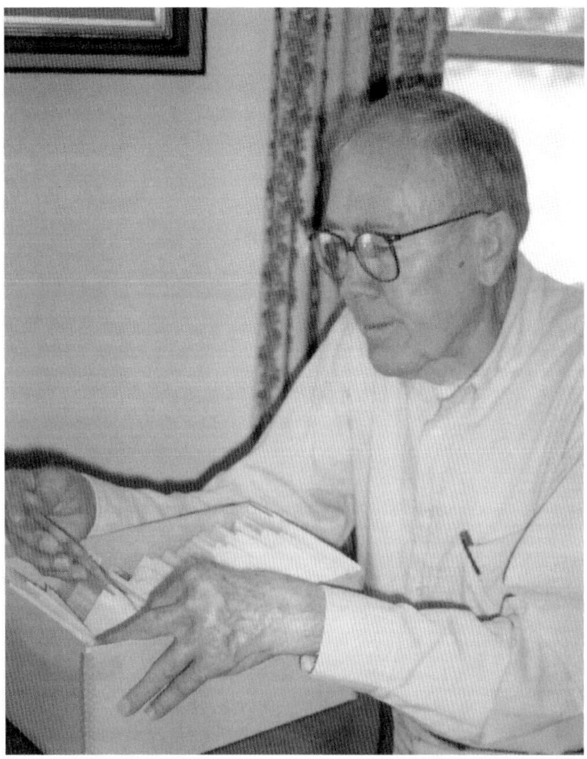

George Lewis (1923–2011)

George Lewis used his camera to document changes in town for more than five decades. Raised in Wayland, he knew every nook and cranny and eventually became unofficial town historian. He taught in the geography department at Boston University, was a founding member of the SVT, and served on numerous boards in town. He received a Bay State Historical League Local Hero award for lasting impact in activities not limited to local history.

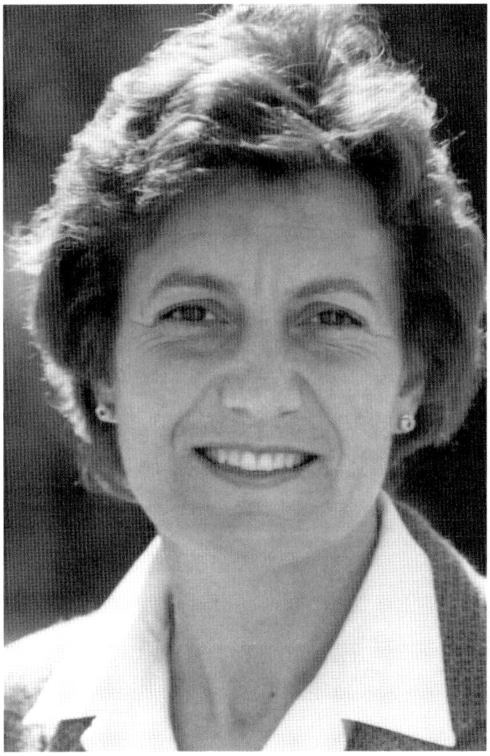

Lucile Hicks
Lucile Hicks served in the Massachusetts House of Representatives from the 13th District for eight years. She was elected minority whip of the House in 1987. She served on three special legislative commissions studying taxation, growth, and divorce. The American Cancer Society named her Outstanding Legislator of the Year in 1988. A former high school teacher, she was a member of the Sudbury River Citizens Advisory Committee and the Sudbury Business and Professional Women's Club.

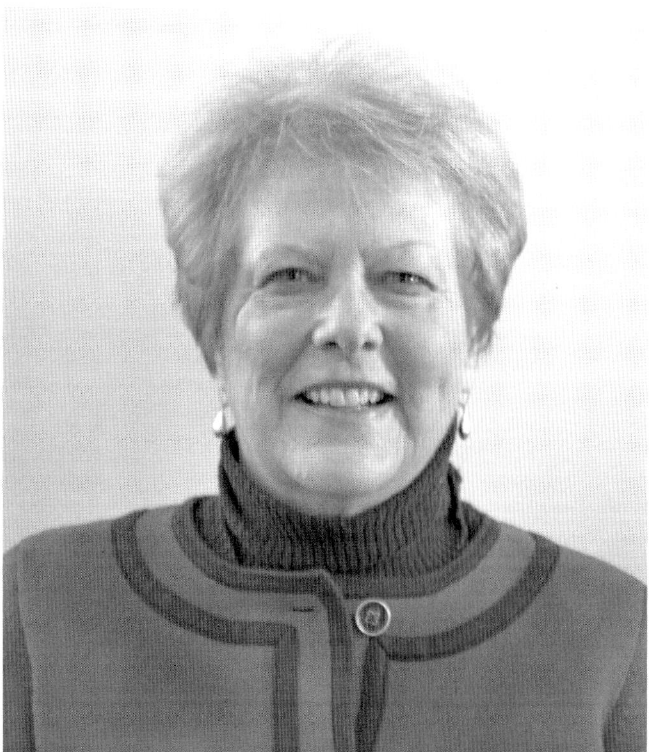

Susan "Sue" Pope
Sue Pope found her dream house 44 years ago, next to a working dairy farm where Holstein cows grazed outside her window. While raising three children, she was for many years a selectman, school committee member, and a Massachusetts state representative. In her retirement, she is head of Friends of the Council on Aging, trustee for Parmenter, corporator at Emerson Hospital in Concord, and a longtime member of SVT. (Courtesy of Dorothea Callen.)

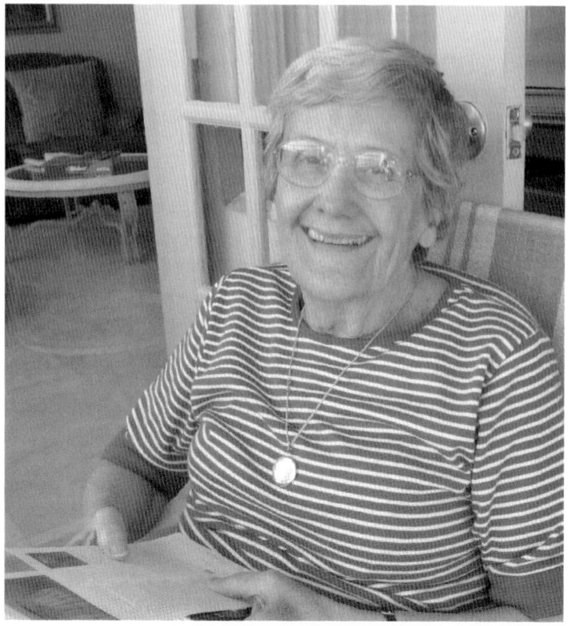

Mary Trageser

Mary Trageser spent four decades in Wayland, raising four children and working both full and part time at the Wayland Public Library. In 1944, she worked in London and Germany for the Office of Strategic Services, forerunner to the CIA, and later for the state department. After World War II, she worked in Paris for Averell Harriman, chief negotiator of the Marshall Plan in Europe. (Courtesy of Richard Hoyt.)

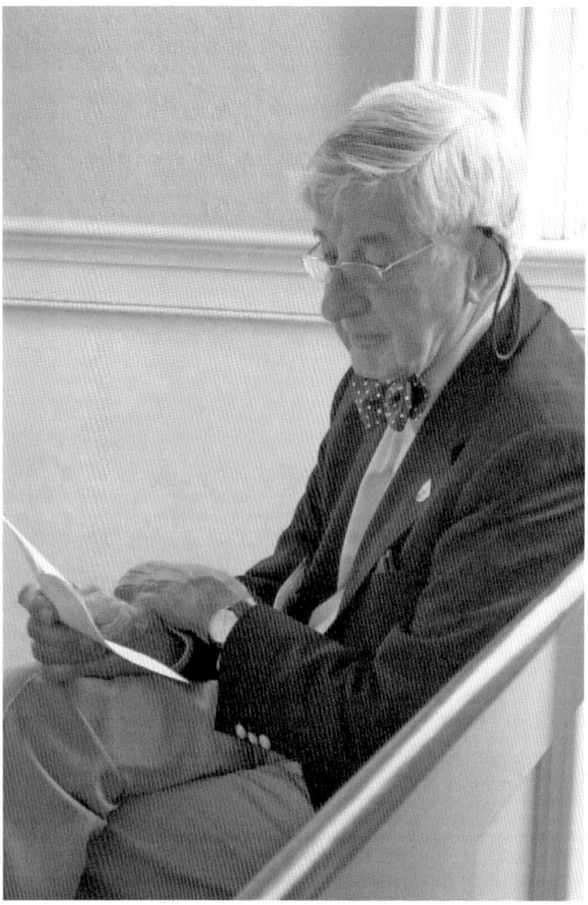

Perry Hagenstein (1931–2008)

For almost four decades, Perry Hagenstein walked regularly to the library and post office from his home on Bennett Road. After a long career in the field of natural resource policy and economics, he volunteered many hours with First Parish Church, Wayland Public Library, Historical Society, and Conservation Commission. Admired by all, Perry left an indelible mark on the community. (Courtesy of David Lang.)

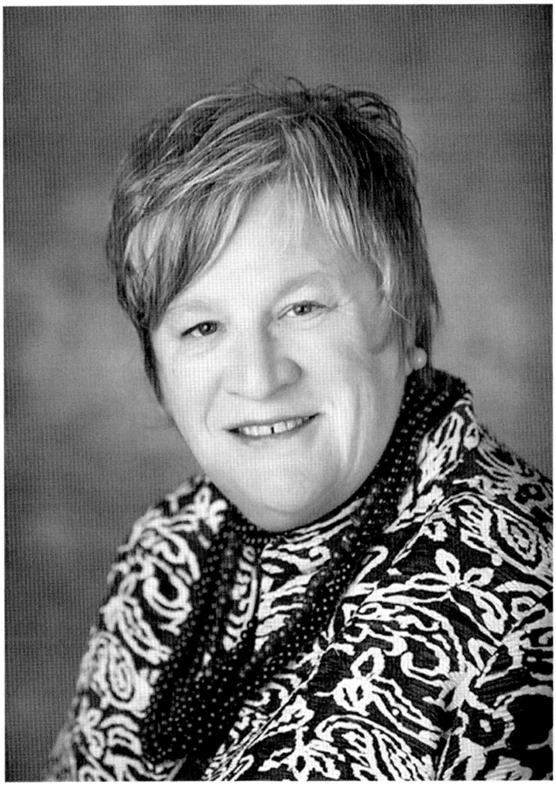

Elaine Sweeney
Elaine Sweeney spent two decades volunteering in the town's schools while raising a son and daughter. A lifetime member of the National School Board Association and featured speaker for the Massachusetts Association of School Committees, she served as Wayland representative to the Minuteman School Committee for 12 years. She helped establish the boat rental program at the Wayland town beach. She is currently a successful real estate broker with Barrett Sotheby's in Lincoln, Massachusetts. (Courtesy of Elaine Sweeney.)

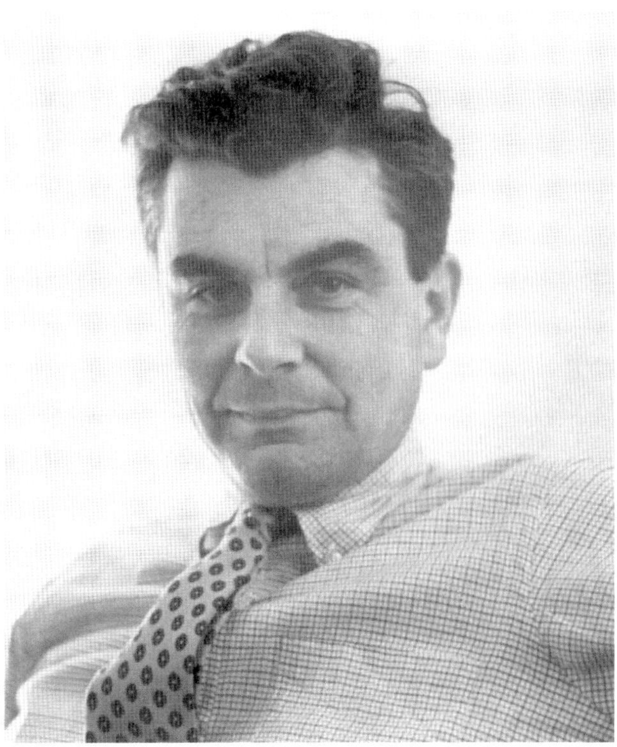

Robert Swain (1928–1988)
Bob Swain served seven terms as chairman of the town's Finance Committee from 1968 to 1987, creating financial stability during a period of economic growth. He guided the financing of the town as it embarked on many new projects, supporting a high-quality school department and acquisition of conservation land. Anticipating the advent of Proposition 2.5 and a new era of tax limitation, he helped develop a local tax cap to soften the impact on the town.

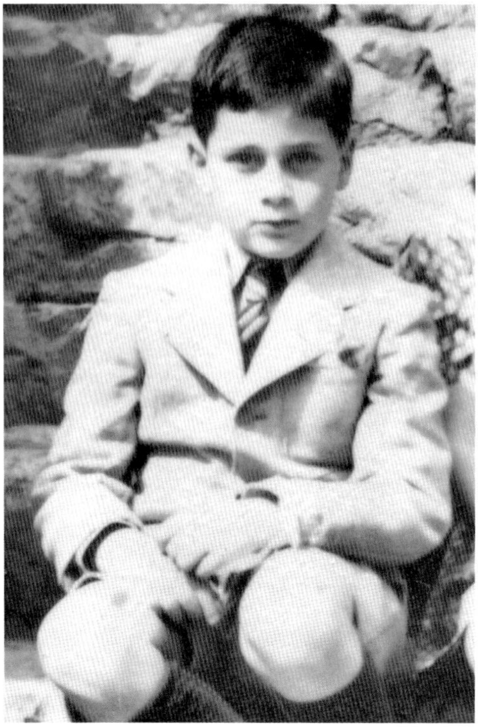 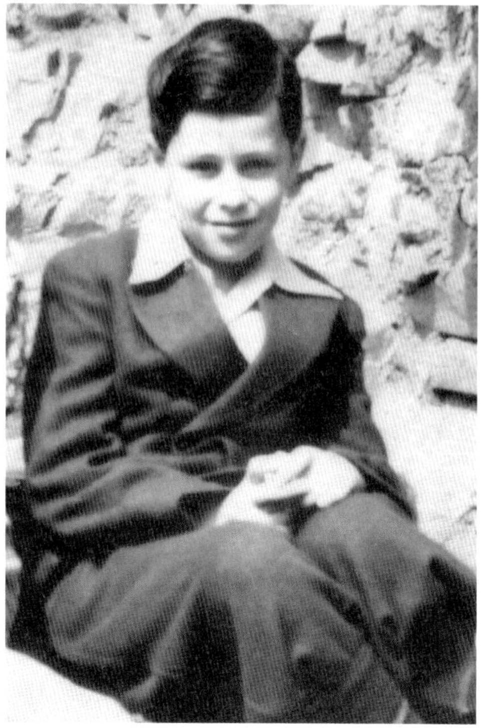

Werner F. Gossels and C. Peter R. Gossels (ABOVE AND OPPOSITE)
Born in Germany, the Gossels brothers were saved by the heroism of their mother, Charlotte Lewy Gossels, who somehow arranged for them to escape to France on July 4, 1939, when they were only five and eight years old. Kind strangers first moved them from Quincy, near Nazi-occupied Paris, to rural Chabannes in unoccupied Vichy, France. Then, in September 1941, they left France through Spain and Portugal to safety in the United States. Peter (above right and opposite at right) was first taken in by the Singal family in Brookline, Massachusetts, but was moved to a group home in Mattapan after a few years. He attended Boston Latin School before graduating from Harvard College and Harvard Law School. Peter and his wife, Nancy, arrived in Wayland in 1961, and raised their three children there.

Werner (above left and opposite at left) was taken in by the Glaser and Gordon family, who raised him and made it possible for him to go through the Brookline School system and on to Yale University. In 1964, he settled in Wayland with his wife, Elaine, and five children. During their 50-plus years in Wayland, both men and their families have involved themselves in the evolution of the town. Peter served on the Finance Committee, was town counsel for 11 years, and moderator of town meetings for 30 years. Werner served on the Planning Board, was a longtime leader on business zoning matters in the Wayland Business Association, and served on both the Intertown Committee with Sudbury that designed and built the Joint Septage Facility and later on the Operations Committee that ran the facility. He was one of the founders of Wayland Beautification, which for the past 16 years has worked to improve the appearance of public spaces in town. Elaine Gossels served as president of the Committee for Advancement of Performing Arts in Wayland Public Schools and as treasurer on the Board of the Wayland Public Schools Foundation, which has done much to keep Wayland Schools on the cutting edge of public education. In 1990, after their children had graduated, they endowed the Gossels Family Fund for Academic Excellence in the Wayland Public Schools, to provide Wayland's children with the quality of education their children had received, equal to that normally available only in private preparatory schools. At the Wayland Public Library, Werner and Peter established the Gossels Family Fund for Human Dignity in honor of their mother, aunt, and grandmother who were murdered by the Nazis in the Holocaust. (All, courtesy of the Gossels families.)

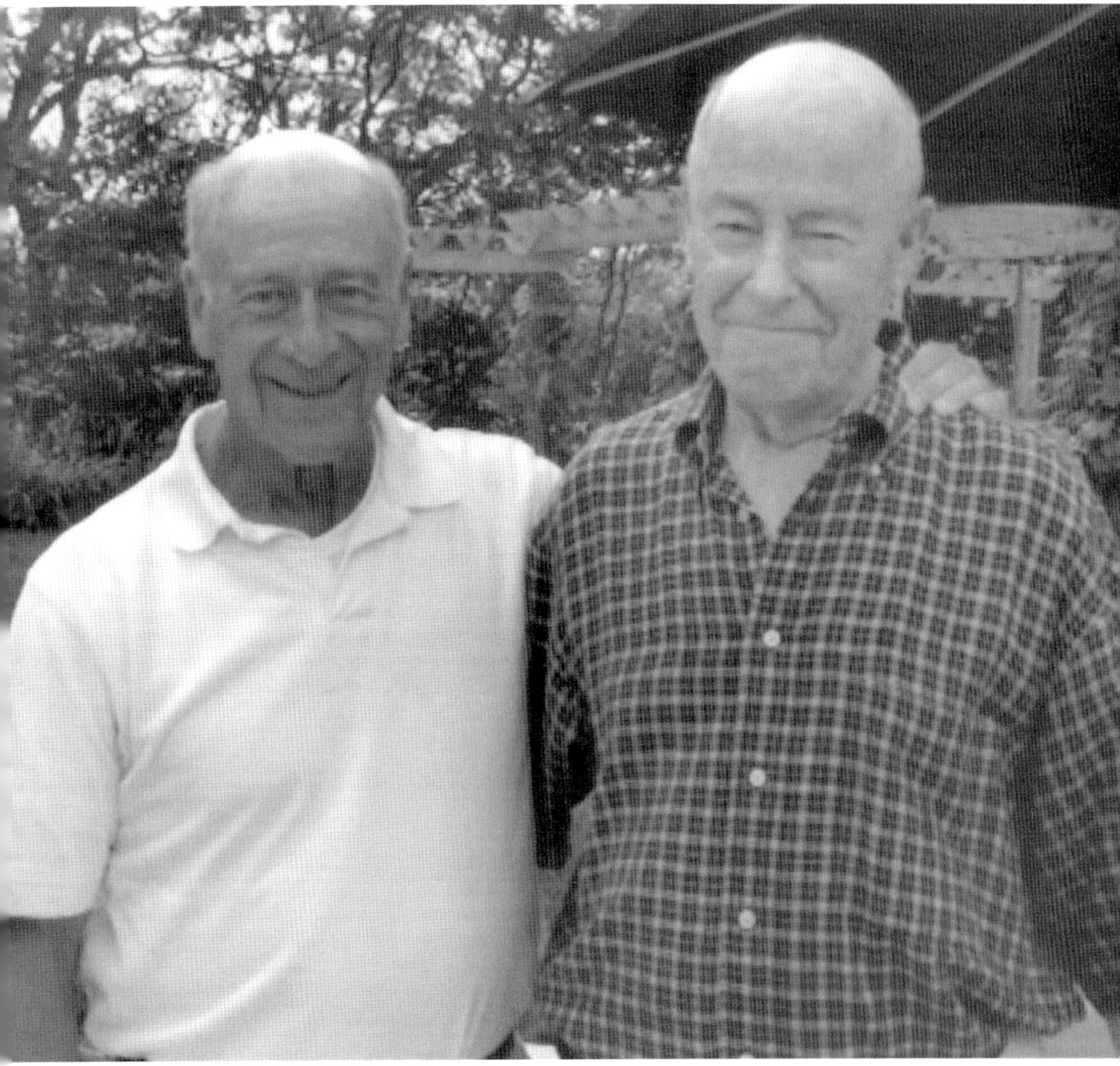

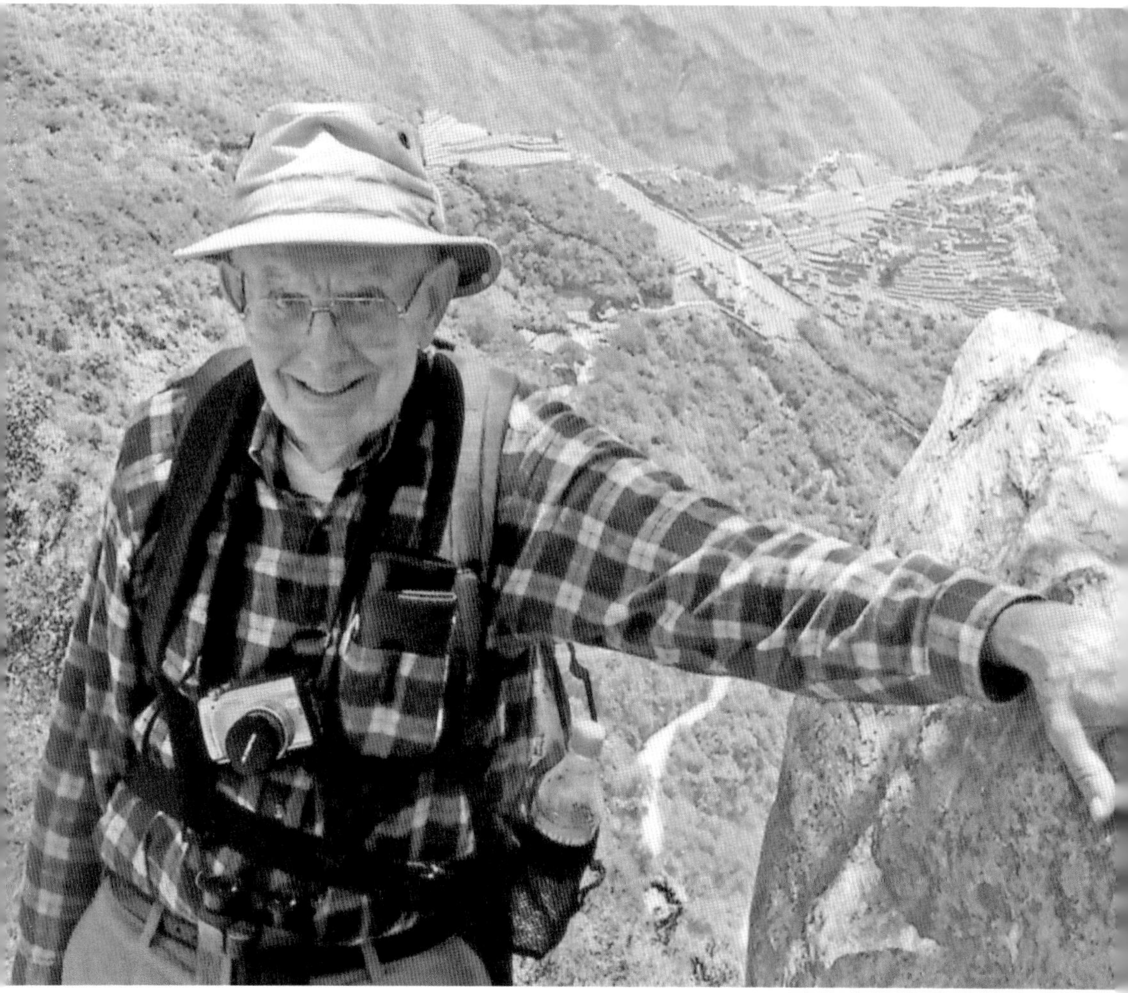

Henry "Hank" Norwood (1930–2011)

Hank Norwood was best known for his leadership in the annual Concord Christmas Bird Count, which he coordinated for 51 years. He helped people of all ages learn about birds and join the annual bird count. He also initiated and supervised a hawk watch, collected statistics on the decline of common nighthawks in the SUASCO River valley area, and co-authored a scientific paper on the influence of El Niño on bird migration patterns. He was on the board of directors of the Friends of the Assabet River National Wildlife Refuge, the region's newest federal wildlife refuge. (Courtesy of Peggy Norwood.)

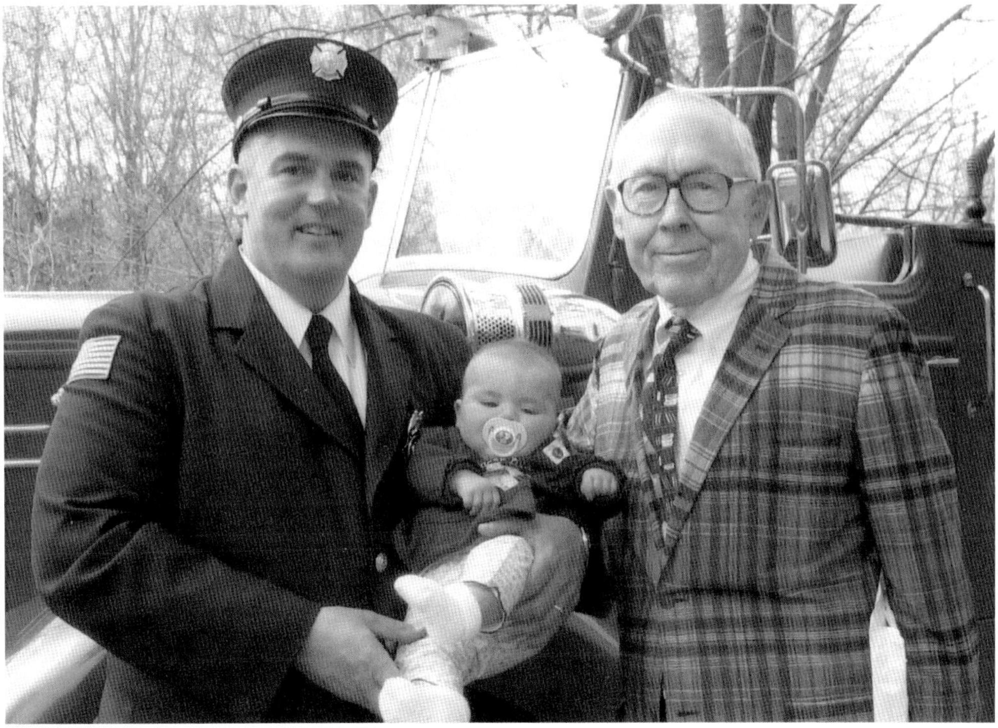

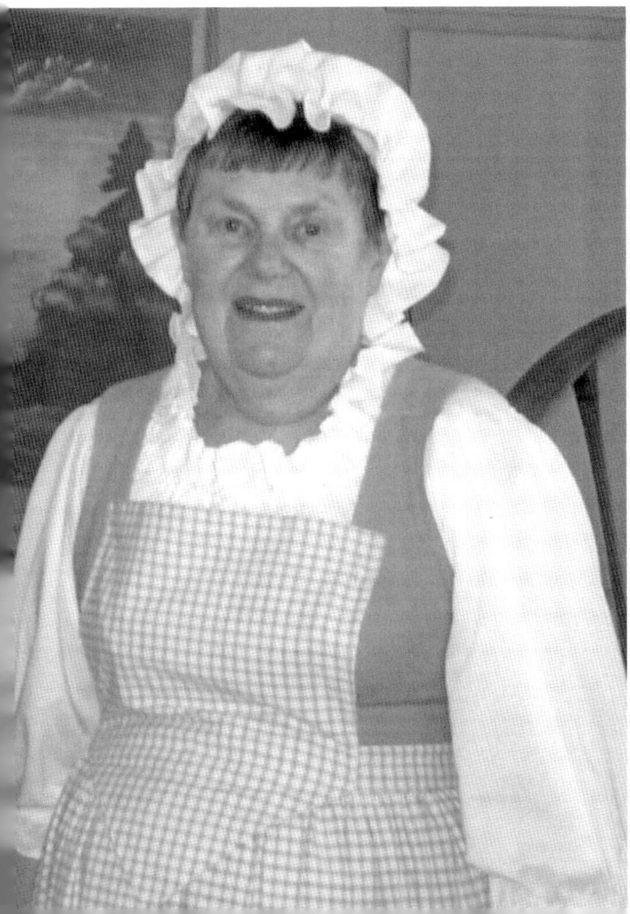

Robert "Bob" Dorey
Bob Dorey (left), a firefighter who grew up in Wayland, brought the town's shiny 1953 fire engine to help celebrate Wayland Historical Society's 50th birthday. Many society members dressed in period costumes for the celebration. Bob's daughter Sarah (center) came along, as did George Lewis (right), who had been present at the society's organizational meeting in 1954. (Courtesy of Heather Dorey.)

Gloria Backman
Gloria Backman moved to Wayland in 1952, when the town was starting to evolve from a rural to a suburban community. In 1985, after raising five children, she became active in the Wayland Historical Society. She is the society's costume curator, responsible for documenting and storing the society's extensive collection of clothing and textiles. In addition, she participates in the society's after-school history program dressed in authentic colonial clothing.

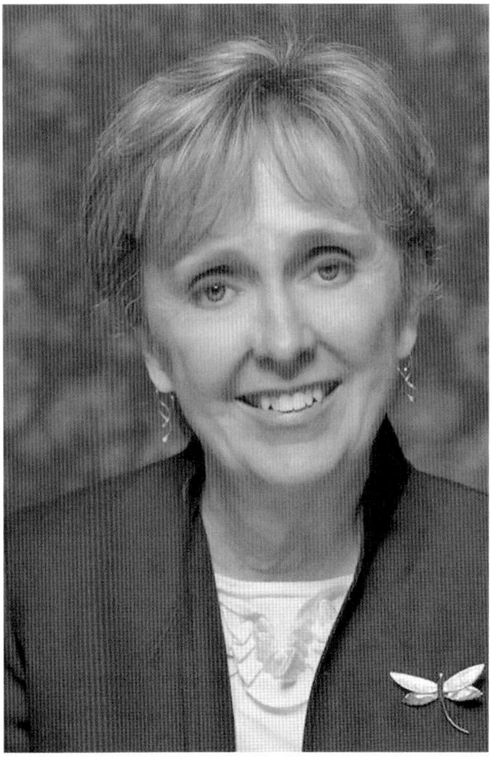

Cynthia "Cindy" Mayher

Cindy Mayher has been the executive director of Parmenter Visiting Nurse Association and Community Care Inc. for the past 25 years. She has directed the operations of the organization's home care and public health programs and implemented important health and social services for the community. She has overseen the development of a Medicare-certified hospice program, the creation of the Miriam Boyd Parlin Hospice Residence in Wayland, and the establishment of an award-winning children's bereavement program. Cindy has been instrumental in raising funds for un-funded and under-funded services that Parmenter provides for the community. (Left, courtesy of Jessamyn Mayher; below, author's collection.)

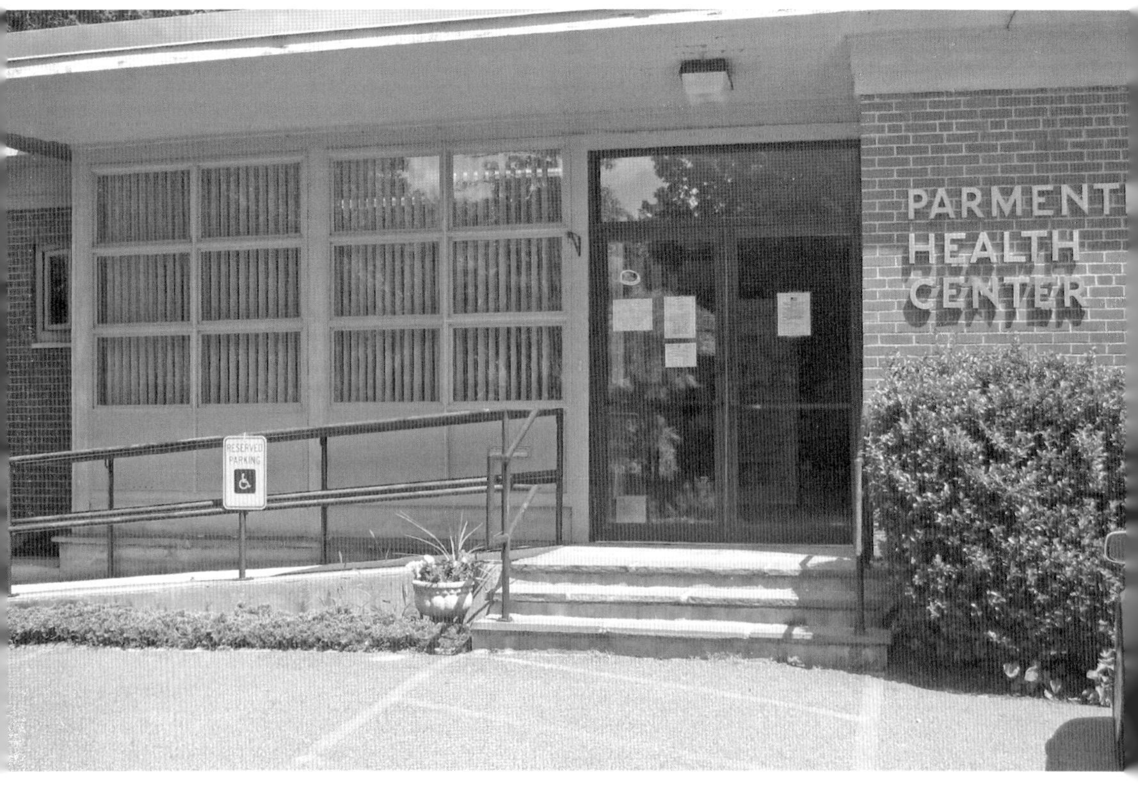

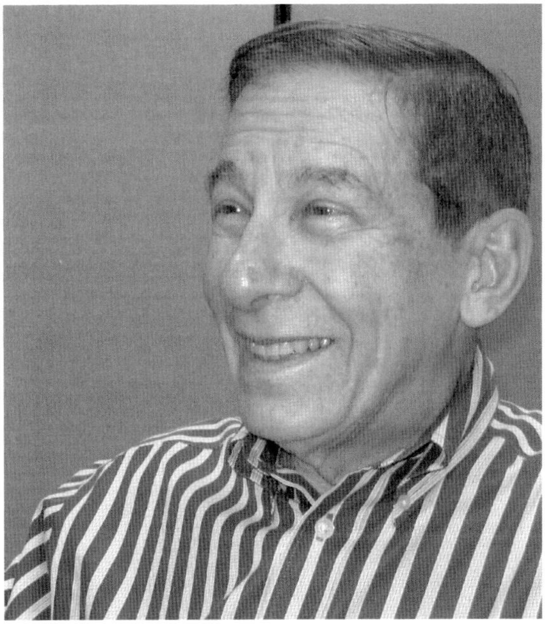

George H. Harris
George Harris served six years on the town's park and recreation commission and almost a decade on the board of selectmen. In 1981, he and a number of citizens filed and won a suit to overturn an unlawful Special Town Meeting vote to take vacant school land to build low-income housing. To improve government's transparency, he has been a staunch defender for over 30 years of the Open Meeting Law and the Public Records Law. (Author's collection.)

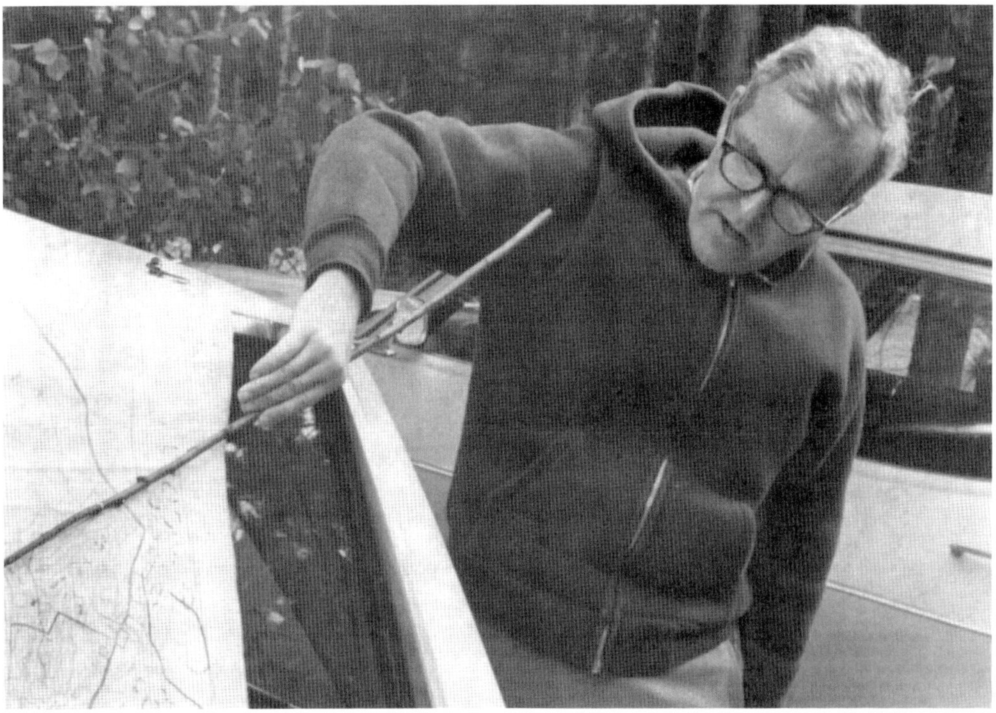

Kenneth "Ken" Moon (1925–2010)
Ken Moon was a dedicated land preservationist who worked tirelessly to maintain Wayland's many conservation lands during his 50 years in town. He served on the Conservation Commission for 25 years, building bridges and removing beaver and muskrat dams along many popular trails. He received citations from both the state Senate and House of Representatives. In 1995, he was honored by the town and received an award from the SVT three years later.

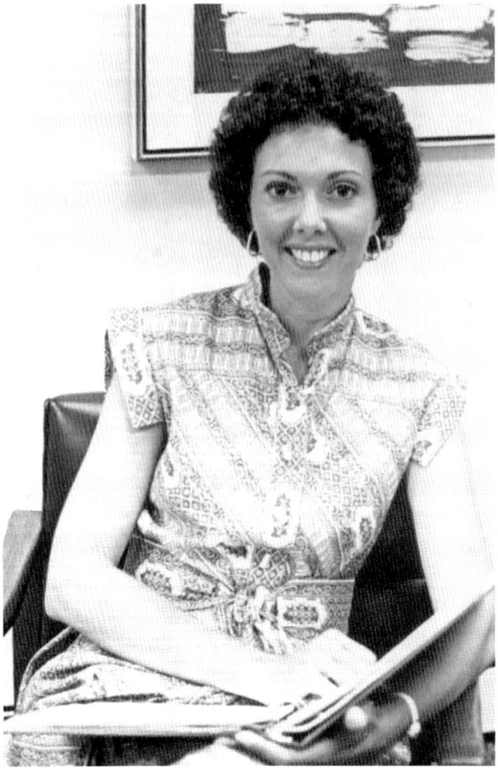

Louise Brown

Louise Brown was on the staff of the Wayland Public Library for 37 years, serving for 26 years as director. She directed all services, including the supervision of a large 1974 addition to the library. In 2004, she was inducted into the Massachusetts Library Association Hall of Fame. Now retired, she continues to volunteer on local projects, as president of her class at Simmons College, and as a tour guide at DeCordova Museum in Lincoln, Massachusetts.

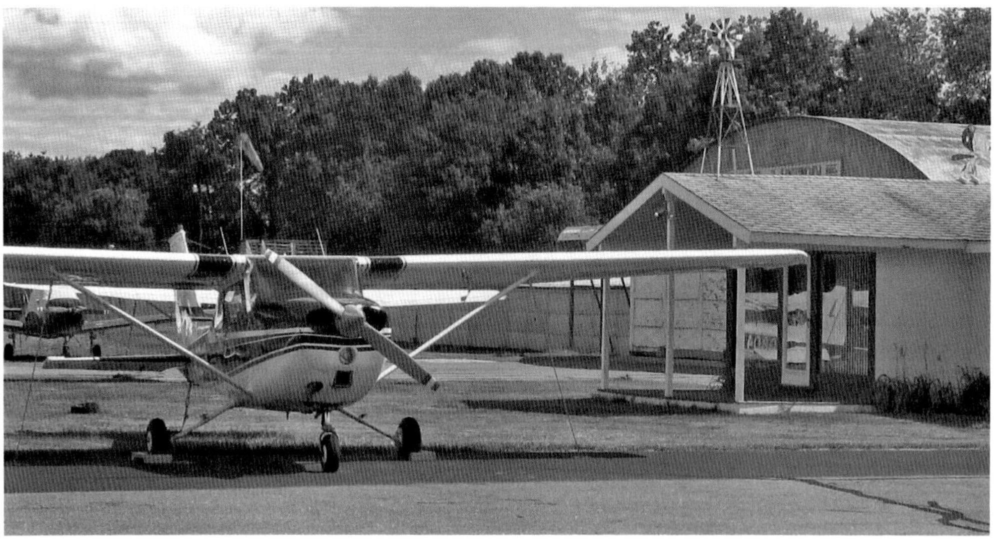

Carol Stites (1921–2007)

Carol Stites had more talents than she had time. She flew gliders, was a flight instructor at Marlborough Airport, and was licensed to fly 727s as well as sea planes. She and her husband, Frank, built a wooden tandem aircraft, a car, and a small boat in their back yard. When she was not flying, she was playing tennis, teaching pottery, or conducting art classes. Her art was often displayed at DeCordova Museum in Lincoln, Massachusetts, and Vokes performers depended upon her artful hand for their makeup. (Author's collection.)

Dr. Eva Pereli (1919–2004)

Dr. Pereli, born in Budapest, was practicing internal medicine when Soviet troops invaded Hungary to suppress an anti-communist uprising in 1956. She graduated from the University of Hungary with a degree in music and played classical piano before earning her degree in medicine. Dr. Pereli could speak seven languages and could recite the Latin works of Ovid, Cicero, and Virgil. She opened her pediatric practice in Wayland in 1975 and was known for treating many indigent patients without compensation. She would enthrall legions of Wayland schoolchildren and adults with stories of her life in her native country, which began as a child of privilege and ended with her daring escape. One of her favorite stories was that of her first taste of American peanut butter, given to her when they crossed the border into Austria. She served on the Wayland Board of Health and as physician for a school in the area for troubled boys. Dr. Pereli organized a number of clothing collections for Transylvania, a former part of Hungary, when the Romanian dictator Nicolae Ceausescu was razing his country. As a naturalized citizen, she loved everything American.

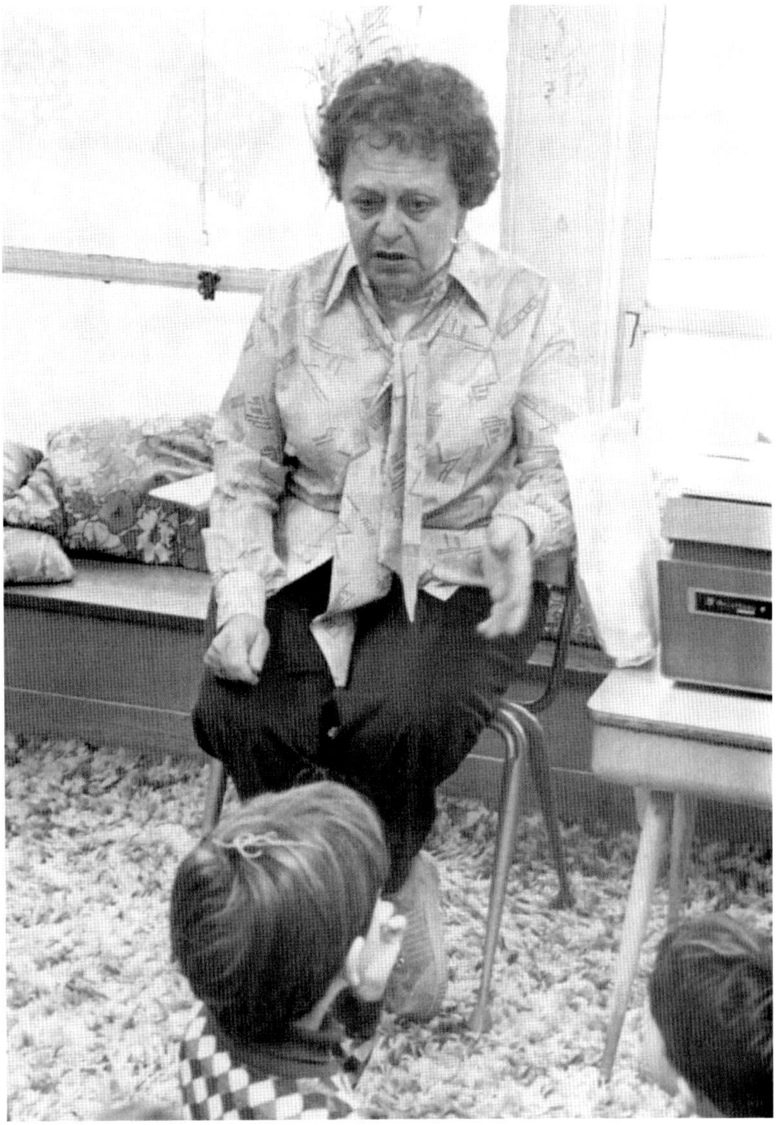

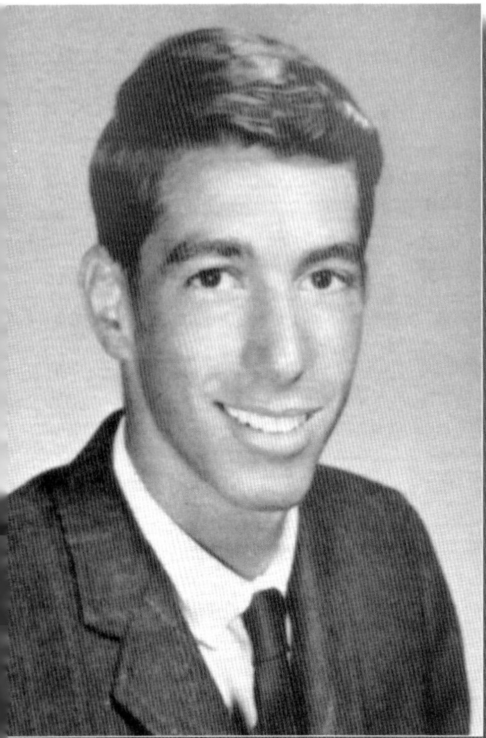

Jan Richard Schlichtmann

Schlichtmann graduated from Wayland High School in 1969, going on to the University of Massachusetts, Amherst to earn a bachelor of arts degree and a law degree from Cornell University. He was admitted to the bar in 1977 and specializes in personal injury law and toxic torts. He became famous in the 1980s as a result of his lawsuit against W.R. Grace and Beatrice Co. (Anderson v. Cryovac) alleging that chemicals from these companies had contaminated drinking water in Woburn, Massachusetts. Eight Boston-area families battled against two corporations they held responsible for their childrens' deaths. In 1996, Jonathan Harr wrote *A Civil Action,* a book based on the case. A film by the same name, based on the book, was released in 1988, starring John Travolta as Jan Schlichtmann. Schlichtmann's passion for justice cost him many years of his life and millions of dollars. He once said, "Rich isn't difficult. Famous isn't difficult. Rich and famous together aren't difficult. Rich, famous, and doing good—that's very difficult." (Both, courtesy of Jostens Publishing.)

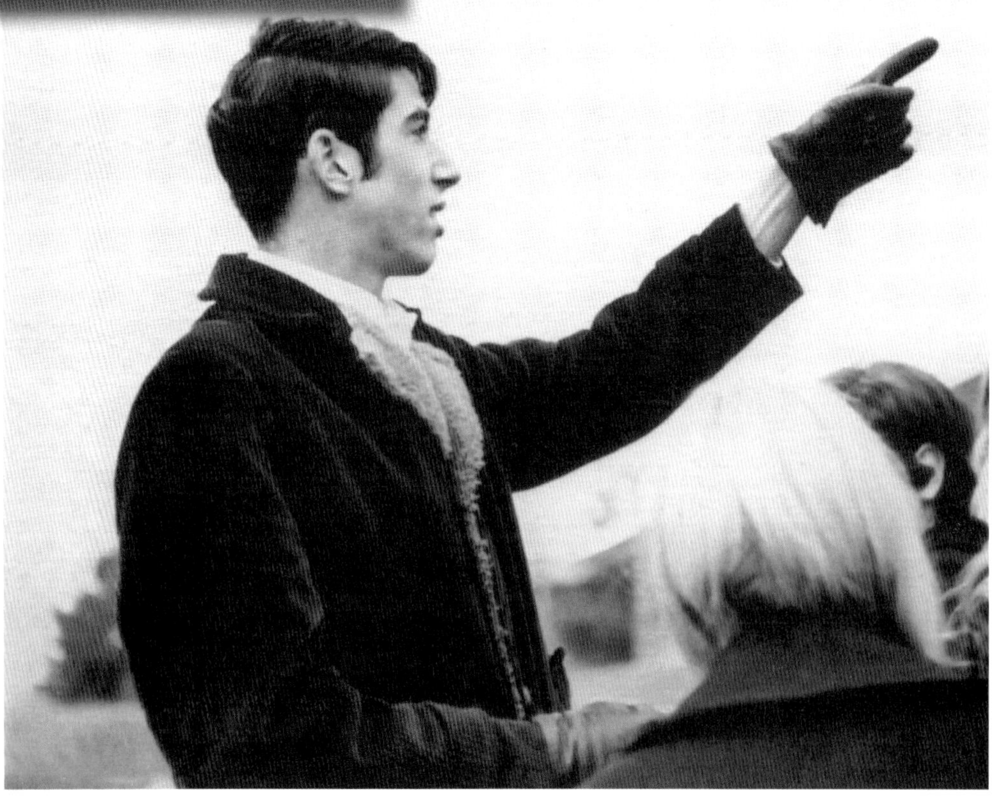

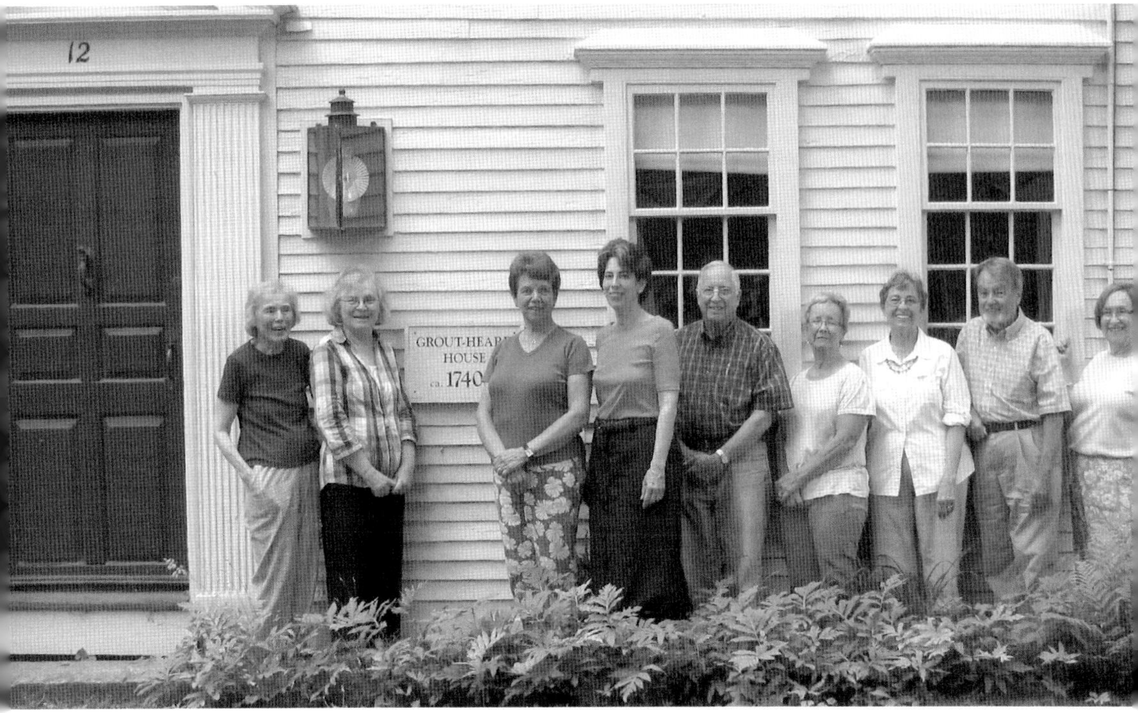

Wayland Historical Society Museum

The Wayland Historical Society was incorporated in 1954, two years before Raytheon Corporation donated the Grout-Heard House to the society. The house was located on Old Sudbury Road on land Raytheon had purchased to build a new facility. It was originally built in the town center, on land granted Thomas Cakebread of Watertown as incentive to join Sudbury Plantation as their miller. Ownership later passed to a relative, John Grout. John's grandson, Jonathan Grout, built the oldest part of the house about 1740. After the Revolutionary War, blacksmith Silas Grout bought the property, and with additions and changes, it remained in the family until the 1950s. The house had been moved to Old Sudbury Road in 1878 to make way for a new town hall. After a fundraising drive in 1962, the house was moved back to the original site, which was again available. The Historical Society collections include books, maps, documents, photographs, furniture, paintings, housewares, and other items pertaining to Wayland's history. The house now contains the memorabilia of generations of caring and generous residents. Curator Lois Hanssen Davis is in charge of the collections and research; her husband, Don, maintains the society's website, waylandhistoricalsociety.org; museum manager Joanne Davis helps maintain the house, assists with research, and conducts tours; and costume curator Gloria Backman maintains clothing and textiles. Currently a committee of volunteers is inventorying collections as part of a project to use the museum software PastPerfect to organize information and eventually digitize the archives. A totally volunteer organization, the society offers programs for the general public, works with the schools to enhance their local history curriculum, and operates as an excellent research facility. The society's board of managers meets monthly. The Grout-Heard House Museum at 12 Cochituate Road is open to all, free of charge, from 9:30 a.m. to 12:00 p.m. on Tuesday and Friday and by appointment. Volunteers, pictured here from left to right, are museum manager Joanne Davis, curator Lois Davis, directors Katherine Jenny, Aida Gennis, John Heckscher, Molly Faulkner, Jane Sciacca, treasurer George Ives, and president Jan Dunn. Not pictured are Margery Baston, Carol Repose, John Beard, Jim Ashkar, Debby Jones, Roger Backman, Richard Hoyt, Robert Mainer, and Don Davis. (Courtesy of John Schlafer.)

INDEX

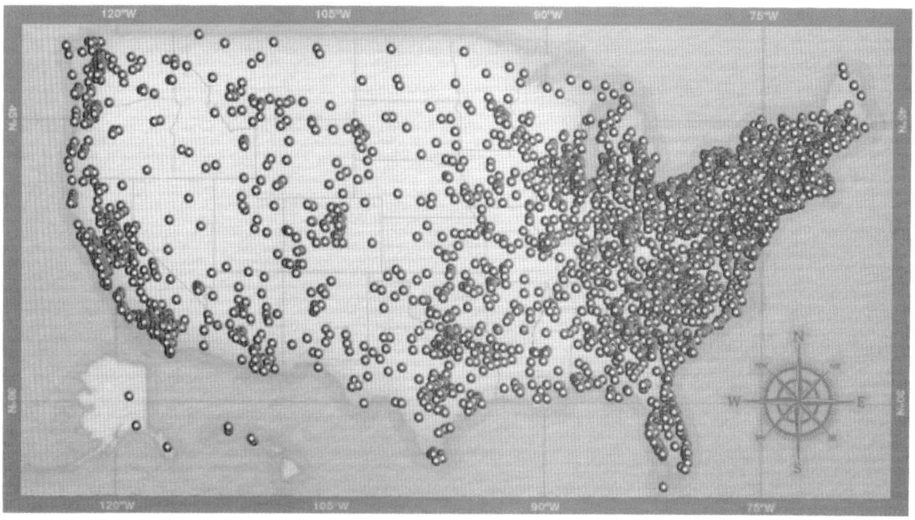

Consistent with our mission to preserve history on a local level, this book was printed in South Carolina on American-made paper and manufactured entirely in the United States. Products carrying the accredited Forest Stewardship Council (FSC) label are printed on 100 percent FSC-certified paper.

MADE IN THE USA